THORNTON McCAMISH is an Australian writer based in London. A regular contributor to Australian newspapers, he was an editor of the *Big Issue Australia* for two years and is the author of several plays. Thornton has been an inveterate traveller, mostly through Africa and Europe, ever since the insurance money for his stolen saxophone came through.

SUPERCARGO
A JOURNEY AMONG PORTS

Thornton McCamish

LONELY PLANET PUBLICATIONS
Melbourne • Oakland • London • Paris

Supercargo: A Journey Among Ports

Published by Lonely Planet Publications

Head Office:	90 Maribyrnong Street, Footscray, Vic 3011, Australia
	Locked Bag 1, Footscray, Vic 3011, Australia
Branches:	150 Linden Street, Oakland CA 94607, USA
	10a Spring Place, London NW5 3BH,UK
	1 rue Dahomey, 75011, Paris, France

Published 2002
Printed through Colorcraft, Hong Kong
Printed in China

Edited by Meaghan Amor
Designed by Margaret Jung
Maps by Natasha Velleley
Author photograph by D.J. McKinlay

National Library of Australia Cataloguing-in-Publication entry

McCamish, Thornton.
  Supercargo: a journey among ports.

  ISBN 1 86450 346 7.

  Voyages and travels. 2. Harbors. I. Title. (Series:
  Lonely Planet journeys).

910.45

Text © Thornton McCamish 2002
Maps © Lonely Planet 2002

LONELY PLANET and the Lonely Planet logo are trade marks of Lonely
Planet Publications Pty. Ltd.

For Sarah

CONTENTS

ACKNOWLEDGEMENTS

When you're writing a book about sentimental travel, it doesn't seem too grand to aim for truth rather than narrow fact: this is one reason most of the people who appear in this book won't recognise the names I've given them and the ships they sail in. The main reason I've changed them is to protect them from insult and me from injury.

That said, it hasn't been possible to avoid facts entirely. As well as the books mentioned in the text, I am indebted to Ernle Bradford's *Mediterranean: Portrait of a Sea*, Fernand Braudel's *The Mediterranean and the Mediterranean World in the Age of Philip II,* Alan Ross' *Reflections on Blue Water*, Alan Villiers' *The Monsoon Seas: The Story of the Indian Ocean,* Miles Bredin's *The Pale Abyssinian,* and *Nathaniel's Nutmeg* by Giles Milton. Much of the historical background for the latter parts of the book was gleaned from Richard Hall's magnificent *Empires of the Monsoon: A History of the Indian Ocean and its Invaders.* Any errors of fact or interpretation are entirely my own work.

Thanks are also due closer to home. I would never have attempted a book without encouragement from Simon Castles, Paris Lovett and James Button; without Susan Keogh at Lonely Planet, I may not have been given a chance. Tristan Gemmill and Alastair Ritchie gave this book their sweat, dialogue and some tough games of Twenty Questions. I also want to mention IRH, Laura, Dave Palser's fry-ups and sage advice, and all those people who kindly refrained from suggesting I should get a proper job, not least my parents, who passed on the travel gene and have borne my wanderings with grace ever since. Dan Fitts and Sarah Sandaver read an early draft and wisely advised me to cut most of it. None of these people is in any way responsible for the 260-or-so pages that remain, but my heartfelt thanks go to them all.

My greatest debt is to Sarah Carlisle, who inspired this book, paid for most of its research and stuck with it – and me – through long absences. No ship of mine could ever sail without her.

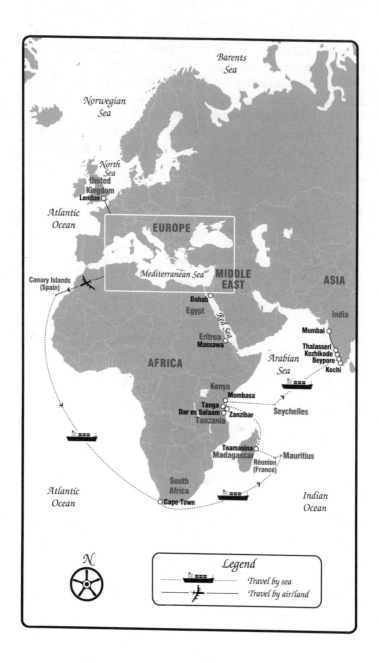

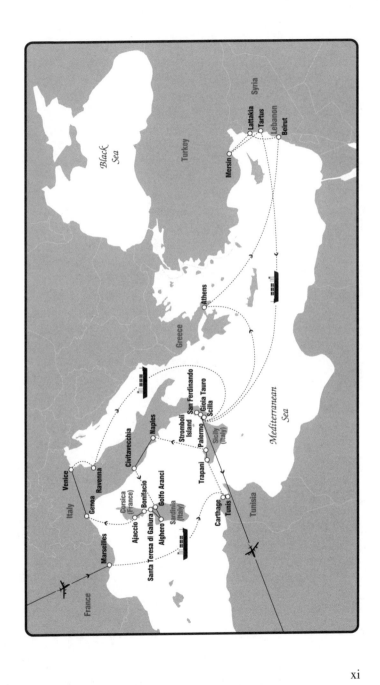

ZIBIB AND BRUCE'S MAGIC CARPET

> The camel driver . . . thinks of all the ports, the for-
> eign merchandise the cranes unload on the docks,
> the taverns where crews of different flags break
> bottles over one another's heads, the lighted,
> ground-floor windows, each with a woman comb-
> ing her hair . . .
>
> Italo Calvino, *Invisible Cities*

MASSAWA, 1997

Real places are never as good as imaginary ones.

Or so I was thinking as I sat in the hot shade of a harbourside café with Piers and Bill, drinking Eritrean beer and trying to avoid eye contact with the one-legged pool player who was staring at us across the room. I didn't know what Massawa was supposed to look like, but surely it wasn't this.

The thirty-year war of liberation that ended in 1992 was, the Eritreans say, their ultimate triumph over tragedy. But in the frank sunlight, it was the tragedy that stuck out: the shelled-out buildings, bullet-holes punched through concrete walls and the chipboard lining of the phone booth I had tried to call home from; the pot-holed streets, the rotting sandbags of the machine-gun posts dug into ridges overlooking the road from Asmara. Not much of it had been patched up in five years of peace.

At the end of the street, a freighter flying the UN flag was tied up at the docks, unloading a shipment of goods from the First

World: tonnes of food aid and medicine, and perhaps fertiliser for the new agriculture scheme on the mainland.

All I knew about Massawa was that the Scottish explorer James Bruce arrived there in 1769 on his way to the fabled Ethiopian court at Gondar. This part of the world had not been visited by Europeans for 150 years – not since a party of Portuguese Jesuits had arrived on an ill-starred mission to convert the Orthodox court and most of them had been killed or sold into slavery. The inhabitants of the area had grown savage in isolation, Bruce believed, 'growing every day more barbarous, and defied, by rendering it dangerous, the curiosity of travellers of every nation'. He didn't have a very good time there. While he waited for permission to pass into the interior, Bruce idled away the brutally hot days fishing and writing in his journal. When the locals began using the harbour to dump the bodies of smallpox victims, he gave up the fishing.

I watched Brent laughing with a group of young men behind a row of battered Fiats. I marvelled at his energy. Some people have a genius for travelling. Brent was one of them. His travels were unweighted by regrets or expectations. He mingled with his new pals with ease, giving them turns looking through his video camera, demonstrating its digital playback facility, and asking them where he could meet girls around here.

He called me over to distribute a packet of Marlboros I'd bought duty-free at Johannesburg airport for situations just like this one. A chance to befriend the locals with a small gift from Philip Morris, another little something from the First World to go with the food relief being unpacked on the docks. I wandered over, smiling like a corrupt missionary. I tore off the foil tab and held out the pack. I was instantly surrounded, then, as polite eagerness collapsed into a mad scramble for cigarettes, gang-tackled. The pack was emptied in seconds. A boy who didn't get one ripped the pack out of my hands and stomped on it. They wandered off, instantly alight, laughing among themselves and blowing smoke into each other's faces. Brent laughed so hard he could hardly hold the camera up. 'I hope you didn't want one, buddy.'

An elderly man who'd been supervising a young boy fishing in the harbour marched over. He scowled. 'What you do?'

'Just making friends,' Brent grinned, filming away.

The man shook his head. 'It not allowed to make camera here.' He pointed at the port.

'Don't worry,' said Brent. 'The president knows we're here. It's all cool.'

'Give a cigarette please,' said the man.

I pointed at the ravaged packet on the ground. 'That's all there is. Sorry.'

'Fucking idiots,' the man said. I watched him stride off, muttering to himself in Italian. Then I realised that I had to find a toilet. Fast.

For a fleeting moment, as I sprinted groaning to the nearest bathroom, I wished I'd stayed home and just read about Eritrea instead. I'm not proud to say that, but it's the truth. Character flaws are formed early, and my preference for fantasy travel probably began when I was six. I blame Marco Polo.

Not the real Marco Polo, a pretend one. It was my first-ever favourite book: *Marco Polo's Adventures*. Or something similar. The story was a loose adaptation of history, basically the tale of a very young Marco Polo making his way east from Venice through the ports of Arabia and India to China. Not for this adventurous child the hard-nosed commercial imperatives of the real Polo. This was a children's story, in which ships, pirates and ports were rendered in two sunny dimensions only. There was no syphilis or port tax in it; there were no corrupt immigration officials, or stowaways dying of thirst in iron containers. Young Marco's outfit, pirates' culottes with a jaunty little vest, owed more to *Treasure Island* than to the dress of Venetian merchants of the early thirteenth century.

The very last image in the book was the stuff of delicious nightmares: a terrible storm blew up and Marco's ship was smashed to pieces. Marco survived the storm, but he was left alone, frightened and waterlogged, draped over a smashed wine barrel. He was drifting into the mouth of a sinister-looking harbour where junks lurked in the shadows cast by glowing braziers. I could almost smell the salt water in the old leather of Marco's sodden slippers and the fishy stink of the port. I could see the flicker of galley fires through the portholes of galleons. What was he going to do? Would he drown? Would he be sold to a slave-merchant? Boiled for stock in a Cantonese kitchen? The book didn't say. It ended, like an episode of 'Batman', with its hero dangling on the brink of doom.

Happily, it turned out that the story of Marco's amazing adventures continued in a second book. I begged my parents until I was taken back to the newsagent in Mooroopna, the nearest town to our home, where the first half of Marco's story had washed up. I demanded the sequel. The nice man in the newsagent wasn't sure which book I was talking about. So I described it for him, outlining Marco's adventures, how he'd dined with sultans, ridden on their flying carpets and fought off brigands. The newsagent went into his storeroom. He rummaged around for a while in some cardboard boxes, among remaindered copies of *Carrie* and *Steppenwolf* and back-issues of *Truth* newspaper. He didn't have it. But he'd be happy to order it for us. Every Saturday morning after that, when Dad drove us into Mooroopna in the ute to get bread and milk and the newspapers, we would ask after *Marco II*.

I remember counting down the days. Months passed. Gradually the book's non-appearance became the kind of topic that wasn't for discussion in front of the kids: death, divorce and *Marco Polo's Adventures, Book II*. Eventually, this policy had the intended effect, and I forgot all about it.

In Massawa we checked in to a hotel, showered and found a place to eat. I was in Eritrea tagging along with Brent, the Melbourne-based painter Piers Bateman and the Sydney photographer Bill Moseley. Piers was painting, Bill was working on surrealist themes. Bill had brought several props with him, including a fairly realistic severed hand made out of rubber. As we drove around the country, Bill would ask shepherd boys to pose with the hand, then photograph their bemused expressions with his antique Hasselblad camera. In the capital, Asmara, a quiet, solemn city with wide streets and elegant Italianate villas, we'd met plenty of Eritrean émigrés who had flocked back to their homeland after the war. One, a young photographer called Yadav who'd escaped Eritrea ten years earlier as a boy, latched onto Bill straight away and proudly chaperoned us around his beloved capital. He took us to restaurants where he flirted outrageously in Tigrinya with the waitresses and tried to hide his hurt when they struggled to under-stand his expatriate accent. As if Eritrea didn't look wonderfully bizarre enough already, we drank a lot of *zibib*, a numbing spirit which is a distant relative of the ouzo family.

That night in Massawa, we drank more *zibib* with some of the pals Brent had made in the afternoon. I was enjoying myself again. I spoke to a Swiss schoolteacher called Miguel. He told us he'd been going to Zanzibar almost every year since 1970. His was the kind of sun-leathered face that creased into rugged handsomeness with middle age. The problem with Zanzibar, he said, was that the old neighbourhood of hippies had been pushed out by the tourists. So this time he'd come to Eritrea instead. I guessed that Miguel had been trying to be anywhere but home for most of his life. He had the unearthly air of a galactic hitchhiker who had travelled widely and found himself vaguely unsatisfied by planet Earth.

An Eritrean man perching on a drum in the corner told us that during the massive bombardment of 1990 he'd fired rockets at Ethiopian jets from the roof of the smashed Governor's Palace; rockets smuggled, so he said, across the Red Sea from Yemen in little boats. The more beers he drank, the more jets he remem-bered having personally blown out of the sky. His friends laughed and rolled their eyes.

We paid and stepped out into the night air. We headed back to our hotel on the harbour. The narrow dirt streets were lit with oil lamps and glowing cigarette tips. Children played in the shells of buildings that hadn't been repaired since the war; buildings with doors and windows boarded up and buckled Italianate balustrades hanging from the second floor. People sat outside their stone houses flapping at the sweet smoke of coke briquettes with scraps of corrugated tin. Above, wooden window screens were thrown open to the breeze. There was a smell of hot nuts and popcorn.

When we arrived back at the waterfront where we'd started that day, I could hardly believe the transformation. Old Massawa – the islands of Wushti Batsi and Taulud – is connected to the mainland city by a causeway guarded by three Russian-built tanks captured by Eritrean troops and re-used against the Ethiopians during the final terrible battle for the town in 1990. But facing out to sea, on the ancient harbour of Wushti Batsi, I felt as if I were on a magical island cut off from the twenty-first century altogether.

All dreamy travellers have an idea of what the world should look like. In most places they go, they have to narrow their eyes and block their ears to blot out the Portaloos, hot dog stands and the rumble of jet engines overhead, and try to imagine what it might have been like once. Not here. Night had revealed Massawa as a town that was no longer from our time at all.

Massawa at night was the most fragrantly atmospheric place I'd ever been. The docks stank of oil, mud, dusty children, fish, and wicks spluttering in oil lamps. Italianate palazzi and Ottoman villas built out of coral bricks were dimly reflected in the still black water. Further around, on the other side of the bridge to Taulud I could see some kampong-style huts with thatched and tin roofs perched on stilts above the water. A motorboat idled below. Two men were unloading wooden crates onto the pier while another man in a turban and white kurta pyjamas stood in the boat running the beam of his torch over the crates and pier.

Just along from where we'd distributed cigarettes that afternoon, a large two-masted dhow with a raised deck – a classic Persian Gulf *boom* – had tied up below the gunwales of the UN ship. We wandered over to have a look. It was crewed by a large Arab family. The women were out of sight below, cooking the evening meal. I could smell chillies frying in hot oil. The men negotiated with a pair of immigration officials who had sauntered down from the customs buildings further along. The officials made a cursory inspection of the boat's hold and filled in some forms. The boat had come from Port Sudan and was bound for Aden. After Aden, they'd probably follow the winter monsoon down the coasts of Somalia, Kenya, Tanzania and even Mozambique before returning six months later. These people were true caravanners of the East African coast. Except for the electric riding lights taped to the top of the stemposts, this boat could have sailed into Massawa straight from the tenth century. Sinbad the sailor would have sailed in a boat indistinguishable from this one. In fact, judging from the crumbling caulking that seemed to be holding the sewn hull together, he might have done time in this very boat.

Like most of the ancient seaports lining the Red Sea, Massawa has more history than it really needs. It was a major seaport for the ancient and sophisticated civilisations of Abyssinia for at least two millennia. For centuries it had been a major trading centre, exporting pearls, ivory and slaves to Arabian traders who sold them on via Persia to Damascus and Venice in one direction, and China in the other. But the sea also tooketh away. Within the last five hundred years invaders had streamed through this harbour: Portuguese, Arab, Egyptian, Turkish, British and Italian. During the Italian Abyssinian campaigns in the 1930s nearly 300,000 Italian troops passed through Massawa's docks, dragging packs heavy with tins and smelly cheese and photos of their mammas.

I was back again the next night, wandering in a happy daze through the town. But it was a guilty kind of bliss. It seemed perverse to be so excited by the bombardment aesthetics of one of the world's poorest countries, to have found a wonderland whose picturesque medieval soul had only been revealed by a terrible war. When he was stationed in Italy during World War II, writer Norman Lewis saw the past returning with a hideous vengeance, rising out of the rubble of Naples. 'The Middle Ages had returned to display all their deformities, their diseases, and their desperate trickeries,' he wrote, describing a city that stank of charred wood and had no water, a glorious city bombed back to the hellish aesthetic of Hieronymus Bosch. Eritrea's resurgent middle ages

7

weren't like that. Massawa's waterfront had the rambling exuberance of a Breughel canvas. Life was flourishing here; people were friendly and there was humour and optimism about the future.

To me, mistily *zibibbed*, the waterfront of Wushti Batsi oozed mystery. It looked like the kind of place in which you could buy anything if you wanted it badly enough, where you could lose yourself forever among the Arabic archways and winding alleys. This was as close to the edge of the map as I'd ever been. Not a modern map either, an old one. It was, I fancied, the last place I'd ever seen young Marco.

EGYPT, 2000

Three years later I sat on the waterfront of the tiny traveller's camp of Dahab on Egypt's Sinai peninsula, picking a fly out of a lukewarm glass of Nescafé. Dahab's modern history as a backpackers' hide-out began after the Six Day War when young Israelis had started to come to dive and snorkel on the stunning reef walls just metres offshore. The hippie ethos they had brought with them survived intact, particularly in the old Bedouin village of Assalah, a makeshift line of jerry-rigged cafés and cheap hotels, all blissfully unimproved by the Sinai tourist boom. In the evenings, I sat on the upper deck of the boat-shaped Tota restaurant ('branches in Dublin, Ireland, and Dahab') and watched cargo ships parade along the Gulf silhouetted against the mountains of the Saudi shore opposite.

I was reading Paul Theroux's travel book about the Mediterranean *The Pillars of Hercules* in which the author quotes his friend and renowned writer on maritime matters, Jonathan Raban, on the nature of the seaside:

> . . . the seaside became known as a place of extraordinary license . . . [The sea] lay outside of society, outside of the world of good manners and social responsibilities. It was also famously the resort of filthy people – low-caste types, like fishermen . . . It was a social lavatory, where the dregs landed up.

I looked around me at my fellow-travellers with new interest. Filthy people? I saw badly sunburned Europeans, some American trust-fund types monitoring the NASDAQ on the Internet between dives, confused day-trippers and a smattering of Egyptians. Some of the long-termers here were so relaxed they seemed to be in a delicious coma, like well-fed crocodiles, letting the months slip by on only one or two heartbeats a day. They smoked joints, slurped milkshakes, swam, then lay in the sun until their skin peeled away in Band Aid–sized scabs.

Then I remembered Massawa. Plenty of human flotsam had washed up there. The sinister guys unloading crates from the motorboat by torchlight – smugglers? Or arms dealers? I thought of all the people we'd met: dissipated expats, war veterans and travellers looking for the final frontier; the American Peace Corps girls Brent had befriended who had given him ear-curling accounts of the recreational licence they took on friends' pleasure boats; the American speculators who sat in cafés all day drinking cassava juice spiked with hip-flask whiskey and trying to work out how to get involved in Eritrea's nascent tourism industry. And then there was us, with our rubber hand and probing video.

Raban was right. It wasn't just the voyeuristic curiosity about the devastation of the war that made Massawa so fascinating; nor was it the vicarious thrill of recent violence in this new-old place. As Raban wrote, it was the sea and the human driftwood that had washed up here over the centuries. Maybe this was how all ports used to be before they were pasteurised by modernity. My epiphany in Massawa had been about the sea, not the ruins. The sea, that repository of dreams and dregs, had brought Massawa's ancient port culture floating back. How many places like that were left in the world?

LONDON, 2000

Ports. That's what I told people. Not port cities in themselves, but *portiness*. I would travel among ports, treating the water-fronts of each place as part of a continuous culture of the oceans. I would visit ports where the piers were encrusted with centuries of barnacles and brine, sniffing the harbour air for the ancient ghosts of the sea's past I thought I'd glimpsed in Massawa.

I didn't want to follow in anyone's footsteps, particularly; I didn't want to re-enact any great sea journeys. I had a simpler mission. In my mind's eye, I saw myself holding forth in a series of dockside dives between London and Malacca. I would keep company with dissipated missionaries, exiled Anglophiles, sea dogs, pimps and saints. The whiskey would be vile rotgut. There would be a piano in the corner with keys sticky from spilt absinthe on which I might, if the mood was right, play 'Bound for South Australia' or the theme from *ET*. It would be a purely whimsical trip, an attempt to find a culture that may have already disappeared. Best of all, it would give me an excuse to go back to Massawa and see whether I'd made it all up.

I found a cruise agency in London which specialised in booking passage on cargo freighters. A lovely Swedish woman called Ada was put in charge of my case. Ada was tall, glamorously blonde and extremely friendly. None of this had stopped her working as a cook on a Yugoslav freighter for six years. If anyone knew how to get places on a freighter, it was Ada. I gave her a list of ports I wanted to see. She said she'd do her best. I believed her.

After I'd dropped in to check on Ada's progress one morning, I caught the tube into Soho and bought a huge map. I took it to the nearest café, a Starbucks, and wrestled it flat. I pored over the map, exultant: Mediterranean, Levant, Africa, Indian Ocean. I felt like William Boot, the unwitting hero of Evelyn Waugh's *Scoop*, preparing himself for a journey to a country he barely knew existed. He too had dreamt of Abyssinia. Admittedly Boot didn't contemplate his unexpected journey in a Starbucks.

These days maps aren't the joy for adventurous travellers they used to be. Every year the tourist industry bites new chunks out of Africa, Asia and South America, and the map on which travellers plot their adventures shrinks. In Luxor, Cairns, Toledo and Cape Town, the scene is the same: travellers lingering miserably at the back of the package-tour crowd, guiltily straining to hear what's being said by the multilingual tour guide clutching the Prada bag with one hand and waving her pink 'Quickie Tours' paddle with the other.

But my map seemed perfect, and not just because the coffee I promptly spilt all over it gave it an aged look. Ports were lining up on the map as if they'd been waiting for me. They seemed connected by a magical isobar that drew history and Marco Polo together into a coherent trajectory through space and time. I would head east. Freighters would get me to more out-of-the-way ports, but I also wanted to wander on the docks of some of Europe's great port cities. It would be easiest to do this on ferries, because I would be able to hop on and off according to my own schedule.

I decided I'd begin by doing a lap of the Mediterranean, taking in Marseilles, Tunis, Naples, Genoa and Sardinia, then pick up a cargo ship in Venice for a voyage across to the Levant. From there I would either connect to a ship for the Red Sea, or join a Dutch ship in Tilbury heading down the West African coast.

It was a sentimental quest, I knew that. But then, sentimental travelling was the kind I was best at. Before I was twenty-one, my only experience of overseas travel came in the form of Bruce Williams' slide nights. Bruce was a bachelor friend of the family, an English teacher with the travel bug. With his engrossing commentaries and splendid moustache, he was – to me at least – the Phileas Fogg of our times. He made several epic journeys in the school holidays of the late seventies; each one was ritually re-enacted in the weeks after his return in the form of a slide night at our place.

When the lights went down and the projector's cooling fan began to whir helplessly in the still heat of a summer evening, the sensible wall-to-wall flooring of our lounge room was transformed into a magic carpet. I can't remember now any of the places Bruce went to; I vaguely recall that increasingly they involved classic train journeys. But I remember clearly how exciting the world beyond Mooroopna looked. Watching Bruce's tour of Bali or Peru or Thailand, I longed to tumble through the plaster wall where the fragile images were projected, into these places made of trembling squares of light; Thai jungles and Indian train carriages perfumed with the odour of the hot slide projector.

But life is not a slide show. Anyone who has a nostalgic idea of travel knows how crushing it can be to actually visit the places you dream of. To arrive is to discover that the place is not the dream, partly because no-one is serving dry biscuits and cubes of cheddar while Bruce changes the slide cartridge. I don't think Bruce ever went to Massawa, probably because the railway built by the Italians between 1887 and 1912 was destroyed in the war and hadn't been rebuilt. So there was nothing much for him there. If he *had* gone, Massawa mightn't have seemed so perfect to me.

At the time, I was working as a subeditor on the foreign desk of a national daily in the heart of London's historic docklands. As I sat picking the raisins out of my cafeteria lamb stew one night, I remembered Raban's idea about the dangerous edge of the sea; the dregs of society banished to the littoral. From the wall-to-ceiling windows on the twenty-second floor I couldn't see much evidence of this watery substratum of danger and vice, unless you called office workers throwing their beer bottles into the water transgressive.

The problem with London's docklands was modernity. I had lived most of my life in Melbourne, a port city at the other side of the world which is rarely thought of as one, whose docklands had faded in size, importance and character over the last century. All around the world, docks were falling into disrepair or being turned into loft apartments, cinemas and generic fish cafés.

Still, London was the right place to plan a trip into the past. When you have seawater on the brain, all of historic London comes to seem like a giant hydroponic coral living off the subconscious reservoir of its maritime history. The city's antique stores and junk shops are a haven of nautical salvage. There are hoards of maritime detritus hidden away throughout the city: brasses, models of ships, compasses and barometers, foghorns, sea chests and paraphernalia from the days of Blue Riband Atlantic runs and P&O liner routes. At Greenwich Market, in the shadow of the London Maritime Museum on the Thames, every print shop has a fat rack of etchings and lithographs on marine themes. Like recognising at first sight a relative you've never met, there is an odd familiarity to the London which emerges as you flick through them. These lithographs are like grey-gauze windows overlooking the eighteenth and nineteenth centuries: the days when ships sailed all the way up to the centre of London, as far as Limehouse Dock on Regent's Canal and Execution Dock in Wapping, where the corpses of condemned criminals were strung from gibbets; when the Isle of Dogs thronged with commerce and the entire river, from Wapping to Blackfriars Bridge, stunk of tar.

That world has utterly vanished from London now. Trying to imagine it is like trying to draw a *Punch* cartoon with maritime clichés. Three hundred years ago, when England was approaching the heights of its maritime glory, the stretch of the Thames between London Bridge and the Tower of London was known as the Pool. This narrow section of water was the world's greatest cultural entrepôt and housed its largest concentration of capital. Thousands of ships of different flags crowded into it on a first-come, first-served basis. They were caulked, re-masted, fined, painted, loaded and unloaded. In the early eighteenth century, it was estimated that a quarter of London's population was bound up with the commerce of the seas. In masters' cabins on the ships and alehouses off the quays, sailors, merchants, bankers and owners signed up, signed off, traded and told wild lies about the things they'd seen, where they'd been and how many Polynesian wives they had. The decks of the vessels crawled with customs officials and slaves. Thriving alongside the tremendous volume of legitimate trade was a booming black-market economy oiled by embezzlement, fraud, collusion and payoffs. Most of the proceeds were funnelled through the capital's gin shops and whorehouses.

Since then the ships have evolved into the enormous iron vessels which come no closer to London than the modern docks at Tilbury; and all the sin and industry that once thrived on the riverbanks has drifted north into the glass towers of the City of London. Now and then you see a barge or a party boat, but as for the rest, time has washed it away.

My plans began to come together. I had the beginnings of an itinerary. I had time off. I had rolls and rolls of slide film. But the news wasn't so good at the newspaper. That winter I found myself subbing depressing stories on the renewed fighting between Eritrea and Ethiopia, whose governments had been allies in the war against the former communist dictator Mengistu. The Massawa I remembered from my visit three years earlier was being freshly demolished under a new bombardment. The ancient sea culture I thought I'd tasted as I sat on the docks was being re-buried by another round of terrible violence.

In an antique print shop at the Church Street Market I found an advertisement for P&O trips to Australia dated May 1960. The copywriters noted the chance to learn to play shuffleboard and deck quoits; emphasised the interesting people you might meet aboard ('journalists, soldiers, scientists, Dons'); and provided some tips for the forgetful packer ('Don't Forget the Wife!'). The passage then was around six weeks. Six weeks! An ocean of time, a sea of blameless idleness.

It was at that point I decided to recruit a travelling companion for my jaunt through the Mediterranean. Really Tristan selected himself, mostly because, as an actor between jobs, he was used to blameless idleness. But he also seemed an ideal travel companion in several other respects: he loved food; he had a brilliant memory for trivia; and he boasted a comprehensive recall of the rules of hundreds of card, board and parlour games. He also spoke fairly fluent French, which would be very handy in the Mediterranean.

One day we visited Tristan's agent in Notting Hill, then took ourselves off for a coffee on the upstairs balcony of a café on Portobello Road. Tristan lit a cigarette and exhaled a lungful of greasy smoke. Neither of us was a smoker. But Tristan had been driven to it by recent heartbreak. 'You know,' he said, staring down at the street, 'this trip couldn't have come at a better time. I really need to get out of here for a while.' Two weeks laid out on the sundeck of Mediterranean ferries would be just the ticket.

'We actually have to live the life, you know,' I said lightly. 'It's not a pleasure cruise. I'll need you to get into fights in sailors bars. Gamble for the barmaid with Portuguese sail-makers, that kind of thing.'

Tristan stared at me, red-eyed, through his smoke. 'You realise that together we sound like an interior decorating firm, don't you?'

'What do you mean?'

'"Thornton and Tristan". How does that sound to you? If we meet any Portuguese sail-makers they'll be laughing too hard to beat us up.'

He was right. 'What about pseudonyms? I usually use Harry as my party name. It's easier.'

'Whatever,' said Tristan, slumping in his seat with infinite weariness. 'What. Ever.'

Ada was having some difficulty with my schedule beyond Genoa. The problem with travelling on freighters is that they are notoriously unreliable. In the twenty years since Gavin Young wrote his classic sea journey *Slow Boats to China*, booking his passage as he went, the waterfronts of the Indian Ocean had become places even less receptive to the wanderer. Most of the ships on which he secured passage had long since been recycled as Iraqi washing machines or as tin roofing in Mumbai. As far as Ada could tell, they hadn't been replaced.

It was obviously going to be difficult to stitch together a continuous journey from freighter segments; the ships never hook up where they're supposed to and refuse to offer any guarantee that they will be where their schedule says they will be. The only ship that could connect me between Alexandria and the Red Sea was expensive and unreliable. It was a shame, Ada said: there was a French cook on that one.

I continued trawling second-hand bookshops for sea lore. Jonathan Raban got his sudden need to take to the sea like 'an attack of eczema'. He wrote in his beautiful story 'Sea-Room':

> The idea of taking ship and heading off into the blue is, after all, a central part of the mythology of being English . . . In the books, the English are always running away to sea. The ocean is the natural refuge of every bankrupt, every young man crossed in love, every compromised second son.

In the light of this thought, Tristan seemed more and more suited for the first leg of my trip: I was Australian and married, but Tristan was English, crossed in love and probably close to bankrupt.

The only fragment of sea writing I couldn't dig up in London's second-hand bookshops was *Marco Polo II*. I don't know if the second part of Marco's adventures ever even existed; it certainly never arrived at the newsagent's in Mooroopna. Perhaps the publisher hadn't sold enough copies of the first one. Or perhaps Marco just existed in a parallel dimension. The same dimension as sea monkeys, those miniature-humanoid sea-creatures advertised in generations of American comics in the days before laws about misleading advertising, which were supposed to frolic in rockpools and were only available by mail order from a postal address in New Jersey. According to the ads, sea monkeys would prosper in an ordinary goldfish bowl – but none of my pleading letters to New Jersey was ever answered. Maybe they never existed either.

TWENTY QUESTIONS

> Ah! These commercial interests – spoiling the finest
> life under the sun. Why must the sea be used for trade
> – and for war as well? . . . It would have been so much
> nicer just to sail about with here and there a port and
> a bit of land to stretch one's legs on, buy a few books
> and get a change of cooking for a while.
>
> Joseph Conrad, 'A Smile of Fortune'

When Evelyn Waugh's unlikely scoop, amateur ornithologist
William Boot, headed off to be a foreign correspondent in
Abyssinia, he packed forked sticks. He knew that forked sticks
were used to carry messages in the Abyssinian mountains
because James Bruce had seen them in use two hundred years
earlier. I took no sticks, since my dispatches weren't going to
be needed in a hurry. Instead, I took books; lots of books. Evelyn
Waugh and Joseph Conrad, Alexandre Dumas, Eric Newby and
Paul Theroux, D.H. Lawrence, Dea Birkett, Dorothy
Carrington and Gavin Young. And John Irving. I had books
about sea travel, books about Marseilles, Naples and Venice,
books about rats and plague. I was carrying about twenty kilo-
grams of sea lore.

When I met Tristan at London's Liverpool Station, I saw that
he had brought only a small backpack. A very small backpack. I
was concerned about this. I was lugging a laptop and a camera
bag as well as my library. I'd hoped that Tristan would shoulder

some of the weight of my reading now and again. Or at least his share of the guidebooks.

'Pretty nifty, eh?' he gloated, showing me how the minimalist space inside was neatly packed – full – with undies and suntan lotion. 'It's sort of Swedish, don't you think? Sexy.' He surveyed my several bags. 'And *light*.'

'But there's no space in there.'

'I don't need it! Look! It all fits!'

There had clearly been a misunderstanding somewhere along the line. I shifted my considerable weight to the other foot. I searched for the right phrase. 'You realise you're only here to carry my hatboxes, don't you? You're supposed to be the expedition packhorse.'

Tristan frowned.

'I mean, where are your lederhosen? You look like a Swiss yokel on a school trip.'

'That's funny,' he said, exhaling the grey smoke of the day's first ciggy. '*You* look like David Boon after an unusually large pizza.'

There are several ways to approach Marseilles. We had chosen the only way of arriving which didn't in fact involve Marseilles at all. It turned out that the only problem with buying the cheapest possible flight from London to Marseilles was that we wouldn't actually land anywhere near Marseilles. We would land in Nîmes. How we got to Marseilles was not the concern of Ryanair, though we were told ground staff would be glad to point us in the direction of the municipal bus running the sixteen kilometres or so to Nîmes railway station.

We finally arrived in Marseilles by train at a quarter past seven. We felt some trepidation. Marseilles knows how to deal with people who come looking for a bit of dockside rough. If they're unlucky, it beats them up. If they're lucky, they get strong drinks and a flavoursome bouillabaisse. This was the place where the Mediterranean's various races and fish came together to make a great soup but a dirty and poor city; where scurvy-ridden old sea dogs went to eke our their days, spending their pensions in ten-franc bordellos and fish-soup cafés. It was violent, racist, depressed, and bullishly proud of it. At least, that's what the tourist literature said.

From the moment we stood at the top of the monumental stair-case that led down from the railway station, Marseilles looked better than it was supposed to. A sweeping vista of huddled *belle époque* buildings and elegant boulevards lay before us. In the hazy distance, between us and the sea, we could see forts, cath-edrals and the radar masts of giant ferries.

Time to find a place to stay. We were determined not to book anything in advance, in case we should miss out on an unexpected opportunity: an invitation to someone's home, for instance, or a night in the police cells. We wanted to be flotsam on the warm salt current. Which meant that, in Marseilles on a Friday night in the middle of summer, we had nowhere to stay.

There was something special going on around the old port area, too, which was stuffed with noisy motorcycles, strings of arm-in-arm pedestrians, belching lorries, people licking ice creams and workers erecting scaffolding. It felt celebratory and welcoming. We might as well have been in Cannes for all the menace we felt. Fearing the worst, we turned our backs on this party and plunged into a lane with a beguiling stench of uncol-lected garbage.

Eight hotels turned us away. Then, finally, in a dimly-lit street with an arcade of piss-stains low on the walls, we found the Hotel Monte Cristo.

As far as I knew, we were the only people who were staying in the Monte Cristo that night. In fact, we may have been the only people who stayed in the Monte Cristo for longer than an hour since the shower curtains were put up around 1950. The staircase up to our room wound around the cast-iron lift well of a con-demned elevator. My boots clung to the sticky linoleum. It was narrow and dark.

Our door opened without the assistance of the key. It was dark and bare, except for two beds and a greasy pink shower curtain that concealed what appeared to be a shower head. A hank of grey lace hung in the window.

This was the Marseilles of my dreams. A neon 'HOTEL' sign hung vertically on the wall outside our window. Leaning out, we could see that the first four letters glowed through a matting of spiders' webs and seagull guano, but the 'L', which swung within reach of our window, was dead. This 'L' was the key to our escape from this fleapit in the event of fire, which actually seemed a pretty likely event. We calculated that from the 'L' we could drop to the ledge on the floor below, and that from there we could drop all the way to street level without doing any damage more serious than breaking our legs.

Tristan looked at me and caught me grinning. 'You have to admit it's a steal at £7.50.'

'And,' I said, pointing at the window, 'we know for sure we can survive a fire. *If* we get enough warning. I don't see an extensive fire alarm system here.'

But Tristan was off. He loved it. 'And what else is there to worry about? The sheets are clean.' He skipped into the corridor to check out the facilities. 'The toilet could be . . . *slightly* worse.'

An inspection of the door revealed that there was no lock. Tristan turned serious. Cogs were turning. He slapped me on the back. 'Well, old boy, if a big hairy man breaks in at three o'clock and insists on buggering one of us to within an inch of our lives, I'm sure I'll have time to swing off the 'L'. You, on the other hand, well, you'll just have to deal with him with your wit.'

'But I don't speak French.'

Tristan coughed. 'I wasn't being serious about your wit. I think you'll just have to grin and bear it. Mark it down to experience.'

The proprietor gave us a pitying look when we came down to tell him we'd take the room. Perhaps we were rent boys fallen on hard times.

Outside, the warm air was spicy with clove cigarettes and the smell of fish. The party was gathering momentum down at the marina. The oldest part of Marseilles huddles around a small enclosure of yachts and speed boats like an ancient crab guarding its dinner. We watched a few Eurotrash *pleasuristas* stepping off their yachts with ponytails and gold-rimmed Gucci sunglasses slung over their chins. The sight of these people, with their haloes of ill-gotten wealth, was a reminder that port cities were sometimes shaped by the bad things that come off boats. Such as the plague, for instance, which arrived in Marseilles from Syria early in the eighteenth century and killed half the population. I could see why they'd built such impressive forts to keep out unwanted elements.

Marseilles was an important pleasure port by the beginning of the nineteenth century. With Napoleon safely tucked away on the island of Elba in 1814, Europe was once again safe for the grand tourists who'd been so busy catching syphilis in Italy and France in the previous century. Advances in technology – and the legacy of Napoleon's engineering works throughout France and Italy – meant that by 1830 tourists heading for the cultural treasure house of Italy could take a regular steamship service from Marseilles to Genoa, Livorno, Civitavecchia and Naples, which cut travelling time by about a third.

Time for soup. We found a busy restaurant in Place Thiars and scoured the menu. Bouillabaisse, indigenous to Marseilles, is, with Vietnamese *pho*, one of the world's greatest soups. What they have in common is their potential for metaphor. Staring deep into a bowl of either, I can't escape the feeling that the secret to life is floating like a distant memory in its depths. Tristan advised me to drink some water.

I ordered a version of bouillabaisse with 'rust' sauce, several slabs of what was supposed to be rockfish but actually tasted a lot like cod, some bits of potato and a forlorn, upturned crab with no flesh in it. It was evidently a garnish.

'How does your metaphor taste?' Tristan asked smugly. His crab looked much more recently alive.

If Marseilles was still capable of exerting night terrors on its visitors, then most of them, I suspected, emerged like a malevolent genie from a bottle of Ricard pastis. That night I tossed and turned and thought of all the despairing sailors and prostitutes who'd holed up in this room over the centuries. Mosquitoes grew drunk on my aniseed-flavoured sweat. People screamed in the street. Later, an endless stream of trucks seemed to build to a terrifying pitch of acceleration and, just when it seemed inevitable that they would smash into the building and kill us all, they would roar past like enraged bulls that had missed the matador's cape. It was like playing a game of mental chicken all night, popping in and out of my uneasy dreams for cover from the murderous roar of the trucks.

In the morning, I expected the cobblestones to be caked with the dried blood of the murder victims I'd heard gasping their last during the night. There was nothing. We bought fresh croissants, stoked up on a couple of stiff espressos and set out for a tour of the city's back lanes.

Maybe we'd overestimated the city's badness. After all, Evelyn Waugh was mocking Marseilles' terrible reputation as long ago as 1929. Another book I was carrying was *All Around the Mediterranean* by Warren H. Miller, an American journalist who also visited in the 1920s. He described Marseilles' notorious main thoroughfare, La Canebière, not as a sink of titillating iniquity, but as 'the one modern Forum in all the world: it is lined with luscious cafés and here the whole 800,000 Marseillais gather at the *apéritif* to discuss everything under the sun . . .'

Crime syndicates may thrive there, but Miller was still right – Marseilles would be a great city for the boulevardier. Paul Ricard invented his eponymous pastis drink in Marseilles in 1932, and no self-respecting intellectual *manqué* has since failed to write a novel without first drinking quite a bit of this horrible aniseed-flavoured aperitif. People were still drinking it at café tables in virtually every street.

Some cities have that ability to weather time in such a way that the peculiarities of modernity are somehow absorbed into the history of its streets. Marseilles is like that. In the smoky lanes lined with tobacco shops and chemists, each with several floors of packed-tight flats above, you could be in any city, the sort of

generic European city you get in black-and-white post-war photographs. We passed streets lined with the 'smokepot tenements'
noted by Jack Kerouac fifty years earlier. Many of the wooden
window shutters were missing slats. The leathery fishwives who
leant out of the windows to watch boys playing football below
were missing teeth. We peered into dark shoebox bars, carefully
avoiding the eyes of men – possibly foreign legion veterans – sitting at the tables outside with their warm glasses of pastis.

I was exhilarated. I couldn't possibly have felt further from the
Provence of the Sunday supplements, that Anglo-American terri-
tory of truffling pigs, home-made hock and wonderful French
schools, all pickled in the formaldehyde of early retirement. The
city we'd found was bleaker than that.

Still, by the time we'd capped off another utterly peaceful day
with more fish soup, we were beginning to feel restless. After dinner we made our way up to higher ground trying to find a view.
High up somewhere in the Algerian quarter we ran into a gang of
seven-year-old soccer players who looked like they might have
liked to beat us up, so we bought them off with cigarettes. We
climbed up to the heights above the main fortress protecting the
mouth of the old port, the Fort d'Entrecasteaux, and looked across
the city. A boom box somewhere on the marina was playing
'Jailhouse Rock'. We'd found no sailors bars. In fact, there didn't
seem to be any authentic-looking sailors anywhere.

Finally, desperate to find something resembling the Marseilles
of legend, we headed up to the La Pleine Quarter and walked into
the first sex shop we found. It was as bright as a butcher's shop.
Racks of videos with pink and white flesh on their covers were
laid out under grim fluorescent light and classified by genus:
'scat', 'hetero', 'S/M'.

'Er, sex show?' Tristan asked the guy behind the counter. 'You
know, er . . . *Les Folies Bergères?*'

He didn't seem to understand.

'Les filles sans vêtements?' I said, trying to paint a picture of
the sort of place a hard-up sailor might go to drink lethal drinks
and behave badly. I tried to think of the French for 'opium den'.

'Ici?' he said incredulously.

'Oui, en Marseille.'

The man exchanged glances with his colleague, who was fussing with a display of plastic penises on a stand by the door. 'I don't zeenk so,' he said. 'Ze nearest streep show would be Avignon. But I'm not certain.'

Back at the hotel, we opened the windows to air the room. A formation of mosquitoes gratefully entered.

We opened a bottle of cheap red. Tristan settled on his bed to write some postcards. He'd been suspiciously cheerful all day. I was glad that he seemed to be getting over his heartbreak, but regretted that he hadn't, so far, expressed any interest in night-long rampages through sleazy bars. Now and then he chuckled at what he'd written.

'Who are you writing to?'

'Just a friend,' he said, then giggled at something else he'd written.

As I lay there listening to Tristan amuse himself, I began to think about the young Polish Ukranian, Teodor Josef Konrad Korzeniowski, who'd come here at the age of eighteen, in 1876, seeking a career on the sea. Gavin Young wrote that Korzeniowski spent his time in Marseilles 'Coasting, gun-running and gambling'. And certainly the man known to us as Joseph Conrad showed more entrepreneurial flair in this city than you'd normally expect from a novelist. In *The Mirror of the Sea*, Conrad recalls meetings in a tavern on the old harbour quay of the *Tremelino* syndicate, a group of four young men who co-owned a sixty-ton balancelle taking charters for coastal trading. 'The antique city of Massilia,' he brags, 'had never, since the days of the earliest Phoenicians, known an odder set of ship-owners.' There were ladies involved at these meetings, *all sorts of ladies*, 'some old enough to know better than to put their trust in princes, others young and full of illusions.' Nominally, Conrad's ship carried cork and fruit, but it seems that more interesting items occasionally found their way into the hold among this unexceptionable cargo. Conrad was at the helm when it was decided to drive the

Tremelino onto rocks and deliberately wreck the ship in order to avoid being intercepted by Spanish coastguards.

I slept fitfully again, awoken occasionally by the sound of someone being beaten up or murdered in the street below. The mosquitoes grew so fat on my blood that they were grounded and dragged themselves around on my back instead. In the morning I saw that I'd squashed several of them into the sheets where they had burst open like ripe raspberries.

The *Carthage* towered over the buildings on shore. It was a great, blunt brick of a ship, with dead straight sides, and barely a pucker in its front end for a prow.

'All travelling becomes dull in exact proportion to its rapidity,' John Ruskin wrote; he meant that it got worse the faster you went. I hoped he was right. There were faster ways of getting from Marseilles to Tunis, but this seemed to me the best way to see both places as seaports.

Tristan and I stood at the taffrail and looked down at the wedge of water opening between the *Carthage* and the docks. It widened until the flanks of the great hull were no longer touching the dock. I noted that the water of Marseilles harbour, which Conrad described as the 'decoction of centuries of marine refuse', was precisely the same colour as last night's rusty bouillabaisse.

As we passed the Château d'If, a tiny island fort in which the hero of Alexandre Dumas' novel *The Count of Monte Cristo* was imprisoned for so many years, Marseilles pulled itself together and became a fantasy city again, with a fantasy façade. To fish, it must look like the City of Oz. In the shimmering midday haze, Marseilles gleamed like a pile of engraved bones. Port cities can do this. They have angles that landlocked cities don't have – and everyone wants to be as close to the waterfront as they can be. But they can never be close enough. The allure of a great port city seemed to hang in the inscrutable space between the view from the hill-top condos and the one from our taffrail.

Soon Marseilles had disappeared, folded into the cliffs. I

25

watched our wake for a long time, a ruffle of grimy white fanning out across the inky dark blue.

It looked like we were the only English-speakers on the entire ship. There were lots of prosperous-looking Tunisian families whose cars were packed into the hold with all the booty from their European raid strapped to roof racks: motorbikes, surfboards, tents and cartons of tinned food. Our fellow passengers explored aggressively. Everyone looked afraid that they might miss out on a secluded Aladdin's cave of duty-free shopping, or a piano bar, or sunbed suite. Tristan and I joined them. Our cabin was small and clean. We were sharing it with a tidily dressed man whom we saw briefly when he arrived, and not again thereafter; the only trace left of him was a French volume of Tacitus lying by his bunk.

With growing excitement we inspected the menus of three different restaurants. In a pleased and complicit silence, we dawdled around the radiantly hot pool deck. By the time we'd located a third bar, back in the bowels of the main deck, we were convinced we had found a floating paradise.

'There are three bars,' I said, my voice squeaking a little.

Tristan gripped my shoulder. 'There is a *disco*.'

'There are very few women, though. Our age, I mean.'

He blinked and looked around him. 'You're right. But heck,' he said, grinning hugely, 'who needs women when you've got a pack of cards?' He slapped me on the back. 'Ever played Spite and Malice? Just the thing we need.'

The sea was so flat its surface seemed to bounce the afternoon sun straight back out to space. At one point we passed a tiny island, which we were later unable to spot on any map, rearing out of the ocean with Disney-like loveliness and mystery. The only cloud we ever saw on the Mediterranean was poised over its craggy head like a question mark. If the ship didn't have a wake that ran all the way to the horizon, gently buckling halfway with the surface currents, you wouldn't have been able to tell that it was moving at all.

In the late afternoon we settled ourselves on the sun deck. There was a pleasantly sybaritic odour of popcorn, Le Tan and hot skin. It smelt like holidays.

I watched a couple of teenaged girls arrange themselves prettily on sun lounges nearby. Within seconds, two boys in their mid-teens appeared, one with his tongue literally hanging out. It wasn't the only thing hanging out: when he perched on a nearby sun lounge, a roll of soft fat folded under his small but pert bosoms. I've never seen a male looking more like a large, greasy fly at a barbecue. This boy was blessed with a complete lack of self-consciousness. He began speaking animatedly to his quarry. The girls listened. They seemed to have been stunned into politeness by his chutz-pah. One gave him a dazed smile. Encouraged, he grew more ani-mated in his movements. He kept tugging his plastic sun lounge closer and closer until his large, sweaty face loomed over them.

Tristan had been watching too. 'How often do you think this works for that guy?'

It was truly a marvel of bravado. The poor kid hadn't been blessed with fine features. He was pudgy, had an oddly shaped mouth and drooly lips. When he laughed, he snorted. I was painfully reminded of my own teenage years.

'I give him five minutes,' Tristan said, whose mood seemed to have soured again. We watched as the boy gamely brushed the arm of the prettier of the two girls, and the girl flinched in undis-guised disgust. 'No,' Tristan said, 'make that three minutes.'

Then, as abruptly as it had begun, it was over. The prettier girl had borne the indignity long enough. She pulled her wrist away from the boy's muttony hand, stood up, and fled across the deck with her giggling friend.

The boy waved them off with a brave face. He reached into his Speedos and scratched himself reassuringly.

'It's like a wildlife documentary,' Tristan remarked, a little unfeelingly.

At about thirty hours, this was to be the longest single voyage on our brief jaunt around the central Mediterranean. I remembered the P&O advertisement I'd hung above the television at home as a good-luck totem, and recalled its promise to passengers of a chance to share the ship with a variety of high-powered people ('journalists and politicians can often be found on board . . .').

I wasn't terribly interested in journalists or politicians, but I hoped an arms trader wasn't out of the question. At five o'clock or so, Tristan and I scoped the three bars and settled for the narrowest, darkest one. Already the barflies had separated themselves from the crowds of families, settling like silt at the bar. Perched on uncomfortable-looking stools, several men sat drinking alone, fidgeting with match wallets and snatching glances at one another in the mirror behind the liqueurs. A few of them nursed striped plastic shopping bags.

'Ah, the open sea,' Tristan sighed, lighting a smoke and settling himself on a banquette with his back to the porthole. 'It's working wonders. Have you noticed that I've only smoked one packet today? I can feel the sea air clearing out my head.'

Every day Tristan gave up smoking with the last cigarette of the night, and took it up again with the first cigarette of the morning.

We ate nuts out of greasy little packets and played Twenty Questions. Tristan strung me out to twenty-one questions as I groped through history for the mystery identity. It turned out to be Buzz Aldrin, which annoyed me. I pointed out to Tristan that Buzz Aldrin contravened the 'Three Musketeers Rule', which disallowed people who were part of a group of equally famous others – in this case the three crew members of *Apollo 11* – and whose ability to hide inside that group could cost the guesser several valuable guesses.

'I've never heard of that rule.' Tristan is a stickler for rules.

'It's standard Twenty Questions match play.'

'You just made that up.'

'I'm telling you,' I said, 'if you pulled a stunt like that in a Houston speakeasy, you'd be horribly beaten.'

This was quite crafty of me. Of course, I *had* just made it up. On the other hand, Tristan had, once, nearly been beaten up in a

Houston speakeasy and this reminder had unsettled him, as I had intended it to.

'What,' said Tristan, folding his arms, 'is the "Three Musketeers Rule"?'

'Think about it. Without the "Three Musketeers Rule", it's effectively a game of Eighteen Questions, isn't it? Because I might have narrowed it down to the Three Musketeers by question twenty, and, unjustly, am forced to lose because I'm forced to guess among them. Is it Athos? Porthos? Or whatshisname, the other bloody musketeer?'

'Aramis. Plus D'Artagnan. But you can't have fictional characters anyway.'

'It's just the name of the rule!'

Sadly, there was enough time before dinner for another round. Nothing, not even invented rules, could save me from Tristan's next gambit – Anne Frank – who cost me a humiliating twenty-eight questions. Somehow I got stuck after guessing she was a famous Northern European woman writer, dead, twentieth century, famous for one book, non-fiction. It's easy when you know it.

That cheered Tristan up enormously.

After a plateful of claggy pasta from the *bains-marie* of the ship's cafeteria, we climbed back up to the sun deck, now dark and emptied of visible signs of human life. We stretched out on the banana lounges glowing white against the scuffed AstroTurf decking, wedged our feet between the bars of the taffrail and gazed up at the sky. After a bit a deck hand appeared. He swept the poolside area with a stiff broom and gathered up fragments of shattered plastic cutlery, tipping them into a large garbage bag.

'Well, my boy,' Tristan announced, 'I think this is our first truly Conradian moment.' We gazed at the heavens above.

'Look at that sky,' I murmured.

'Yes,' Tristan sighed, 'at last, here we are, gazing *à la belle étoile*.'

Actually, we couldn't see the stars because of the thick scarf of brown engine smoke unfurling overhead, but I knew what he meant. It felt profoundly right to be lying with the vibrations of the deck at our backs, the timeless night sky above us and a paper bag of pistachio nuts on the deck between us. The tip of Tristan's cigarette flared red intermittently. I cracked the smaller, stubborn nuts between my back teeth and flicked the shells out into the ship's wake. I've always been irrationally terrified of the sea at night. I got a slight sense of vertigo watching the shells flutter in the light from the windows below, then drop away into darkness.

We had actually escaped the 'fast farcical furious real life of this roaring working world', as Jack Kerouac put it, somewhere in my backpack library. Not only were we heading away from the real world, but we were heading away *slowly*. This seemed to imply that when we had to come back, it would take a long time.

Tunis didn't look right from the start. The ferry eased into a wide, flat and unprepossessing modern harbour. The water, however, looked better than the bouillabaisse of Marseilles' harbour; here it was a murky jade colour.

On the evidence of a brisk trip through Tunis' outlying sub-urbs, there seemed to be little connection between the city and the commercial port. The city itself, which radiates out from its famous medina, felt thoroughly landlocked.

We settled in at a clean and cheap hotel. We showered. Tristan did some push-ups. Then we headed for Carthage.

To get there we had to take a sweaty local train to Carthage Hannibal, an exquisitely pretty station with red and lilac flowers and attractively tiled waiting areas. The whole suburb was white and blue. Several sharply dressed young Tunisian men hovered by BMWs in the shade of garden walls. Chauffeurs or assassins? It was certainly the right kind of area for a chauffeur; sloping sub-urban blocks in Mediterranean blue and white, draped with incan-descent bougainvillea and flowering trees and featuring Moorish carved doorways. Tristan waved at one of them. The man-child's scowl wavered for a bit, then he broke into a grin and returned the wave. 'The friendly assassin,' Tristan grinned.

The Cathedral of St Louis was hideous. It squatted at the top of

Byrsa Hill as if dropped from a great height to flatten the memory and spirit of the temple of Eschmoun, the Phoenician god of health and healing, which crowned the Carthaginian citadel two and a half thousand years ago. The whole site is now well beyond the healing powers of Eschmoun.

We stood next to a newly minted Roman column and took in the view. Below us lay the Byrsa Quarter ruins, the only Carthaginian remains substantial enough to be classed as ruins; beyond them, the postcard sweep of the Gulf of Tunis, flat and glazed in the afternoon sun. The sprawl of suburbs was neatly trimmed where they met the beach. Between 1560 and 1570, when the Barbary pirates were at their zenith, this bay would have been cluttered with the sails of the corsair fleet. It's not just history which is written by the victors; it's geography too. In Rome, which was sacked and burned several times after the Punic Wars, the classical bone structure can still be clearly seen beneath the accretion of more recent history and the riot of smog and building sites; in Carthage, ancient history has been obliterated. Thanks to the Romans, there remains no evidence that ancient Carthage ever existed. You get a much better view of ancient Carthage from Gustave Flaubert's description of dawn breaking over the peninsula in *Salammbo*:

> The conical roofs of the heptagonal temples, the stairs, terraces, ramparts, gradually took shape against the pale dawn; and all round the Carthaginian peninsula pulsed a girdle of white foam while the emerald-coloured sea seemed frozen in the cool of the morning. Then as the rosy sun spread wider, the tall houses tilted on the slopes of the ground grew taller and massed together like a flock of black goats coming down from the mountains. The empty streets lengthened out; palm-trees, rising out of the walls here and there, did not stir; the full water-tanks looked like silver shields abandoned in the courtyards, the lighthouse on the Hermaeum promontory began to grow pale.

More reconstructions of Carthage can be found in the National Museum behind the cathedral, among a staggering collection of amphorae and Roman-era mosaics. Best of all were delicate models of the Punic ports before the Romans got to them: they showed a high-walled, circular fort built out of wood, the Cothon, surrounded on the landward sides by massive wooden walls, which could provide shelter for 150 quinqueremes at a time. At its centre was an artificial islet which served as the headquarters of the Carthaginian admiral and his staff.

We walked down to the Punic Ports. These ancient rings of water, from which Carthaginian navigators had departed on voyages taking them all the way around Africa 2000 years before the Portuguese managed it, could have been irrigation dams on the bottom paddock at home in Mooropna. They were squalid little saltwater ponds, choked with reeds in which rubbish gathered. Scipio ordered his soldiers to fill them in when he razed Carthage in 146 BC, and the job they did lasted forever.

Several families were poking around in the reeds for shellfish, probably mussels. An old man tried to get us excited about the port, in his slow, rasping French, but Tristan wasn't interested in chatting, mostly because the old man had a barrow-load of scrap metal he was obviously hoping to sell us.

The wide world has never seemed more like a played-out goldmine, well past its boom days, than it did that afternoon. The fluorescent glare of the African sun killed off any possibility of imagining this place when it was the most important naval base in the Mediterranean. As I stood there, shading my eyes from the light, I thought of Bruce Williams' slide nights. The thing about the slides was that they showed Bruce to be utterly, transcendentally changed by travel. At home, Bruce seemed unusually urbane, but otherwise fairly normal. Not when he went away. In Bruce's slides, you could see his very person glowing in the halogen sunshine of Bali, his body turned into primary colours by the Kodak iridescence of Hawaii or Chile. Like Flaubert, Bruce understood the magical qualities of the light of dawn and dusk. The low slanting light of his pictures seemed to hint at adventures and wonders just out of the slide's frame, off in that bit of jungle there, or deeper inside that cave.

The train back to the medina provided another opportunity for Twenty Questions. I did the late Christopher Skase, the corrupt Australian businessman who fled from fraud charges. Tristan stumbled across it with a flukey question about criminal activity. He replied with the late, great West Indian fast bowler Malcolm Marshall, whom I only just caught with my twentieth question, having fumbled around for ages nailing his nationality.

At a station on the way back to central Tunis a passenger was arrested with minimum fuss and removed from the train. 'A stowaway I'll bet,' Tristan said, straight-faced. 'A wharf rat with drug interests all around the Mediterranean. From a long line of corrupt wharf rat types. Probably a murderer, too. Maybe you should talk to him.'

When you pack your suitcase for a place you only *hope* exists, you risk travelling the world and seeing nothing. You risk travelling badly. This is how location scouts for historical films must see the world, of course. They do this kind of thing all the time, trawling the globe for shapes, smells and angles of sunlight that exist only in the pages of books they've optioned. In effect, they audition the places they see for the role.

The great medina in Tunis is a treat for the senses of anyone with any imagination at all but it didn't get the part.

It should have seemed wonderful. It was a place where small-time con artists operated from 1000-year-old shops, where you could hear unrecognisable languages in each covered street and buy goods from all over the world. We found a quiet souq where we had a smoke and a coffee and watched the waiter preparing glowing slugs of tobacco on a small brazier for the water pipes the men were smoking all around us. Barbary pirates probably smoked their *chichas* in this very place. But it didn't help to know that. Our exchanges became increasingly terse. We were navigating using a French map.

'It's just miles and miles of tat, isn't it?' Tristan complained, disappointment taking its toll on our good humour along with the heat. 'It's all just *tat*. Why would you come to Tunis so that you can buy a plastic shark made in the Peoples' Republic of China?'

The shark was the only thing I liked.

At night we ate a perfunctory meal in a café that didn't serve beer. Our legs were exhausted. We stalked the city streets for another hour, hunting for a nautically themed bar. 'Preferably with maritime floor mosaics,' I said. 'Fish, triremes, that sort of thing.'

Tristan gave me a bitter smile. 'So Tunis is going to be a big chapter in your book, is it?'

'Somewhere in this town,' I said grimly, 'is the flavour of the sea. Somewhere here is a trace of the Barbary corsairs. We just haven't found it yet.'

'So are we looking for ancient sea dogs who want to share tales of hashish smuggling? Or just a bowl of convincing couscous à la marinara?'

He was clearly taking the piss now. 'If a bar has a ship's wheel stuck on the door,' Tristan continued, looking for the first time that day as if he were enjoying himself, 'does that count as nautical flavour?'

'Yes,' I said.

We returned to the hotel in heavy silence. Our footsteps echoed hollowly in the five-storey stairwell.

The next morning we bought ferry tickets to Trapani in Sicily. After strong espressos at Café Zem-zem, Tristan sent off another postcard to his friend and we took a taxi out to the ferry terminal. A youngish inspector rifled through our gear. It turned out that he had lived for a while in London. He and Tristan then began chatting about Chelsea's prospects in the premiership next season.

Our inspection tour of the *Flaminia* lasted about twenty-five seconds. All ferries feel a bit like airport departure lounges, but the *Flaminia* felt like an airport where all flights had been cancelled for the foreseeable future, where there was no catering and the toilets didn't work.

Most of the ship wasn't even open for our crossing to Trapani.

At one point, an Italian sailor shouted at a passenger who had unwittingly tracked a smear of human shit onto the lounge room carpet. The shit had floated out of a toilet which had backed up within minutes of leaving port. I hadn't noticed any odour because it was masked by a heady stink of diesel. The cafeteria opened for precisely fourteen minutes. We found enough lira in our pockets to pay for risible pasta and a salad of artichoke hearts.

Tunisian families had claimed the one lounge area begrudgingly opened by the management, so we passed the afternoon on the top deck, trying in vain to catch stray zephyrs that might have gotten lost out here. We didn't talk much. To pass the time I gave Tristan a riddle – as a fan of parlour games, Tristan loved riddles – but it was too hot for thinking, and he gave up after a few unsuccessful guesses. We lapsed into silence. A little later Tristan looked up from his *Hello* magazine with troubled eyes. He blinked a couple of times.

'What's the matter?' I asked. 'The artichoke hearts repeating on you?'

'Did you see what I think I just saw?'

I glanced around: a blank universe of sky, heat and baking metal. Nothing.

'Unless I'm very much mistaken,' he said, in a low voice, 'I think I've just seen our first ship rat.'

'Really?'

He pointed at a loosely wound fire hose at the far end of the deck. 'Over there. It's about a metre long.'

We gazed at the fire hose for a while, waiting for the rat to reappear. It was hard to imagine a rat that had fallen so far in the world that it was reduced to working the decks of the *Flaminia* for a living.

Thanks to Hans Zinsser's magnificent tome published in 1935 *Rats, Lice and History,* which I was hauling around in my backpack, I knew that Tristan's rat was almost certainly a black rat, *Rattus rattus.* This was the rodent which had given Europe the bubonic plague, typhus, horse flu and many other serious diseases after it arrived from Persia in the first few centuries AD. After a brilliant career of spreading disease and destroying crops and buildings, the black rat's reign ended with the arrival, around AD 1500, of the bigger and considerably more vicious brown rat. So successful was the new predator that the black rat found itself squeezed into the margins of the rodent world, reduced to scrapping a living on wharves and ships where it still enjoys a degree of success thanks to its superior talent for climbing. If the seaside is, as Jonathan Raban suggested, a last resort for the dregs of society, then it is also the place where the dregs of the rat world hang on for dear life.

No sign of the rat after ten minutes. 'I tell you, it was the size of a small alligator. Only furry. And with ears, you know, and a stringy tail.'

I believed him. 'Probably the first of many.'

Trapani's waterfront had the feel of a place that had been in steady decline for longer than anyone could remember and had become comfortable with it. Pirates used to operate out of this port in the sixteenth century; small-time crooks and chancers mostly, out-of-work fishermen scavenging a living on the edges of a sea ruled by the Barbary corsairs, dabbling in kidnapping, a bit of contract killing, maybe mounting the odd shore raid in small, undefended harbours. When we arrived there were a few fishing boats swinging gently on their anchors outside the harbour. Our ferry docked after manoeuvring around a half-sunk trawler. The Italian immigration people came aboard: young men all of them, with Dolce & Gabbana sunglasses perched on their chins and fleshy muscles straining through tight polyester shirts.

We bought a map from a silently staring man in a newsagent which specialised in porn and football magazines, and found our way to a hotel. From the outside, it looked like a villa suffering from psoriasis. Generations of paint were peeling away in plate-sized flakes. We pushed past the ten-foot-tall, heavy-bolted door, crossed a dark courtyard with a depressing, musty smell of rising damp and crumbling plaster, and scaled several flights of concrete stairs. At the top we found a family apartment which had been converted into a hotel at minimum expense. A woman with strong, meaty arms and what looked like a washcloth tied around her head showed us a large room with cool concrete floors, two prison beds and a shuttered window which over-looked a side street. In the alley below, boys were kicking a football and hawking spit onto the cobblestones.

Delighted to be off the ship and safely installed in a Sicilian hotel, our moods lifted at once. They improved even further with the addition of some Peroni beer and lots of pizza in an open-air restaurant on Piazza Saturno. We wandered around the old town for a while afterwards, trying to find a bar fitted out with some old pirate loot, where old sailors might get together to reminisce about days before the mast. We found nothing. Nightlife in town was strictly bring-your-own Vespa, or else was taking place behind the locked doors of mafia palazzi. So we walked to the end of the spit that hooks around the old town, Torre de Ligny, and perched on rocks at the breakwater.

In 241 BC, in the dark water beyond the breakwater floodlights, the new-look Roman navy defeated the Carthaginians in a terrible sea battle which pushed Hamilcar Barca's army out of Sicily for-ever. It was said that the strait was dyed red by the blood of the Carthaginian sailors.

But we didn't want to dampen our mood thinking about that. Instead, I coughed my way through a cigarette while Tristan com-piled fantasy cricket teams, drawing mostly on the cricketers we'd grown up watching in the 1970s. By the end of the night we had a Mustachioed XI, featuring a lot of cricketers from Ian Chappell's 'Ugly Australians' side and a Gravely Overweight XI, also featur-ing a disproportionate number of Australians (including legendary beer-lovers David Boon and Greg Ritchie), but captained by the great Pakistani stroke-maker Inzamam-ul-Haq. They were both formidable sides, which probably says a lot about cricket.

In the morning, breakfast took place in a shady lane in the old part of Trapani. The waiter was a man with a pronounced hump and loose flesh on his hips. His son, who was maybe twelve, had already begun to learn the old man's walk that he would have forever: a phlegmatic, seigneurial waddle. As he dawdled among the tables he sighed and squinted up at the narrow band of blue sky between the buildings. The croissants he delivered with a yawn were warm and filled with jam.

Suddenly pleased with everything, we loitered for about an hour and a half. There was nowhere for us to be. Sometimes just sitting in the sun drinking coffee feels like a religious vocation. This was one of those times. 'This is how it should be,' Tristan murmured. 'We're here and just about everyone else we know is working. Do you realise that?' I thought about it. It was a Sunday, but I knew what he meant. 'They're earning money,' I reminded him. Tristan smiled tolerantly. 'When you're an actor you learn to let go of all that stuff.'

Before we left, Tristan wrote another postcard to his 'friend'. Just thinking of his friend's reaction at receiving these postcards made him laugh to himself. All signs of heartbreak had now faded. This was great news, of course, but I had some misgivings, too. This trip had been planned as a hard-living study of the rough edges of the Mediterranean rim. That's what Tristan was there for: watching my back in grim dives run by shrewd mammas and playing dice with gunrunners in shady alleyways. Instead, we were trotting around in the spring sunshine like a couple of glad-hearted dowagers. If there was a way of looking at port towns without getting stuck on the tourist treadmill of pensioni and cute cafés, we hadn't found it. I had another sweet croissant while I thought about this.

We took the bus to Palermo, a lovely two-hour drive through the north-west corner of Sicily through a landscape of abandoned stone houses, orchards and eucalypts. I saw a couple kissing passionately next to a motorbike on the side of the highway, both in mirror sunglasses, both clasping helmets. The sun sparkled on the bike's chrome. They'd pulled off the road so that they could kiss properly, standing up, holding one another in their arms.

Gratifyingly, every rubbish bin in Palermo smelt like it was stuffed full of rotting flesh. Tristan didn't waste the opportunity to make a lot of bad-taste jokes about the Cosa Nostra and what they might have done with the rubbish collectors, who had clearly neglected their job for several weeks.

We were just skipping through on the way to Naples, so as we walked around, Tristan read aloud details of all the things we wouldn't have time to see. Sunday is never terribly lively in Catholic countries, but Palermo seemed to have stalled like an overheated hearse. We bought tickets for the night sailing to Naples; followed a flock of young nuns for a while; and backed out of a few sinister dead-end streets where unsmiling men smoked and leant against the doors of their trucks.

Just along from the container docks, where the cranes slumbered in the sun, there was a graveyard for fun park equipment. Among the junk we spotted defunct merry-go-rounds, slides, shooting galleries with their coloured globes smashed, a large, colourful fibreglass dwarf, a section of big dipper railing and a decapitated merry-go-round horse. We couldn't find its head. 'Some poor bastard probably woke up with it in his bed,' Tristan said grimly.

It didn't take us long to realise that we were in trouble on the ferry. Our cabin was on the lowest of nine decks. We jiggled open the door to our cabin, the lock of which was bent and scratched and had clearly been forced several times. We peered in. It was a two-decker coffin with hospital pillows.

'We're below the water line,' Tristan marvelled.

'We're below everything.'

Tristan put his palm against the far wall. 'We're next to the engine room.'

He was right. The thin walls were already shaking and the roar we could hear at that point was merely the sound of the engine idling. We took turns dumping our packs in the cabin, as there was only room for one of us in there at a time.

In a dull voice, Tristan said, 'Did you see those tanker trucks driving on? Those trucks are right above us. We are between the trucks and the deep blue sea.'

He slumped on the lower bunk, trying to fold his body into the tiny space allowed for it. Beneath the rumble of the engine, there was a strange squeaking sound. It may have been the sound of Tristan crying.

It wasn't just that we were in a room smaller than any cell in any prison in the world. It was that there were five very narrow staircases and a lot of corridor between us and the nearest lifeboat. If the boat sank from critical failure of the car deck doors we'd be on the seabed before we'd even managed to jemmy open the lock of our cabin door.

'What are you thinking about?' Tristan asked in a scared voice.

'Rats,' I fibbed, trying to be comforting.

Tristan flinched. 'I can't believe we're a lower priority than the trucks. I just can't get over that. If the floor gives way we'll be crushed.'

'That would be a blessing,' I pointed out. 'If we sink, not only will we have to swim vertically up five floors of stairs, past hundreds of other third class passengers, but we'll also have to swim through a layer of fire created by the burning fuel in the trucks.'

Tristan looked up at me with moist eyes.

From the sun deck we watched the lights coming on across Palermo. Palermo looked better from the water anyway, but after what we'd seen aboard the *Pride of Messina* it suddenly seemed like a vision of unearthly beauty; it beckoned like a city of gold beginning to gleam in the dusk. Tristan turned to me. 'Let's get off,' he said suddenly. But it was too late. The decks had begun to tremble as the engine strained to push us away from shore.

Around us the sun deck was swarming with family groups jealously guarding garden furniture tables and plastic plates and cutlery. We checked a deck plan riveted to the wall behind the purser's desk. It looked like a naval architect's humorous attempt to map

Dante's nine rings of hell. We could see one bar, two restaurants and a lump of dried chewing gum. We headed for the bar.

The bar was more of a passenger lounge with a kiosk attached. The carpet was a vile military grey designed to absorb stains. There were low racks of tubular chairs across which the more experienced passengers were proprietorially sprawled. Children screamed and kicked footballs among artificial potted plants.

Presiding over this grim scene was a massive Italian sailor who stood behind the cash point with a disgusted smile on his face. We paid and he sighed through his long, hairy nose before handing us a chit with which to purchase some beers at the bar. The beers were duly poured into plastic cups.

'Well cheers,' Tristan said. 'Are we having fun yet?'

The ship began to rock quite heavily around ten in the evening. We drank on, postponing the moment when we would have to descend into the ship's wretched bowels. Tristan killed the hours by trying to recall the details of as many ferry disasters as possible. It was truly a marvel how many nuggets of information about ferry sinkings Tristan had tucked away in his head. Biggest loss of life in a peacetime maritime accident? I didn't know. The Filipino ferry *Dona Paz*, which sank in 1987 with the loss of more than 4000 lives. He was also particularly well informed about the *Estonia* disaster.

We spent the night with our heads jammed up against the cardboard-thin walls separating us from the three-storey-high engine. At least I was finally experiencing a traditional Mediterranean ferry passage. Forty-five years after Jack Kerouac's ferry crossing from Africa to Marseilles, our own ferry had the same stale smell of vomit and diesel and a general sense of misery. Kerouac also had a cabin 'horribly placed next to the upsurging fires from the engine room'.

We were dried out from drinking horrible beer and from the horrendous temperature. Sleep only came in brief intervals. Each time I was near sleep, a fresh rivulet of fretful sweat would run down my forehead onto my cheeks. The tenor of the engine kept changing, as if it was about to give up altogether, or explode, or simply plunge through the bottom of the ship. Every person who went to the toilet left the door open, which swung on its hinges with the menacing creak of a derelict saloon door. At four o'clock in the morning, I dragged on my boots and climbed the stairs to the drinks machine on the main deck. Water helped. But by the time we got to Naples we never wanted to see a ferry again.

A BRIEF HISTORY OF SYPHILIS

We didn't arrive in Naples in a good mood to savour the joys that might be taken from the ferry port. We staggered off the ferry, grim and hungover. It was still cool at six-thirty in the morning, but the dawn sky was clear. Another fiercely hot day in the making. Before us lay an oil-stained concrete apron rigged with cranes, crossed intermittently by forklifts and lorries. It looked like the end of the world had happened overnight and now they were cleaning up.

Tristan had the map. He stared at it, his pert little backpack sagging for the first time on our trip. I tried to speak. I think I croaked something like, 'Here we are, in the home of spaghetti.' Tristan turned and gave me a terrible look, equal parts disgust and wonder. 'Don't,' he said, 'speak to me again until I've slept for twelve hours.'

Traffic was already snarling the small roads between us and downtown Naples. None of the hotels we'd picked out of the guidebook were answering their buzzers. We slumped in a café on Piazza Bovio, at the western end of Corso Umberto I. At the cashier's stand was an elegantly groomed woman in her mid-thirties. I tried to imagine how we must have looked to her: like stowaways, probably, or crumpled foreign tramps. When Tristan paid for our coffees, she was careful not to touch his hand. She shuddered with duchessy hauteur at the way he pronounced '*caffè*'.

We finally settled in a small hotel close to the Piazza Garibaldi. It wasn't exactly on the waterfront, but by then I was past caring.

Sometime around eight o'clock, Tristan returned from the bathroom and photographed me lying on the bed, with my cheeks jammed between the pages of the guidebook I had been using to plot out an ambitious schedule for the morning. We got very little done that day.

On paper, Naples is one of the Mediterranean's great port cities. It has an ancient harbour; it has a famously beautiful aspect on the Bay of Naples; it has a harrowing war record. Through its ancient harbour have come kings, knaves, soldiers and spies.

For British grandees, Naples was a crucial leg of the 'Grand Tour' in the eighteenth and nineteenth centuries. Once the excavations at Pompeii began in 1755 many travellers felt obliged, given the self-improving spirit of the Grand Tour enterprise, to inspect the ruins but mostly Naples was for pleasure, providing a chance to relax after the grinding didactic itineraries of Rome, Florence and Venice.

It took only a few hours wandering the city to realise that the sea and the hordes of tourists it continued to attract hadn't diluted the city's air of cheerful desperation. The high watermark of sin left by the sea on Naples' concrete waterfront had not been scrubbed away. When he was stationed here during World War II, travel writer Norman Lewis found himself marvelling at the resilience of the people. 'It is astonishing to witness the struggles of this city,' he wrote, 'so shattered, so starved, so deprived of all those things that justify a city's existence, to adapt itself to a collapse into conditions which must resemble life in the Dark Ages.' War, disaster, cholera and a long history of bad luck have meant that Naples has always been dingy. It still unmistakably is. Some of the people who visited two centuries ago were so dismayed by the poverty they saw that they took solace in its cut-rate pleasures of the flesh, which might explain why syphilis has such an outstanding track record there.

The first major outbreak of syphilis in Europe was recorded in Naples when the army of the French king Charles VIII invaded the city in 1495 and a particularly virulent form of the disease rapidly spread throughout the city and surrounding areas. The 'French' disease was much nastier then than it is now. The ulcerations resulting from pustular eruptions 'covered the body from the head to the knees,' noted Zinsser, in a *tour de force* passage. 'Crusts formed, and the sick presented so dreadful an appearance that even the lepers avoided them. Extensive losses of tissue in the nose, throat and mouth followed the skin manifestations, and in the train of these came painful swellings of the bones.' Pirates and sailors soon spread it around the entire Mediterranean basin.

When American troops landed at Anzio in 1944 and arrived in Naples shortly afterwards, they brought with them a new strain of syphilis so virulent that British intelligence decided to use it as a biological weapon of war. Norman Lewis described the plan, which, to the intelligence officers who came up with it, must have seemed brilliant in its simplicity. Take some extremely attractive Neapolitan prostitutes already infected with the exotic gonococci and drop them behind enemy lines where they could spread the infection among willing German victims, who'd been kept mercifully free of disease by strict controls over brothels and army hygiene. For their heroic service the women would be paid in gold coin, to be carried, army intelligence proposed, in the rectum. Not surprisingly, the prostitutes in question weren't keen, mostly because they knew the lira was worth even less in the north and once they crossed the line they wouldn't be able to get back. Their pimps paid off the relevant authorities and the plan was forgotten.

Neither of us felt inclined to explore history via a nasty case of syphilis. Instead, we took to the streets. I felt restored straight away. Partly it was the release of walking, partly the delight of being alive in a city which has dealt with so much death and destruction. Neapolitans seemed to have felt this way too. During the last war, the cemetery was the lovers' lane of the city. For many couples living with their families in cramped flats, it was the only place they could go to get some privacy. Some doctors cashed in on this cheerful accommodation between life and death, sin and church, and began specialising in replacement hymens.

Their services proved necessary if the graveyard sex was of a pre-marital kind and virginity was later required for marriage.

We headed back to the waterfront. I had unfinished business there. Naples was on my itinerary because this was the spot where, twenty years before us, travel writer and sailor Eric Newby had taken a long, unhappy look at the oil-spattered concrete on the docks and declared that ports were finished; dried up. In the Mediterranean, at least, the old culture of the sea had gone, he announced, and was barely a memory: 'What was obvious was that as far as being a place of interest to travellers . . . Naples, as a port, like Barcelona, Marseilles, Trieste, the Piraeus, Iskenderun, Beirut, Haifa, Alexandria, Tripoli, Tunis, Algiers and Tangiers, was finished.'

Perhaps modern globalism is the final insult to old-fashioned ports, by-passed by air travel and reduced to gross functionality by efficient, high-volume trade. Modern docks are unsightly and, being unsightly, are usually tucked out of sight on cheap industrial land. They seem tacked on to the backsides of cities which try to look the other way. Some, like London's, have drifted downstream from the city as though downwardly mobile, and have settled on the shores of estuaries where they can sprawl in all their functional ugliness.

Not in Naples. There you can stand on the spit of land occupied by the Castel dell'Ovo and take in the entire six-kilometre waterfront: to the east, giant bulk ships berthed at the commercial harbour, the ferry terminal and the yacht marina; to the west, the hydrofoil marina and small boat anchorage.

I wasn't going to argue with Newby. He's a man who knows his port culture. As a young man he crewed on one of the last sailing ships in the Australian grain trade, circumnavigating the globe in a square-rigged barque.

But the ferry terminal wasn't so dismal in bright daylight. The docks were a lively bunfight, not least between the smells vying for dominance in the air: rot, rubbish, strong perfume, almond pastries, petrol fumes and sun screen. We watched, fascinated, as the fast ferries from Capri arrived and disgorged their load of Italian high society. The *dolce vita* set stepped onto the asphalt in their gold lamé and Lycra glory, as if from the high-gloss pages of *OK!* magazine, blinking at the abrupt ugliness of the terminal and looking around irritably for paparazzi.

Around us, dock workers strode around shouting and laughing; drivers honked constantly and made elaborate and rude-looking gestures to one another. It was clearly no accident that the first ethnographic study of gesture was written about Naples. Nearly two hundred years ago the classicist Andrea de Jorio published his *Gesture in Naples and Gesture in Classical Antiquity*, a work which carefully catalogued Neapolitans' hand signals for a particularly Italian range of meanings, including lust, scorn, cuckoldry, rage, love and money. I'd never seen a copy, but we didn't need an ethnographer to interpret the finger flipped in our direction every time we got caught in a seizure of mad traffic, which was often.

Circling back towards our hotel we passed quickly through the squalid alleyways of the Quartiere Spagnoli, stepping over the burnt-out corpses of at least four different Vespas, and hurrying away from the more obvious hustlers and pick-pockets. We found a cinema which seemed to be entirely devoted to the output of Italian porno star and director Rocco Siffredi. One film poster appeared to show three actresses beaming at the camera through dribbles of semen. The less sordid reality loitered at street level. A couple of matronly women sitting in shaded doorways opposite called out to us as we made a couple of amazed turns past the cinema. One of them had taken practical steps to overcome the language barrier between her and potential clients: she sat on her stoop with a handwritten price list resting between her thighs.

We ate dinner that night at a place whose dining room consisted of a dismal lane behind a building site. Before dinner Tristan had written another postcard to his 'friend', who now had a name – Emily – and was in high spirits again, smoking like a funeral pyre and ordering up a feast. 'I like it here,' he said expansively. 'Naples, I mean. It has an earthy feel.' He paused, a flap of pizza halfway to his mouth. 'A dirty, slightly slutty, anything-goes kind of feel. And it has Italian food. I think this is your city, old fruit.'

He was optimistic about our chances of picking up a yacht trip from the marina further along the waterfront. I wasn't. I knew a South African woman who had gotten work for a couple of seasons on an Italian charter yacht. Tall, beautiful and smart, she had at least two advantages on me, but I think a third – the fact that she was prepared to wear a tiny pair of white shorts while she served food and scrubbed out the head – was the decider.

'I see you in that role,' I told Tristan. 'Let's put that beefcake to work.'

'But what about you?'

'What if we said that I was your pimp? That way the captain wouldn't take too many liberties with you.'

Tristan chewed thoughtfully. 'Why don't we say that you have tuberculosis? You're a writer; writers have tuberculosis. That way, they'd know you weren't going to eat anything.'

'Do I look like I've got tuberculosis?'

Tristan dug a caper out from between his front teeth. 'No,' he said after a moment. 'But you do look a bit like Greg Ritchie.'

The next morning we headed for the yacht marina. We dodged traffic on the Via Francesco Caracciolo and crossed a desolate strip of underfunded park. A big top-heavy man sat smoking and staring at a burst soccer ball bladder lying on the ground while another man sewed ink into his back with a portable tattoo needle. The man's shoulders were already swarming with mermaids and swords. The new one looked like a Pokémon. A moist breeze stirred chocolate bar wrappings in the grass. There was a fun park here too, just like the one in Palermo, except that this one was nominally functional. A man sat very still in a ticket booth next to a merry-go-round, which scraped on its concrete mounting with each rotation. He may have been asleep. Or dead.

During the last war, professional storytellers, the *cantastorie*, would set up in these gardens, their canvas backdrops painted with bloody scenes from the crusades, and recite in verse the glorious deeds of Charlemagne and the paladins to rapt audiences. The *cantastorie* concertinaed history according to the tastes of their audience, which cared nothing for more recent kings or conquests or revolutions. I liked to think that the shows were halfway between Homer and Bruce's deft handling of the slide projector at home; stories whose sails were filled with the great spirit of exaggeration and whimsy blowing off the bay.

We lingered hopefully by the yacht club. Bosomy men with bellies the colour of medium-rare steak hosed down their power-boats. Someone was playing 'La Macarena' on a boom box some-where. There were some more elegant yachts tethered to the marina further around, but the gate to the jetty was locked. Searching for a notice board of some kind, we entered the yacht club where a stubby, squinty little man in floral boardshorts pursed his lips at us, closed his eyes and waggled a forefinger. *'Privé!'* I thought he said. So we left and perched for a while on the sharply edged boulders on the harbour wall.

Gradually we realised that we had stumbled across Naples' gay beat – there were some couples, but mostly thin, tanned boys with abs that could have been stapled on, draped like Caravaggio rent boys across the steaming rocks. One or two looked quite interested in Tristan. 'Maybe some of these guys own boats,' I whispered.

'I doubt it. Not enough gold jewellery.'

He was right. It was a long shot anyway. 'Looks like it's going to be a ferry to Sardinia.'

'To be honest, I don't think I was really prepared to do the nec-essary anyway.'

We climbed up the Vómero hill through a series of cool stone lanes lined with tall and narrow stone houses. Afternoon sun lit the tops of the brick houses above us where shadows of stockings and singlets lay pegged to the bright walls.

We sat on the walls of the Carthusian monastery, the Certosa di San Martino, and let the view soak in. The city lay below us like a wave of delicate stone that had flooded in from the sea and calci-fied between us, the slopes of Vesuvius in the distance and the curve of the bay. The bay had turned a soft, hazy blue mottled here and there by patches of deeper water. I thought of the Chilean poet Pablo Neruda who spent a few months on Capri in 1951 and who recalled his time on the Amalfi coast as a period of bliss, long days 'perfumed by the Mediterranean onion'. I thought I was beginning to understand what he meant. It was very pleasant just to sit on the warm stone walls with the sun on our backs and look.

We both woke in foul moods. We managed to get up, shower, breakfast, pay for our room and get aboard a train to Civitavecchia without saying a word to one another. In Civitavecchia we had several hours to wait before our ferry arrived to whisk us over to Golfo Aranci in the north-east corner of Sardinia.

Tristan regarded the main strip sourly, then laid himself out under a palm tree. 'I am going to sleep here until our ferry leaves,' he told me calmly. 'I do not wish to be woken up. Because while I am sleeping, I am going to have an idea for a board game which will make me very, *very* rich.'

It was hard to put a finger on what was so awful about Civitavecchia. There was another bare-bones fun park above the beach, but it looked like all the fun had rusted out of it years ago. I spent the afternoon using the McDonald's toilets, keeping an eye on Tristan's recumbent form, and avoiding the unfriendly stares of some guys who were nominally doing roadworks on a kerb, but were mostly whistling at sweaty female backpackers and throwing a Frisbee for their yapping dog.

There were no bars aboard our ferry, just kiosks selling bitter doses of coffee in paper thimbles. Our games of Twenty Questions had been growing rancorous lately, so Tristan pulled out his cards instead and beat me soundly at a game of Spite and Malice.

We arrived in Golfo Aranci at nine o'clock that night. A man selling lotto tickets to passengers informed us that there was no bus running that night to Olbia, the largest town nearby and our destination, which lay about fifteen kilometres away by road. Its lights were tantalisingly visible across the bay from Golfo Aranci itself.

Tristan's afternoon nap under Civitavecchia's shadiest palm tree had worked wonders on his mood. Radiantly chipper now, he led me down the main street of our Bethlehem, past a boarded-up hotel and a deserted railway station. 'This is going to be brilliant,' he enthused, peering into closed-looking restaurant windows. 'I've got a great feeling about this. How many people do you know who have spent the night in Golfo Aranci?'

'None.'

But he wasn't listening to me. 'This is so . . . *excellent*.'

To my surprise, we found a little hotel that was open, clean and even had a room we could use. Tristan quickly closed a deal on the room with the proprietor, a friendly woman in pantsuit and pearls who would have given it to us for nothing by the time Tristan had finished with her. Travelling with Tristan was like that. It was like walking alongside a ripple in the crowd. In the streets, people of both sexes would stare at him in surprise, then their eyes would flicker away from him to make sure that they weren't missing out on anything in my direction. Reassured, their eyes returned to dwell with expressions of envy, desire and resentment on Tristan, and especially his torso which looked as if it was carved out of a flawless slab of caramel toffee by an incorrigible liar.

We strolled down to the water at the end of the street and followed the shore around. No-one had seriously applied themselves to developing the beach at Golfo Aranci; some of it seemed to belong to the large houses that backed onto it; other parts looked like they might have been the province of a weekend sailing club. It looked like a pleasant little fishing town that doubled as a low-rent seaside spot for people who couldn't afford summer in a place with a proper beach. It probably scraped a living out of things that fell off trucks coming in and out on the ferry. Further around was a cosy marina sheltering several smallish fishing boats.

That night in the town's only open restaurant I was struck by the familiar feeling that the closest I'd come to the elusive port ambience I sought was when I was eating and drinking in places like this, seafood restaurants overlooking black water; the smell of deep fried fish; rustic timbers in the ceiling and floor; and a salty breeze negligently blowing through an open window.

Tristan must have noticed my eyes misting over. 'The calamari a bit rough, is it?'

51

'No. Just getting a little sentimental, I guess.'

Tristan refilled my glass. 'Let it out, old cheese.'

'I was just thinking that this is about as close as I'm going to get to what I'm looking for, isn't it? I mean look at that model.' I pointed to a beautifully made three-masted barque on the mantelpiece, tacking across a steady gale of cigarette smoke from the next table. 'There's the spirit of the trip, my friend, that's the world of ports. That's it. That's what's left.'

Tristan took a deep draught of beer. He looked like he was about to say something, then thought the better of it and took another swig instead. 'I sense disappointment here. I get the feeling that you wish you'd gone somewhere else. But I also feel that this is probably the beer talking.'

I sensed Massawa and my helplessly unspecific goal drifting away from me here in the Mediterranean. Now and again I tried to revive the spirit of our quest. From one of the books Tristan refused to carry, I had read out that afternoon a description of a Hogarthian scene of slough and wickedness observed by Charles Andersson on the southern Atlantic island of Ichaboe during the height of the guano rush there in 1861:

> The scenes of drunkenness and debauchery would have disgraced the lowest house of vice. Spirits in much greater quantity than were allowed by the regulations were issued to the men, with the connivance of the mates, though not with that of the masters, and bacchanalian orgies were held in the encampment abominable beyond belief, which would call up a blush on the face of the most abandoned.

Tristan bore all this with grace. If he privately wondered what it was I thought I could contribute to an orgy, he didn't say so. 'Are you going to this place?'

'Ichaboe? Of course not. But if I end up taking the Dutch freighter to Cape Town, we'll probably sail within about 400 kilometres of it.'

'Close,' Tristan said kindly.

After dinner we sat on the tiny fishing pier. The pebbled concrete was still warm. 'Piers,' wrote John Betjeman, 'provide a walk on the sea without the disadvantage of seasickness and are havens of fresh air and freedom.' After dark, they also let you perch above the mystery of night water without any risk of falling in.

There was only a wedge of moon out, but the water was as still as a fish pond, and so clear that we could make out a tyre and a barnacled sewing machine lying on the bottom. Further down the pier, a couple of guys were fishing with glowing lures, jerking them through the water like flowing sparks. A swarm of translucent whitebait pulsed in the water below us.

'Give me another riddle,' Tristan said. So I gave him the one about the dwarf who comes home, goes inside, picks up a stick and realises that he might as well kill himself.

We had no luck, but plenty of tasty dinners and strong drinks in the pretty fishing ports of Sardinia. Wandering along the waterfront at Alghero, I was struck again by the restlessness of ports. Something about their impermanence and the wideness of the sea was an invitation to keep going. The temptation to jump onto a ferry to somewhere else, to anywhere else, could be overwhelming. Some days we moved on to the next place simply because we were able to do so. Most of the ferry terminals had all the charm of a Greyhound bus depot, but the ferries themselves seemed to point out into the flat blue sea of the Mediterranean summer with infinite promise.

We saw no sea dogs or wharf rats. In Santa Teresa di Gallura, on the northern tip of Sardinia, we got talking to a couple of American girls backpacking their way towards Greece. They fell about laughing when we introduced ourselves. 'Tristan and – what? – *Thor*-don? You're kidding, right?'

Still, we had something in common: they too had experienced the horrors of the *Pride of Messina*. They then asked what my book was going to be about and I tried to explain how I was travelling between ports, searching for traces of a port culture; romance, stories.

'Have you found it?' This was the quieter, dark-haired one with intense eyes. Her friend, who was wearing a lot of make-up, was much more outgoing and much drunker, and had attached herself to Tristan, who was trying to watch the Euro 2000 semi-final on a television behind her head.

'I don't think so,' I said.

'You need to get on a cruise ship for romance,' she advised me and proceeded to tell me a story about seducing Filipino deck hands on the *QEII*. 'My friend and I got drunk and we picked up a couple of guys and invited them back to her cabin for a drink. Then she and her guy started going at it, right there in front of us. It was real embarrassing, but I couldn't leave because she had the key to my cabin in her pocket. It was like – "Ah, excuse me, Julie? Do you think I can have my key?" She was so drunk she didn't even hear.'

She stopped abruptly. She seemed to be waiting for me to comment.

'Gee,' I said.

'Anyway, it was a big mistake. Usually the crew aren't even allowed on the same deck as you, they really keep their distance. But after that we got pestered every day by these guys who had heard we were up for it.' She grinned. 'That's a story for your book.'

'Thanks.'

'No problem.' She glanced casually at Tristan. 'Is your friend with someone?'

It was time to get further east.

In the morning we took the ferry to Bonifacio, in Corsica, then made our way overland to Ajaccio, where we found a cheap room in a 150-year-old hotel run by a man who claimed to be the last in a long and proud dynasty of hoteliers to have run the place. Why the last? Because his son was a television journalist and his daughter was a dentist. 'I have been too successful a parent!' When he laughed, his eyes disappeared. His body radiated an historic imprint of body odour. The only people who lived there seemed to be him and his dog, Horloge, who was black, slobbery and massive. Later in the night, when Tristan tried to get behind the rococo reception/bar area for a photograph, the dog growled a warning from behind a curtain of moth-eaten brocade. 'Ah,' Tristan muttered, backing away on tiptoe, ' I zeenk he is an alarm-*Horloge*.'

Our room had a ceiling scene of two fairly ugly *putti*, and wooden shutters which opened onto a pebble-mix balcony and a view of Cours Napoléon below.

After dinner, we wandered down to the marina. We walked around to the yacht jetty and joined a small crowd of people staring at three superyachts conspicuously moored closest to the promenade. Each one was at least thirty metres long, with deep, curved haunches, millions of dollars worth of polished teak and high-tech sonar. On one, a young couple was dining self-consciously on the deck right above the marina. They were being served by a tall, rippling man with no shirt and a glossy ponytail. The crowd hung on every mouthful like it was a Punch and Judy show.

'Dot.com millionaires,' someone murmured.

'Porn stars,' said someone else.

Further around the pier there was a marina for humbler craft. We sat at the end of a jetty. We could hear the murmur of a television on one of the yachts, and the slap of the water on fibreglass hulls.

We sparked up cigarettes. 'My last one,' Tristan promised. We decided to spend our last few Tunisian coins buying some good luck off Neptune. We tossed them into the water one by one, toasting the sea, us, the seaworthiness of the ships we'd been on, the seaworthiness of all the ships ahead of me and the possibility that Tristan might soon land a lead role in a Hollywood blockbuster.

Massawa felt a long way away. I needed a way in. I needed to arrive in each port with a group of people who understood them: I needed to get on a ship where I could meet the sailors. I needed my first cargo ship.

This was our last port together; Tristan was heading back to London the next day and I was heading to Venice via Genoa.

VENICE FACES EAST

I travelled to Venice by train. Ada's instructions had come through. In Venice I would board the *Anneke Schliemann*, a Luxembourg-flagged container ship en route to the Levant.

We shunted out of Mestre station, the last stop before Venice, at walking-pace. I was sharing a compartment with a group of noisy young soldiers. They asked my permission to smoke. I mimed that no, I didn't want a cigarette, then changed my mind and tried to mime that actually, now you mention it, I think I might have one after all. But the soldiers suddenly stopped laughing and stared at something through the window behind me.

Three men in fluorescent work vests and sunglasses were standing between the rails of the next track. One was wiping his forehead with a blue handkerchief. Another was talking on a mobile phone. Nothing more for a hundred metres or so. Then we passed a man kneeling down between the rails, pointing a big, businesslike camera at something further up the line. About twenty metres further on we saw what the something was: a corpse wedged between the rails. There was no head, no limbs, just the pornographically inert remains of a body trimmed back to the torso by the wheels of a train. The severed joints were going black in the afternoon sun. The whole scene was surreally matter-of-fact. We continued on at the same funereal pace. Soon we passed the train, which had finally ground to a halt a few hundred metres further on. Passengers were leaning out of their carriage windows, straining to see. There was nothing to say, so I sat in silence with the soldiers, listening to the clack-clack of the carriage couplings all the way into Venice.

My tiny room at a hotel in Dorsoduro conformed to the mean proportions of maritime architecture that I was anticipating aboard the *Anneke Schliemann*. It was a crummy hotel because it could afford to be. There was a grumpy breakfast waitress and woodchip bread. The morning coffee, which is obligatory, was purgatorial and had unpleasant lumps.

But none of this bothered me. My ship was due in three days time and for the first time in my life, I was truly waiting for my ship to come in.

For me, the miracle of Venice was that its charm was impervious to the usually deflating experience of finding yourself in a place that would forever after exist only in reality and no longer in the form of an idyllic vision. I had been to Venice several times before, but nothing I remembered about it prepared me for the happy shock of coming back. Venice was on the way out, of course. Most of it had been for centuries. It could barely keep its cobblestones above the grimy turquoise of the lagoon. It smelt like old vase water. But beneath the crushing weight of tour groups and the laminated multilingual menus, there was still a living city, where European polyglots did business in luxury goods and people pegged their washing on lines strung up between thousand-year-old terracotta eaves. And there was always the sea.

It started raining in the afternoon. Heavy raindrops plopped into the canals. That night I roamed through the dripping alleys, trying not to get too wet or too lost, savouring the packed maze of stone and water, hoping to stumble across somewhere to eat. I eventually settled on a cheap pizza place somewhere in Dorsoduro. As I chewed, I reread Jonathan Keates' *Italian Journeys*, a neglected gem of modern travel writing, which contained in just a few chapters the most intimate foreigner's account of Venice I'd read. I managed to get some strings of mozzarella on the pages.

Keates made me nervous. As Jan Morris noted in her classic work on this city, more slush and 'ecstatic maiden prose' has been written about Venice than any other place on earth. I was reluctant to add to it.

Instead, I practised my smoking technique. The sailors on my ship would be smokers, I knew; smokers prefer talking to other smokers and nothing melts the ice between strangers like the complicity of sharing a cigarette. I needed to be ready so that I wouldn't cough and splutter like a fraud over my first Marlboro on board.

Smoking helped me feel less noticeable on my own. I've always felt watched in Venice; I think most travellers do. Everyone seems to be looking at everyone else to see how they're coping with the faintly sinister loveliness of it all. You can see in their faces how disappointed some travellers are with Venice. They're scandalised by the whorish tourist trade, the way that hoteliers shamelessly hike tariffs to the very limit of what holiday-makers can afford to pay for their dream; they hate the way the city feels like a high-pressure system of profiteering which radiates outwards in steadily decreasing degrees of extortion from its epicentre in Piazza San Marco. Mostly they're experiencing pangs of misanthropy brought on by the shock of finding so many others just like themselves crowding their view of the past.

I set about finding Venice's sea-facing heart. I began by calling the shipping agents to check on the progress of the *Anneke Schliemann*. The agent I spoke to was clearly a direct ancestor of the tough-talking traders who'd built Venice out of plunder and profit. He was nonplussed by my suggestion that I come down to his office on the waterfront and 'look around'.

'Why?' he asked, without any attempt at politeness.

'Just to get a feel for the kind of work you do there. Chat to some guys on the, ah, waterfront.'

He seemed to sigh; I heard a palm muffle his receiver, then some rapid talk in the background. '*Parla italiano?* Can you speak Italian?' he asked, returning to the phone.

'Er, *un poco*,' I said.

'What?'

'No,' I admitted.

'Then it's not much use. But come if you want. *Arrivederci*.'

That's the problem with fanciful quests. Their magic evaporates in the rude daylight of people going about their business.

I headed to Piazza San Marco, a place I usually avoided because I despise pigeons. I only ever fantasise about firearms when I'm among pigeons. All of Venice made Charlie Chaplin fantasise about guns: he once declared that he would like to blast the figures off the roof of the Biblioteca Marciana opposite the basilica with a shotgun. Presumably just for the heck of it.

The buildings lining the piazza were always a bit of a surprise; a surprise that they were still there after a century of trippers had soaked their façades onto hundreds of miles of film. With characteristic, bloody-minded inventiveness Mark Twain described Basilica di San Marco as an insect: 'Propped on its long row of low thick-legged columns, its back knobbed with domes, it seemed like a vast warty bug taking a meditative walk.' A scarab beetle, maybe. I was struck again by how oriental it looked: a Catholic cathedral that looks like 'an eastern caravanserai', as Jan Morris put it. And next to it, the Palazzo Ducale or Doge's Palace, which looked like it might have been spirited there by a genie from Cairo or Damascus. It's easy to forget that Venice has always faced east, and how far east its merchants were looking. From the early Middle Ages, Venice made the most of a monopoly on trade with the Orient. Goods came from as far away as China, the long trail of customs duties and mark-ups compounding their value the closer they got to the final bottleneck into Europe. In 1501, the Venetian banker Girolami Priuli estimated that an item bought in Calicut in southern India for a ducat would cost sixty to a hundred times as much by the time it had reached Venice via the Red Sea route.

I was heading east, too. From Venice the *Anneke Schliemann* was sailing south to Ravenna and onto the container terminal of Gioia Tauro on the Calabrian coast; then to Piraeus in Greece; and finally onto the Levantine seaboard: Lattakia and Tartus in Syria; Beirut – Venice's medieval gateway to the great hub of Damascus; Mersin, in Turkey, then Alexandria. It couldn't have been better.

In the afternoon, I bought a copy of Italo Calvino's *Invisible Cities* from an African street trader. Books weren't all he was selling, he told me brightly. He flipped up a corner of his grimy rug to reveal a blur of tartan skirts, lipstick and pink and white flesh. He also had Hungarian pornography. The best there was, so he said. I should take my time, have a look.

What is it with me? Drug dealers never offer me heroin, because, I assume, I'm not thin or gaunt enough. I am, however, occasionally offered Rohipnol, the date-rape drug, presumably because I look like the kind of guy who could find a use for it. Now I was being invited to peruse a dog-eared copy of *Naughty Schoolgirls*.

I stuck with Calvino. His book was a series of fables about travellers' cities: cities lost, found, rediscovered, longed-for. All of them were, ultimately, Calvino's own Venice.

> Kublai Khan does not necessarily believe every-thing Marco Polo says when he describes the cities visited on his expeditions, but the emperor of the Tartars does continue listening to the young Venetian with greater attention and curiosity than he shows any other messenger or explorer of his.

Stories told in ports are less reliable than other stories. That's just the way ports are. Venice in particular, with its atavistic fogs and sinuous narratives of lanes and bridges, is a city that lends itself to fabulous yarns. You could see why Kublai Khan might have refused to believe the tales he heard about this place.

The next morning was sticky and hot. I spent most of it inside, trying to trace Venice's days as Europe's wealthiest seaport in galleries and on chapel walls. There must be acres of painted water hanging on the walls of Venice. It's always there: in the backgrounds of saints' pilgrimages, in heroic homecomings and historical events. In a few pictures, usually the ones in which people are shown swimming in the canals, the water is rendered in a euphemistic shade of pellucid topaz, more like diaphanous silk than water; but in most, the centuries have faded Venice's waterways to the colour of split-pea soup. Time has worked on the actual water in a neat parallel of ageing: the lagoon and canals have accumulated grime of their own until they too have taken on the same colour of unrestored mucky green. Finally, after many centuries, the paintings and the reality match.

That night after dinner, I loitered in the hotel courtyard for a while, putting off the moment when I would have to return to my coffin-like room on the third floor. I idled away the time with smoking practice. I had no talent for it. No matter which way the breeze was blowing, the smoke always got in my eyes.

After a while I heard someone hollering hello as they passed the hotel's reception desk and I listened to them stomping up the stairs to the courtyard. It was a man in his mid-thirties, with a dense thatch of reddish curls and a big, friendly face. He was strapped into a complicated pack that would have sufficed for an assault on Everest. He grinned at me, unbuckled his pack and sat himself at the next table. He sighed and gazed up at the stars.

Eventually he said in an attractive Midwestern drawl, 'Smoking will kill you, you know.'

He grinned at me, revealing a rack of splendid teeth that barely fitted into his head: the giveaway dentition of the middle-class American.

I soon learned that Joshua was a plumber from Montana. He was the second of seventeen siblings. For his trip around the world, Joshua had saved US$33,000. He had been travelling for five months already and had only spent $6000. He loved Venice. The best thing about Venice, he informed me, was the religious paintings.

'Which ones?' I asked.

'You know. The ones with the Virgin and the baby Jesus.'

Just then a vicious fight broke out in one of the rooms on the third floor above us. We listened while two people tore away at each other at an unembarrassed volume, shrieking accusations and competing to see who hated the other one more. A couple of staff members emerged from the kitchen, sleepily shaking their heads and apologising for the ruckus. Apparently the fighting couple came every year and the fighting got worse and worse each time. Someone headed up the stairs to pound on their door with a broom. The people in the room screamed at him to fuck off.

Over the next few days, Joshua and I spent quite a bit of time together. Joshua was a kind soul on a voyage of self-discovery. He was interested in getting out of the plumbing game. He was planning to write a book about humour. He'd already begun to take notes. He showed me a notebook in which he had faithfully transcribed various jokes he'd heard in youth hostels in France and Italy. 'I met some very funny people, Thordon. I been real lucky.' Whenever I attempted a throwaway joke, he'd stop right there in the middle of whatever bridge we happened to be crossing. 'Wait up a second,' he'd say. 'I want to write that down.' And he did. As he took my dictation he nodded like a connoisseur at the ludic architecture of my quip, savouring the miracle of comedy. 'Because laughter,' he said often, 'is a kind of blessing.' He frequently spoke like that, usually after accusing stallholders in the vegetable market of trying to cheat him over the weight of the fruit he bought each day to keep regular. 'You know,' he'd tell me, peeling a discounted orange with his thick plumber's thumb, 'you have a very dry sense of humour. Very dry.'

The next day I mooched along the edge of the lagoon north of Piazza San Marco. In the Museo Storico Navale I admired a nineteenth-century model of a Venetian trireme in which every single oarsman had his own distinctive walrus moustache. By the time of the Battle of Lepanto, in 1571, oarsmen for the republic's galleys were in short supply and were being recruited from as far away as Bohemia, so I guess casting your crew from a Victorian penny dreadful is as plausible as anything else. They peered anxiously out to sea.

The museum was full of models, all of them immaculately fitted out. I paused for a while in the room devoted to the development of Italian ocean liners. The designs clearly demonstrated how liners evolved over the twentieth century to cater for the transition from function to pleasure. This change could be measured in the number of swimming pools designers managed to squeeze onto the decks. The pools stretched out and multiplied as the century wore on, like tropical blue plants dilating in the sunshine.

Now hardly anyone travels to or from Venice by liner, though ferries still track up and down the Adriatic and cruise ships still call in summer. I could only imagine a time, in *la dolce vita* of Italy's post-war heyday, when people crowded the docks to wave off their friends and relatives, or, arriving, searched the faces of the crowd on the shore for a loved one.

I left the café, ducked inland and lost myself in the narrow *calle* of Castello. I listened to my footsteps echo off the stone walls. Someone's shutters rattled closed in the next street. The sunnier it got, the more intense was the moody chiaroscuro effect of Venice's shadows. Behind me a pigeon beat its wings making a noise like someone shaking out their newspaper. I stood on greasy cobblestones right at the edge of a narrow canal and watched the wavelets lap at the sides. During the blackout in World War II, 200 Venetians stumbled into these canals and drowned. It must have been a very black blackout.

After a couple of days, Joshua began to wonder out loud why he was still in Venice. He was finding it expensive. He thought the waiters were sneering. He was looking forward to moving on to Vienna. He had direction. Did I? He thought that perhaps I was a little directionless.

'I'm not,' I assured him. 'I'm writing a book about ports.'

'Why?'

'Because they're interesting.'

'Mmm.' His powerful teeth crunched into an apple. 'So what are you doing here?'

'Well, Venice is a port city.'

Joshua blinked.

'And my book's about, you know, what's left of port culture in today's globalised world. The cities, the sailors, wharfies, sea dogs . . .'

He nodded, squinting in the sharp sunlight. 'I've got a dog.'

I couldn't help reflecting that when some people came to Venice they met Italian duchesses, or architecture students from Santiago, or murderous professors, or retired train robbers. They met Byron, or, if they were unlucky, Tom Ripley. They had fascinating conversations in Harry's Bar. They stole moments of lovemaking under the tarpaulins of gondolas that knocked gently on wooden posts in the lagoon. Me? I had come to Venice and met Joshua.

Finally, three days after I expected it, the shipping agents called me at my hotel and instructed me to make my way to their offices at the Venice ferry terminal where they would arrange my transport to Porto Marghera. Joshua shook my hand firmly and wished me well. My last glimpse of Joshua was as he walked across the Campo San Pantalon, guffawing at some feeble joke I'd made days before.

I humped my pack for two hours. I became horribly lost in Venice's greyest, most colonic streets, herded by backwards signs into cul de sacs and up unnecessary stairs where I found my way blocked by barbed-wire fences. It had to be thirty degrees in the shade. I asked every police officer I saw where the agents' offices were; like riddling sphinxes each officer was more polite and friendly than the last, and each one gave me directions exactly opposite to what the last one had said. After an hour or so, my spine was numb. The weight of the books I was carrying in my pack dug into my shoulders. My arms were shaking so much I could hardly fit the coin in the slot of the phone booth at the Stazione Marittima. My agent was on the phone to someone else; I'd have to call back.

I slumped against the wall of a concrete warehouse, my legs splayed out in front of me. When some blood found its way back into my head, my eyes began to work again. I saw that I was alone on the dock. A huge ferry was tied alongside. I saw rows of orange lifeboats strung along the railing of its upper deck. Passengers crowded the railing. Some of them seemed to be pointing at me. I squinted, my eyes slowly focused, and I saw that they were, in fact, laughing at me.

I wanted to hide. I wanted to take my shamefully bad sense of direction and throw it in the sea along with the rest of my miserable life. But the water was at least twenty metres away. I'd never make it. As I lay like a dying tortoise on my pack, the people on the ferry began waving at me. *Waving*. I couldn't believe it. After a few moments, in which I'd conspicuously failed to wave back, one of them gave me the finger.

I staggered back up to the immigration hall and pushed a few coins into the telephone. This time I got a different guy at the agency who insisted that I call the agent responsible for my ship. It was a mobile number. I wrote it on a polystyrene cup which contained a cigarette butt floating in coffee dregs. When I finally got through to the mobile phone, the man on the other end seemed irritable. What did I think I was doing? Didn't I realise that my ship might have gone without me?

'What should I do?' I howled.

'Where are you?'

I told him. He swore. 'You must take a taxi.'

'But there aren't any taxis here!'

'Then you must walk up to Piazzale Roma. It is not far. Hurry!'

A couple of hours later, after I'd been rescued by a young priest who kindly pointed me in the right direction, I arrived at my first living, breathing commercial port: Porto Marghera.

I'd been anticipating this moment for a long time. In my mind I heard the voice of the young narrator in *Treasure Island*: the 'great multitude of ships and all sizes and rigs and nations . . . old sailors with rings in their ears, and whiskers curled in ringlets, and tarry pigtails . . .' This inner voice faded, rudely drowned out by the bleep-bleep of a truck reversing.

It wasn't what I'd imagined; not even close. Perhaps it was because of the suddenly bleak weather, an indifferent blustery wind, dirty-looking clouds, a strong smell of tar. A few men in blue boiler suits crossed empty plains of asphalt, squinting into the wind. Trucks groaned in reverse and belched exhaust.

My taxi driver was having trouble finding my ship. He roared around the outer suburbs of the docks, treating the great wastes of oily concrete like a skid pan, squealing around stacks of briquettes and concrete pipes. Each new ship we approached looked more godforsaken than the last. As I lay on the bed in my hotel that morning, listening to the couple upstairs row and then have noisy make-up sex, I'd hoped for a ship with plenty of character. I'd dreamt of a ship that had marinated in the brine for a while, a ship crewed by crusty old salts with regrets in every port. But now that I was here, looking at them – at the mercy of them, these listing hulls with great scabs of rust – I began to pray for something less authentic. At each berth, my driver leant out and asked for directions from whoever was standing around. No-one knew what he was talking about. My driver swore happily and roared off again. He pointed at the meter which showed my mounting tariff, laughed and shrugged his shoulders. At the gangway to another ship, a sullen Chinese man looked me over, then spat on the concrete. It wasn't my ship. Not if he had anything to do with it. We kept going.

And then, finally, around a hillock of coal and behind what looked like an abandoned oil derrick, there it was. Not the biggest ship in the port, but big: a low, sleek hull painted green and a superstructure perched like an upstanding cereal box at the aft end. It looked brand new. And beautiful. The *Anneke Schliemann*.

At the top of the gangway a tiny sailor in a grimy boiler suit welcomed me with an ironic salute. 'You passenger, man? We been waiting for you.' He laughed and slapped me on the back. Grabbing my pack, he slung it over his shoulder and gasped. He led me into a gloomy corridor and then up five flights of stairs. Finally he opened the door to a boxy cabin. I noticed a strong smell of disinfectant. There was a small desk with a boom box chained to it, a narrow banquette seat along one wall, a clothes cupboard and a square porthole that overlooked two metres of space between the superstructure and the sheer wall of stacked containers in front. If you fell out of this porthole, you could only hope that Superman might get to you before you hit the bottom. 'I get master,' the sailor said, panting.

Captain Borgman was no Superman. He was an unsmiling bear of a man in his mid-fifties, with a huge, fleshy head. He had a thick German accent and frowned with the obvious effort it cost him to find English words and then arrange them into sentences. He was wearing tight, shiny shorts and a stained white T-shirt. His body was the shape of an upside down pear.

'I guess I just made it in time,' I said, shaking his hand.

'We are not going until tomorrow. There is enough time.'

I got the impression he was expecting someone else. Every now and then he cast me a sidelong glance as if he expected me to own up to my silly prank and admit that I wasn't the passenger at all, and that the real passenger would be coming along shortly. Mr Borgman led me into the officers' messroom, a low-ceilinged room lined with fake-walnut panelling. He showed me where I would sit at mealtimes, in the farthest seat from him, with empty seats to my right. 'You should come for dinner any time you want between five-thirty and six-thirty. What you do is up to you. I don't mind. I don't care what you do. Go anywhere you want.'

He gruffly expressed his hope that I would enjoy my time on the ship, then excused himself. 'I must go now. I have much work to be doing.'

I explored with mounting glee. My cabin was minuscule but comfortable. I wedged my photographs of Sarah into the porthole frame. I unpacked my clothes. The radio was tuned to the American Armed Forces Network. The DJ, a perky sergeant called Red, was fielding a lot of requests to play Britney Spears.

I wandered around on the outside decks, admiring the scale of the ship and glowing with a warm proprietorial pleasure at how clean it seemed, how freshly painted. *My* ship. The superstructure was a narrow iron ziggurat clamped to the ship's stern. There were outside walkways and platforms on each of the decks, connected by interlocking flights of stairs. From the wings on either side of the bridge deck ladders led up to an open deck at the very top of the ship which bristled with antennae and radar aerials.

After dinner in the officers' mess, I climbed back up to the top deck. In the darkness the port was an unearthly spectacle. The port's floodlights misted in the warm rain. Soaring gantries and claws threw mysterious shadows across the ship. They were still loading containers. Suspended from each crane was a flat, iron claw designed to grip the container by the corners, like a hand stretching to pick up a car battery. Stevedores in hard hats stood on stacks, guiding them down, shouting and pointing. The ship shuddered very faintly as each container settled into the hold.

I wasn't the only passenger aboard. After dinner I noticed a woman prowling around the aft decks in a lipstick-red raincoat with a hood, and a Nikon SLR pressed to her face. She was moving carefully among the capstans and winches and the massive hawsers which strained against the winches on the deck. I had heard all about Nadia from Ada. Nadia, the Belgian photographer who was going to publish a coffee-table book about freighter travel.

We went inside for a cup of coffee in the officers' mess. Nadia had an English father and spoke English without any accent at all. We laughed heartily at each other's jokes, the way you do when you're anxious to get along. Nadia had wanted to take a ship to the Far East, but had run out of time and so was on this one instead. She hoped to capture the 'working life of ports' in photographs, she said. 'You're writing a book, aren't you? What about?'

'The same thing.'

'Ha! So neither of us is a real passenger.' She wrapped her pale, long-fingered hands around her cup. Her neat fingernails were painted orange. 'Can you believe how cold it is? I can't. Do you think these cups have been disinfected?'

Nadia seemed to know someone in every single port on our rotation. She must have been one of the best-connected people in Europe. Not for her a three-hour slog through the docks in exhausting heat, either: she was delivered to the ship in Venice port by water taxi. Its owner was a friend of hers, so he brought her over to Marghera for free. In Venice, Nadia had met lots of fascinating people, including a film-maker and an American white-goods heir.

I decided not to tell her about Joshua. 'I hardly met anyone interesting in Venice and I was there for a week.'

She could hardly believe that. 'But the city's buzzing!'

Nadia was a little nervous about the ship. Crew-members had been casually wandering past the open door of her cabin since she boarded that morning, like small boys seeking to confirm a rumour that Santa Claus had arrived early. 'I get the feeling that they don't get many women on these ships.'

I had some concerns of my own. Dinner had been an ordeal. The three officers also tackling the roast duck had said 'hello' as they entered, then nothing more for the rest of the meal. There were slices of half-frozen white bread and plates heaped with cold sausage, but no beer or wine to warm the frigid atmosphere. I kept looking around anxiously to see if there was a carafe somewhere I'd missed. Every time I did so, the Filipino steward leapt forward, plucked his toothpick from his mouth for decorum's sake, and refilled my glass from a cardboard packet of warm reconstituted grapefruit juice.

I'd been below to make myself a cup of coffee in the galley earlier, and I'd encountered a man with a brambly grey beard and pinned pupils. He regarded me with an expression of infinite contempt and weariness. 'Evening,' I said, flicking on the kettle. 'Can I get you a tea or coffee or something?' He looked at me, then he looked at the toaster. He returned his gaze to the plate of cold duck leg he had taken from the fridge. He said nothing.

'Perhaps he doesn't speak English,' Nadia suggested.

Perhaps. But I think he just hated me.

In Venice proper, five kilometres across the water, it was the night of the Festa del Redentore – the Feast of the Redeemer – which commemorates the end of a bout of plague which hit the city in 1577. The captain had urged me to go, but when I asked him the

best way of getting back to town without a taxi, he admitted he had
no idea. In nearly ten years of sailing around the Mediterranean he
had never been to Venice proper, though he had heard it was quite
nice. At midnight, fireworks erupted over the far city like a bonsai
of glittering tracery, rising and falling in the distance.

We left Venice early the following evening. I watched from the
deck above the bridge. We moved down the dredged canal at pro-
cessional speed. I could hear the radios crackling on the bridge
wind below me as the chief officer reported the progress on deck.
The second officer appeared up the ladder, struck the Italian flag
with a few swift tugs and sent another flag ripping up the pole. Mr
Kuerten was a large, pale boy who wore a white T-shirt and over-
sized jeans with a wide, girlish belt when he was off-duty and a
brilliant white boiler suit unzipped to the waist when he was on.
He had a prefect's plump, pink lips and clotted-cream cheeks. We
nodded soberly at one another. The ship's prow headed directly
into the pastel ripples of the setting sun.

'This deck is called the monkey's island,' he said. Perfect
English again. He nodded at the sunset. 'Of course, it is very
beautiful. But I see it many times.'

On the starboard side the massive industrial estates of
Marghera rolled by – chemical plants, storage dams, great rigs of
aluminium pipes – all of them pumping thick chutes of smoke
into the sky. Floodlights fluttered on as we passed. Away to port,
Venice proper lay flattened out against the darkening lagoon. I
suddenly had an irrational idea that I'd never seen it, that I'd
come all this way and only managed to come this close to the
Venice of my dreams.

I wondered whether Joshua had heard any good jokes since
I left.

As we tracked down the coast towards Ravenna a hundred kilometres south, heavy rainclouds appeared over the mountains on
the coast. I stood on the bridge, trying to keep out of the way.
Captain Borgman looked like a genuine old sea dog, except that

physically he more closely resembled a sea-lion, with a great flabby head and neck, his stooping body heavy with strength and fat. His chief officer was a friendly Polish man with a salt-and-pepper beard and a slight lisp.

The rumbling summer thunderclouds that had followed us down the coast from Venice cleared quite suddenly and the night became tremblingly lovely. Around midnight we anchored a few miles off Ravenna, near a row of oil rigs which looked oddly exquisite in the darkness, with intricate skeletons of pipes and steel sparkling under massive arc lights.

'It's incredible,' the captain said. 'People come from all over Italy to have their holidays here.' He pointed to the coast. 'I don't understand. Who wants to lie on a beach and look at an oil rig?'

The chief officer laughed wheezily. 'Ha! Not me!'

'I don't!' said the captain.

'Too much pollution!' added the chief officer.

'Pah!' snorted the captain. 'I can never understand zees people.' I think he meant all people who lived on land.

I ate alone at dinner because I'd gotten the times wrong. The steward set me straight on the correct hours to come to dinner. 'Come befo' si' o'cloh, my man,' he said. 'Thas if you wanna eat some things.' The steward has big baby cheeks, a rounded pot-belly and short muscular legs. He seemed to enjoy playing the role of comical servant. Still no alcohol in evidence. When my glass was empty, the steward slapped my hand away and affably refilled it with pineapple juice from a packet.

Ravenna would have been a terrific port to see 700 years earlier, when the city was actually on the sea. In AD 404, when it was made the capital of the Western Roman Empire, 250 ships could pack themselves into its bay. Today, the sea has receded from the city and is connected to Ravenna's harbour by an eighteen-kilometre canal. The only trace of sea water left in this friendly, slow-paced Italian city is the delicate blue of the tiles depicting the sea in the famous Byzantine mosaics of San Vitale and Sant' Apollinare Nuovo.

The ship's schedule allowed only eight hours in Ravenna, which would have been frustrating for the passengers if both of us weren't already looking towards the Levant ports ahead. We treated Ravenna as a shore-raid. Nadia, who had been traumatised by the food served up in the officers' mess, took the opportunity to stock up on supplies. She bought cereal, rice cakes, dried figs and bags of mixed nuts. I called home and bought some newspapers, rummaging around in the discount tray of an English language bookstore for a while and then took myself off to the church of San Francesco to look at Dante's tomb. The crypt was already at least 400 years old when the Florentine exile was laid out to rest there. It might have been a more profound experience if the crypt hadn't been full of sweaty photographers rigging up flash guns and tripods in a bid to photograph the crumbling floor mosaics.

The man who drove us back to the port in his private taxi wanted to know whether Nadia and I were married.

'Yes, but not to one another,' Nadia said.

Our driver was thrilled to hear this. He insisted on taking us on a scenic detour, several times climbing out of the car to guide Nadia around a park or scenic ruin personally and wondering out loud whether I'd like to go and sit in a café for a while. Perhaps she would like to come and have dinner at his house tonight? His wife was in Bologna with relatives.

'No,' Nadia told him brightly. 'I'm afraid I can't. My ship is leaving tonight.' At the port gates the driver kissed Nadia's hand and gave her his cigarette lighter. 'I don't smoke,' she said, kindly.

'Please! Please take it!'

It was the first of several cigarette lighters.

STARING AT CALABRIA

> The fruit of solitude is originality, something daringly
> and disconcertingly beautiful, the poetic creation. But
> the fruit of solitude can also be the perverse, the
> disproportionate, the absurd and the forbidden.
>
> Thomas Mann, *Death in Venice*

So what is the opposite of solitude? Maybe loneliness. Or perhaps solitude is simply loneliness softened, as Robert Dessaix
has written, by wealth and status and the choices that come with
those things.

I certainly chose this solitude. It was our first full day at sea
and by mid-afternoon I'd spoken about three sentences. All of
them were directed at the steward who offered me delicious-
sounding food options as I entered the mess for lunch, listing the
components of the main course like a carnival spruiker reeling off
the attributes of a sideshow novelty: 'Brussel sprouts, uh? You
like? Very nice. Potato mash? Potatoes all boil up then mash up
good-good? Si. Ya, some chicken stick? You like him?' In the
mornings the steward came by to 'make up my room', by which
he meant he would empty the rubbish bin, flush the toilet and fold
my doona over sideways so that it fitted more neatly on my bunk
bed. I could hear him coming from several flights of stairs away,
his regulation flip-flops slapping on the linoleum.

In the afternoon, Mr Kuerten summoned Nadia and me to the
boat deck for some safety training. He marched us to the free-fall

lifeboat on the third deck, which looked not much like a lifeboat and a lot like an orange fibreglass space shuttle. He invited us to sit in it. 'I'm not getting in there,' Nadia said. 'Yes you must,' said Mr Kuerten. 'For safety.'

Nadia shook her head. 'No way. I'm claustrophobic.' She turned to me for support, laughing, but with a flash of panic in her eyes. 'What if they launch it while we're in there? Just as a practical joke or something?'

'I don't think they'd do that while the ship is sailing at eighteen knots,' I said reassuringly. 'This thing's probably too valuable to lose.'

'Get in,' Mr Kuerten said. He seemed to be enjoying himself now.

We lay strapped into our seats on a forty-five degree angle while Mr Kuerten inspected our buckles. 'So this thing is submersible, is it?' I asked, unable to resist trying to ingratiate myself with the alpha-male Kuerten.

'Yes, of course. It is safe to ten metres or so. But normally, the boat will begin to surface much earlier than that. Don't worry.'

'What if it doesn't resurface?' Nadia asked.

Mr Kuerten looked like he'd never seriously considered this before. He thought for moment, then shrugged. 'The boat would continue to sink and you would drown, I suppose.' I was beginning to think that Mr Kuerten might have a sense of humour after all.

Later, he showed us the pool; a metal void punched like a sink out of the sheet metal of the third deck. It was full with sparkling clean water pumped straight from the Adriatic. 'Free surface effect,' Mr Kuerten noted. Someone had moved the two deck chairs and two banana lounges over to the poolside and arranged them as if dressing a theatre set.

On the bridge I found Mr Fernandes, the third officer, doing watch by himself. 'Good morning, Mr McCamish!' he said, coming to attention. I said, 'Good Morning!', and because that didn't seem like quite enough, added, 'How are you doing?' Mr Fernandes' expression faltered very briefly. 'I am doing sea watch,' he replied evenly. I realised with dismay that he thought

I'd demanded to know what he was doing. I asked very respectfully if I might be able to borrow one of the bridge's pairs of
binoculars and Mr Fernandes insisted that I use the 'good quality'
ones, with adjustable eyepieces, which he was wearing around his
neck, rather than the pair right in front of me.

I carefully scoped the horizon. There were at least five other
ships within range of the binoculars and a couple of islands off
to the east. The sun flashed fiercely on the flat sea. 'No pirates,'
I declared.

Mr Fernandes stared at me blankly.

'No pirates,' I repeated. I grinned stupidly and nodded at the
other ships away to port. 'I think they're friendlies.'

Mr Fernandes crossed his arms. 'There are no pirates in the
Mediterranean. Mostly in South China Sea.'

'Ah. Right. Well, that's good to know.'

I made my way downstairs to the passenger deck where I set
myself up with a coffee and my sketch pad.

I'd brought with me several books to help me understand the culture of travelling on freighters, but the world I read about in my
cabin didn't seem to bear any relationship to the one I was living
in. Freighter travel experienced a small boom in the late thirties,
when freighters and tramp steamers had sprawling superstructures in the middle of the ship and there was space for passengers.
The war ended that. By the time Jack Kerouac booked himself on
a Yugoslav freighter in 1957, passengers were an oddity. In 1962,
the writer Nelson Algren was the only paying passenger aboard
the *Malaysia Mail* when it carried him and a crew of cardsharps
across the Pacific from Seattle to Hong Kong. His shipmates
couldn't believe that anyone would want to pay for the pleasure.

Larry Nixon's *Vagabond Voyaging* was written in 1938 as a
kind of guidebook to the possibilities of freighter travel. Life on
Nixon's vagabond seas bore no similarity to the things I was seeing on the *Anneke Schliemann*. 'On one boat in three you'll meet
a yarn-spinner, a salty old seagoing chap of the fiction type,'
Nixon predicts, 'but these fellows are passing out of the picture.'

Time had made a liar out of poor old Nixon: he also devoted a whole chapter to the wide array of wines, beers and spirits available to passengers. The only beer available on the *Anneke Schliemann* were cases of Stella Artois that you could buy from the slop chest and consume like a lush in the privacy of your cabin.

Farthest from the reality on the *Anneke Schliemann*, sadly, was Norman Lewis's lyrical memory of the ships he had seen wandering among the ports of Arabia and the Red Sea in his book *Golden Earth: Travels in Burma* published in 1952:

> The ships had been wonderful, battered, old relics, full of nautical mannerisms and impregnated with the musk of exotic cargoes . . . Such ships were usually skippered by empirical navigators, captains who lost themselves when out of sight of familiar coastal landmarks. They were as nearly useless as the vessels they sailed in; drank like fishes; went in for religious mania, or for spells of mild insanity in which they were liable to stalk the bridge in the nude. The passengers, too, fitted into the general picture: sword-bearing rulers of a corner of a desert, half-crazed lighthouse keepers, broken-down adventurers scraping a living in any dubious enterprise they could smell out.

Perhaps Nadia and I were part of the problem.

Sometimes I almost forgot that we were at sea at all. When the sea was calm it felt like living in a dormitory above a ball bearing factory where they only let you out of the grounds every few days.

The only officers who ate at the same time as Nadia and I were Dominic, the Romanian second engineer, and Andrej, the ship's Polish electrician. The master – as the captain was known – often took his meals in his cabin, the chief officer seemed not to eat much at all and the chief engineer – the wordless apparition I'd encountered on the first night – only emerged late at night, like a bad-tempered nocturnal mammal, to eat his meals in the darkness of the deserted mess.

Dominic spent a lot of time in the plainly decorated officers' saloon watching Italian television. He had become friendlier since he realised I was on board to write a travel book and not to spy on him. A man who knew his American cinema, he amused himself by calling Nadia and me Lois Lane and Jimmy Olsen. He went to sea because he broke up with his girlfriend and, with a nineteen-year-old boy's cheerful sense of self-destruction, had gone along with some mates and applied for a course in marine engineering. Twenty-two years later, he'd been at sea all his adult life. Andrej was imperturbably easygoing, but his English was thickly accented and hard to understand. 'Having a good appetite!' he shouted every night, as he stepped into the mess room. Together, Andrej and Dominic reminded me of the two old geezers in 'The Muppets' who used to sit up in the dress circle mocking everything that happened on stage.

After a few days at sea, they invited us into the officers' recreation room following dinner to chat and watch television. It was an unprepossessing room with a simple banquette lounge along the back wall and a large television and video player.

Nadia and the others had a good-natured row about biological food. The officers were mocking the organic muesli Nadia ate every night instead of whatever Cookie – as the ship's cook was inevitably called – had come up with in the galley, and she put up a polite but spirited argument for fighting 'Them', the corporations and criminals who poisoned the world's food and atmosphere for profit. Dominic, who claimed to have seen the corruption of communism replaced with the corruption of capitalism at home in Romania, was too cynical to be having any of this. 'Why bother?' he asked, using a toothpick to retrieve a bit of that evening's goulash from his teeth.

'People can make a difference,' Nadia insisted.

'People can do nothing,' Dominic said, 'I've seen it. It's always the same, whatever you call it – capitalism, communism or hippies.'

Andrej agreed with him. 'Iz better to live without thinking,' he said decisively. He seemed happy enough; maybe he was right.

Later I made my way forward hoping to find Nadia. We must have been sailing east because the sun was setting almost directly behind the superstructure. Some angelic clouds on the horizon seemed to glow pink and red, then orange, like puffy light globes, and the air itself seemed to be going purple in sympathy. Life aboard might have been lacking in romance, but I loved everything about the ship. I cherished the Escher-like mesh of gangways and ladders on the aft deck; the low, slanting sun on the rusted iron cables holding the lifeboats to the railing; and the smell of the sea wind, bringing with it that sweetly sad feeling that the wind has come from somewhere else far away and that you are a long way away from wherever it goes next.

Nadia was sitting up on the forecastle deck right at the front of the ship chatting to some of the crew. The guys left shortly after I arrived, claiming they had work to do. Nadia had a real knack for getting the crew to talk to her. No-one listened to them; they didn't even listen to each other. They couldn't believe she was real. Maybe it was like Algren said of the sailors he met on the *Malaysia Mail*: the men had forgotten how to talk to a woman they couldn't buy or borrow. But these guys seemed more playful with Nadia than anything. It was all games. Sooner or later one of them would become infatuated with her, of course, and things would become more complicated.

Nadia and I sat and talked for a while. We were both in need of a debriefing. Nadia was bothered by the captain, who was refusing to say hello to her when they passed in the corridor. 'What have I done?' she wanted to know.

I hadn't seen much of the captain; when he wasn't on the bridge playing Solitaire on the laptop he kept in the chart room, he stayed in his cabin. In the ship's corridors, his bulk blocked out the light. Whenever I heard him puffing along a corridor, I turned around and pretended I was going the other way so that he didn't have to go through the process of backing up, or berthing in a recessed doorway or, worse, trying to squeeze himself up so that I pass.

'I refuse to call him master,' Nadia said. 'Can you believe that we have to call him master?'

I explained what Dominic had explained to me, that *Kapitan* meant something else in German, not a ship's captain.

Nadia wasn't convinced. 'I wouldn't be surprised if he turned out to be a sicko of some kind.'

Food was her other major concern. The stomach-jamming fare had continued to pour cheerfully from the ship's galley where Cookie happily murdered the stodgy Bavarian menus dictated by the captain. For Nadia, who preferred to graze on macrobiotic seeds and pasta made from organic durum flour, meals were a trial. Earlier in the week she had picked three hairs from a bowl of onion soup, and a bowl of rice had yielded a sliver of fingernail. On another occasion she had picked fastidiously at the scraps of dry salad. On the menu were grilled sausages – which were excellent, actually – accompanied by a turret of oily chopped potatoes and a boiled egg. There was cauliflower cheese sauce, too. For me, cauliflower sauce was the acme of British cuisine, its greatest gift to world food. But Nadia couldn't bring herself to touch it with her fork. 'I'll vomit if I do,' she whispered. 'Do you want mine?'

Dominic had told us that the last time there were passengers on the ship, the captain had enjoyed their company so much he had arranged a special party for them with German beer. 'The last time we had a couple on the ship, he makes them a party. He wore a party hat and blew a whistle.'

'We're not a couple,' Nadia told him.

Dominic smiled meaningfully.

'Really, we're not,' I said.

'Besides,' said Nadia, 'I just can't see Mr Borgman wearing a party hat and blowing a whistle.'

'I made that bit up,' Dominic admitted. 'But he will throw a party for you, too, if he likes you. I think he particularly liked them because they were German.'

Nadia wondered how the captain had treated the woman.

'They got on very good,' Dominic told her. 'But she was seventy-five years old, so there was no hanky-panky.'

It was an incredibly peaceful, literally blissful feeling to be riding at the prow of a giant iron tub skimming across the sea at dusk. The water made hardly any sound as it was parted by the teardrop prow and was carved away below the sleek gunwales; just the faint sound of rushing water through the anchor chain portals could be heard. We watched the moon – a huge, dark gold, overripe moon – heave itself over the horizon. Nadia tried to photograph it, then lowered her camera. 'Everything is so spectacular,' she complained good-naturedly.

I walked Nadia back the length of the ship. Refrigerated containers hummed overhead. Now and then we heard a clanking sound in the depths of the ship. She was afraid that the wind, which was picking up by now, might literally lift her off the gangway and pitch her into the drink. She meant this quite seriously. 'I'm just too light,' she said, embarrassed. 'It's happened to me before. I actually was blown over in the street in Amsterdam, once. Maybe I should ask them if they have any weights I could use.'

This seemed like a fairly tall order to me. 'Weights? For weighing down passengers?'

'Yeah. There must be something you can put in your pockets. Just enough to make a difference.'

I promised faithfully that if she ever blew overboard, I'd let the captain know as soon as I could.

Soon, while the northwest squall wrings out its cloud,
    cutter, we'll heave to
free of the sands and let the half-moon do
as it pleases, hanging there in the port shrouds
like a riding light. We have no course to set,
only to drift too long, watch too glumly, and wait,
    wait.

Basil Bunting

Over the next few days, my eye sockets became bruised from the binoculars. When the *Anneke Schliemann* arrived off the tip of the Italian boot shown in the charts, the master announced that we wouldn't be going into port that night. In fact, we wouldn't be going into port for another seven days, which meant that we would be drifting listlessly in the terrible heat, just close enough to the coast to be tantalised by its possibilities, but not close enough to sample them.

Beyond the freshly painted railings, the coast of Calabria ebbed and waned. I became obsessed by the thin strip of sand-coloured land which loomed invitingly out of the haze each afternoon. Each day the ship's master conferred with the chief officer, who stood watch in the mornings, and together they determined the direction of the wind that slowly, at perhaps half a knot, pushed us towards the shore. They then plotted a course in the opposite direction. A call was made to the engine room and the shuddery feeling of the engine awakening spread through the metal deck. Then we would sail for an hour or so, perhaps ten nautical miles, which left us out of eye-shot from shore, even with binoculars. Sometimes, if the direction of the current was right, we motored out quite near to the still-active island volcano of Stromboli. One day we were so close I could pick out individual buildings in the town perched on the mountain's lower slopes. By evening, though, we'd drifted again, back towards the coast.

Gradually the chart on the bridge became crisscrossed with fresh lines of pencil lead, our daily trajectories of sailing and drifting plotted over the ghostly rub-outs of earlier drifts.

Lost in a sea of undifferentiated days, I began to fantasise about Gioia Tauro. At meals, I grilled the officers for information. Dominic and Andrej were my two most helpful sources of information, and they weren't helpful at all. Andrej, who was given to gnomic utterances, said only 'You will see exactly,' and then giggled. Dominic agreed. 'I am staying there once waiting for the ship. I stayed two days. There is one pizza restaurant. And that is all. There is nothing except the beach.'

Andrej mumbled something into his soup, then giggled again.

Dominic translated for me. 'He says it's Africa.'

'Africa? What do you mean?' They watched me with evident amusement. 'But it's Italy, right?'

'No, is Africa.' Andrej in particular thought this was a real hoot. 'You will see,' they said.

On the third day a yacht motored over to have a look at us. Half a dozen people, mostly bare-chested men in jeans and gold necklaces, scratched their bellies and stared up at the bridge, trying to look the ship in the eye. I waved from the bridge wing and about five seconds later, they all started waving back. It seemed appropriate that light should travel more sluggishly out here, where the very laws of the universe seemed to have succumbed to the torpor of our drift.

Dominic was once aboard a ship which nearly ran into a yacht wallowing in a swell off the Dalmatian coast. It wasn't responding to radio calls. The ship's Zodiac was lowered and the yacht boarded. The yacht was found to be utterly deserted, though its dinghy was still attached. I shivered when Dominic told me the story, recalling *Dead Calm*.

'Probably the people had gone swimming and drowned,' Dominic speculated.

'Did you look for them?' I asked.

'Of course not. They could have been dead for weeks.'

They radioed it in and continued on: to a mariner, a drifting yacht is not a mystery, just a potential collision. He told me a story of another ship that came across an inflatable dinghy floating empty on the sea. Its engine was missing, but otherwise it was perfectly intact. The boat was hauled aboard. One of the officers carefully scratched off the name of the ship it had once belonged to and sold it at the next port.

My favourite story about oceanic flotsam had come from the chief officer, who told me that a ship he was on once picked up an Austrian man who'd stranded himself fifteen nautical miles off Gran Canaria on an air mattress. 'I think he fell asleep,' he laughed. 'But then, what can you expect if a person comes from a country with no coast? They have no idea what is the sea!'

We'd now been drifting off Gioia Tauro for six days, a giant hulk of flotsam ourselves.

The ship had become strangely airless as it drifted. The sun poured itself pitilessly onto the iron decks and soaked into the layers of paint so that the ship stayed hot for hours after sunset. Even sitting in the shade at the passenger-deck table, the heat was almost unbearable. I sat at the bench with my back to the main engine funnel reading a book. When I looked up from the black and white of the printed page, I was struck by the brilliant colours: the grass-green of the thickly painted steel decks and handrails, then the insane, empty blue of the sky, and the sparkling, mottled blue of the water, and Stromboli.

The simple rhythms of life aboard were so insistent and regular that the days were very difficult to distinguish from one another. In *The Nigger of the* Narcissus (also in my pack) Joseph Conrad wrote: 'The smiling greatness of the sea dwarfed the extent of time. The days raced after one another, brilliant and quick like the flashes of a lighthouse, and the nights, eventful and short, resembled fleeting dreams.' Perhaps the ship had to be moving in order to create this transcendent effect. For the first time in my life I began to understand, almost physically, why prisoners mark the passing days on the walls of their cells. I found myself making scrupulous daily entries in my journal, just so that I could tell one day of life from the next. I spent a lot of time gazing into the water, which was, according to the chart, 876 metres deep here. I could hear a chain scraping somewhere above us on one of the upper decks. Some days the urge to dive in was unbearable. But no-one swam off the ship. I was laughed at when I suggested it.

With nothing to do in the engine room, even the oilers had joined the deck crew on a painting campaign. Every centimetre of the ship was repainted that week. Crew-members dangled over the water on a plank suspended by thick ropes, repainting the great white letters of the ship's name on the green background. Others carried pails of paint to and fro, daubing railings and steps, smiting spots of rust with swabs of paint. Sometimes, when I was sitting at the picnic table on the passenger deck, fanning myself with my sketchbook and trying to read, one of the crew would appear dragging a hose; he'd smile cheerfully and duck his head in reply to my over-eager hello, and then get on with scrubbing the decks. At night, some of the crew lowered lights on long extension cords, hoping to attract squid to the baited lines tied up to the stern railing. No-one ever seemed to catch anything. It made for an atmospheric still life: several guys leaning in silence against the railing, their faces palely lit by the reflected glow of the bare bulb six metres below. There was nothing to see and nothing to hear but the sound of the black water softly slapping on the hull.

My dream of finding, in the backwaters of the globe, taverns full of men of uncertain reputation seemed to be fading fast in the sterilising heat of the Mediterranean. Nadia suggested that we call a tourist agency in Reggio di Calabria on the ship's satellite phone and ask them to motor out and pick us up. 'Just think! We could be having beautiful pasta and fresh veggies tomorrow lunchtime!' Unfortunately, the ship's phone cost US$5 per minute to use and wasn't receiving a signal from the satellite anyway – I knew this because I'd made a very expensive attempt to call Sarah a couple of nights earlier and failed. Besides, I expected that the Italian *polizia* might have something to say about a couple of 'restaurant refugees', as Nadia called us, motoring past passport control like cocaine smugglers.

On our fifth night drifting outside Gioia, one of the Filipino cadets invited us down to the crew's mess for a drink. I'd heard tantalising snatches of karaoke coming from the crew's mess in the evenings, but I'd never been inside. Here, at last, was a chance to taste some real sea life: if we couldn't visit a seaman's bar ashore, we could visit one on the ship.

Johnny was a chatty guy with a flashy smile and a lean body he was obviously working on in the ship's gym. He introduced me to everyone else; Nadia seemed to know them all already. The scene wasn't terribly promising: ten guys sat at cafeteria tables, a few with cans of Stella Artois in front of them, all facing the television screen mounted on the wall. They looked like they were in detention. Dominic strolled past on the deck outside and stuck his head in through an open porthole. 'What's going on? A party? How come no-one is telling Dominic?'

The reason for that was soon clear: we were here to watch Johnny's home video of an end-of-rotation party aboard the *Paul Schliemann, Anneke*'s brother ship. Now, watching a video of someone else's party wasn't necessarily my idea of fun, but then this was no ordinary party. There was karaoke, drinking and dancing. At one point there seemed to be a mock wedding in progress, with one guy playing a half-hearted drag-queen role, more of a drag dowager, doing lots of foxtrots and elegant dips with various partners. The others lined up to dance with him. Her.

The Filipino guys sitting with us sang along unembarrassedly with the music. They seemed to be enjoying it. It was part karaoke, part misery, part post-modern beer hall.

'This probably seems very strange to you,' Dominic said. 'You can't understand it.'

I told him that I thought I did.

'I know you think you do, but you don't. These boys are at sea a long time,' he said. 'And they have to get out their tensions and all the things that build up inside. You shouldn't be judgemental.'

Why did he think I was being judgemental?

'Because you're young,' he replied.

On the screen, the English captain and his Indian chief officer had torn off their shirts and were now bouncing off one another's enormous bellies. The Indian officer had had more to drink, it appeared, and was taking the bout more seriously. No-one in the crew's mess was surprised when he missed his opponent and went careening straight past the captain, headlong into a fake fern. The captain sent the chief officer up to his cabin to cool off; a few minutes later he was back again, apologising sincerely for his behaviour and taking to the microphone with a touching rendition of 'I Will Survive'. When it was over the Filipinos clapped politely, crunched their beer cans and filed out.

'Do you think we're going to get a party like that one?' Nadia asked.

Dominic grunted. 'I tell you before! There are no parties on this ship. Since this captain took over, the barbecues are all finished. He doesn't like parties.' Sometimes, he said, the tradition was revived for the sake of the passengers if the ship was carrying any; even then it was a miserable affair with strictly rationed beer and lights out at ten o'clock. It was depressing to realise that the captain's attitude towards Nadia and I would be measured by the extravagance of a bleak barbecue.

The captain seemed to be finding our presence aboard a little stressful. The day before he had shouted at Nadia for taking photographs of the crew in their cabins. 'They are not artists,' he complained. 'They are zee men! They are not animals in a zoo!'

Earlier that day I'd been up on the bridge with the master, the chief officer and the second officer. Only the chief officer smiled; the two Germans bade me a stiff good afternoon. I picked up some binoculars and began searching Stromboli for any points of interest I might have missed so far, then crossed to the other end of the bridge and gazed at the scattering of stone houses on the Italian coast caught in its seizure of heat. We had drifted closer than the master usually allowed. It was another brilliantly clear day. I tried to separate the clusters of pale houses and matchbox apartment buildings into the villages marked on the charts. I could make out the gantries on the dock, their vast forearms hooked over the harbour, then the town of San Fernandino behind them, and further south, towards the Messina Straits, the town of Scilla where the six-headed monster with twelve tentacles had given Odysseus so much trouble.

'I am thinking that we will be in the port for Gioia Tauro on Tuesday alongside,' the master said. Three more days away. 'It is a reason I don't know, maybe it is being the stevedores are not wanting to work . . .'

He trailed off into an aggressive pause. He rubbed his temples as though merely speaking to me was causing him pain. Perhaps I'd been gazing too longingly at the land.

'Are we waiting for the mother ship?' I asked. This is what I'd heard from Dominic earlier in the day. I was trying to be helpful. The *Anneke Schliemann* was a feeder ship, which doled out among smaller ports the cargo brought into the Mediterranean by intercontinental freighters. Sometimes feeders had to wait for the mother ships to arrive from Rotterdam or Hamburg.

The master let out a loud groan which gradually formed itself into the first word of another gruelling sentence in English.

'AAARRREGHEEYeeeees, it could the mother ship is we are waiting,' he shouted. He half turned away from me and seemed to look to his junior officers for strength. The chief officer suddenly found something fascinating to study through his own binoculars.

The captain started taking heavy breaths, clearly working himself up to some oratory. 'What I should am telling you is, I don't know. I don't know when we go alongside. Who is knowing this? No-one! No-one knows! And I don't care!' His eyes bulged. They looked like they might actually pop out and start rolling around the bridge's grey linoleum. 'For you maybe it is boring for you here–'

'Oh no . . .'

'–but from my position it is not making any difference! For the seaman it doesn't make a matter, if you are on sea for a week, or a muntz, or what it shall be. Only for passengers!' He spat the word 'passengers' the way he would the name of a virulent bacterium. 'Now you see?'

'Yes, I see.'

'It makes no difference to us!'

'Why would it?'

Behind me, the captain paced the length of the bridge. I felt a bit like Colonel Hogan getting a pasting from an irate Colonel Klink. He marched over to the radar screen, glanced at it, then stared gloomily through the windows at his cargo below. It was another clear, gentle day with a faint breeze ruffling the surface of the sea.

'At least it's very nice weather,' I volunteered. This elicited a giggle from the chief officer.

'It's nice the weather,' the captain grunted, begrudgingly. 'Very fine.'

The master was quite a specimen. He muttered to himself like someone convinced that he was surrounded by fools and was given to stalking up and down the length of the bridge's button-pattern linoleum, squeaking in his flip-flops, damning the laziness of the stevedores and the illiteracy of the Filipinos. Sometimes he took to the bridge wearing only a pair of shorts and flip-flops, thus releasing to public view one of the strangest-shaped bellies I'd ever seen. It was a porridgy pot with an active downward thrust. I felt a perverse desire to prod this pouch with my finger, just to see what the consistency of the flesh was like. When we came into port, however, he became all formal: out would come a pair of crinkled chinos, shiny brogues and a striped shirt with a collar.

From my cabin I could hear him climbing to his cabin next to mine, each step producing an agonised moan of effort. A few times I encountered him clinging to the handrail on the fourth floor landing, puffing painfully, his face a big, unhappy tomato turned with morbid apprehension to the landing above. A couple of times I glimpsed the steward restocking the captain's capacious private fridge, an operation that took almost as long as unloading the containers at port.

Somerset Maugham seemed to have met him in an earlier life. The dullness of the typical ship's captain, Maugham wrote, stemmed from the fact that they had 'seen little more in the ports they visit than their agent's office, the bar which their kind frequents, and the bawdy houses'. One day the captain told me that the last passenger he had had on the ship was an antiques dealer who had bought cases and cases of bargain maritime detritus from flea markets across the Levant. 'He was a *very interesting* man,' the captain said, with meaningful emphasis. 'He made a good business from it. We had many talks.' In contrast, I think he was struggling to see the point of either Nadia or me. He was particularly distrustful of Nadia's camera.

He had visited Melbourne many times during his career at sea. It was hard to believe that when I'd stood on the slopes of Red Hill as a boy and watched freighters edge along the horizon towards Melbourne, Mr Borgman had sometimes been aboard.

Melbourne was a very nice place, he told me. But Tasmania was better because it was like England was a hundred years ago. 'No Asians,' he noted approvingly. He wondered if I knew of any good investments going in Australia. I didn't. He lost interest in me after that.

Further down the chain of command, I was making better progress. I had begun playing table tennis with Dominic in the rec room. I learnt how to play table tennis on the back of a retired shed door made of warped tongue-and-groove planks. Bounce was irregular and a defensive back-handed style quickly became the mainstay of my game. My forehand was a fragile creature that I only took out on the rare occasions that I played someone worse than me. This was not one of those occasions. Dominic's beautifully controlled forehand topspin smashes pitilessly exposed my game's flaws. Sometimes he ricocheted a smash off the low ceiling. 'Great shot,' I was frequently obliged to mumble as I picked the ball out of my hair. He smirked. 'What you mean? It's easy for me. It's nothing.' And indeed, it did seem that he was thinking of something else the whole time he was smashing stinging forehands into my arms, forehead, groin and belly. If I wasn't careful, he would stop wanting to play with me at all. Maybe he was thinking about Nadia. Everyone else on board seemed to be thinking about Nadia.

Sometimes we drank a beer together in his cabin – it had to be his cabin since mine had no fridge – which was only slightly less cramped than my own. He had a rack of pirated DVD movies he had bought out of car boots in various ports. Most of them were Disney animations. His nine-year-old daughter loved them. He loved them too, obviously. 'Forget about *Casablanca*,' he said often. 'Have you been there?' I shook my head. 'The town is shit. No, you wait and see,' he told me. 'In a hundred years' time, *The Lion King* will be the most famous film of the twentieth century.'

Andrej brought some photographs of his family up one night. We swapped: I showed him my pictures of Sarah, which gave him a chance to slip into the old married-man role he and Dominic enjoyed playing so much. They liked to pretend they were glad to have escaped the harridans waiting for them at home. 'How long you been married?' Andrej asked. Only a year. He winked at Dominic. 'You don't know anything yet. It all seems nice, yes, she's very pretty, you happy, everything good. Wait till you are married ten year, fifteen. Then you will see exactly. Then you be happy you can't call your wife!' But I did want to call. That was the main reason I wanted to get ashore.

'I don't see what is the rush,' Andrej said.

'He has to write a book,' said Dominic, rolling his eyes. 'How's he going to write a book from the ship?'

'It's only Africa,' Andrej said. 'You better off write it from your head.' He tapped his temple and grinned. 'I tell you it's better in your head than it is in this place.'

He continued to refer to southern Italy as 'Africa' each time he spoke about it. His little joke never failed to amuse him though.

'What do you mean it's "Africa"?' Nadia kept asking him.

Andrej would giggle some more, flash his wonderful gap-toothed smile, and say: 'You will see. I say nothing, but you will see exactly.'

As we inched into the port, Andrej stood at the railing trying to see if he recognised any old pals among the sailors lining the railings of ships already docked. There was a huge Korean ship already tied up and a mid-size Maersk Line vessel. While the pilot coordinated a laborious three-point turn, Borgman stomped up and down the wing of the bridge five decks above. We could hear him bawling into his radio at the long-suffering chief officer trying to coordinate the Filipino trainees manning the winches at the stern.

Italy was experiencing a heatwave. Dominic, who was monitoring the Italian television news bulletins between the cabaret shows he liked so much, reported that several old people had already died from the fierce temperatures. The heat was also going to the heads of local crime gangs. Dominic had been following with morbid interest a recent spate of Mafia shootings in Reggio Calabria fifty kilometres to the south. 'Every night for the last week there has been a killing,' he told us cheerfully, as we prepared to disembark. 'Hey, don't worry. The mistake most of them make is they sit at a café table outside. I don't know why these dons are always sitting outside. It's stupid. That's where they always get shot by somebody on a Vespa, bang-bang, just like that. My advice is you should sit inside.'

Gioia Tauro is one of the largest container ports in the Mediterranean. Yet when people imagine historic ports perfumed with the scent of frankincense and saffron, harbourside villages redolent with memories of sailors' brawls, places marinated in the sweat of ancient mariners, they rarely think of Gioia Tauro. You wouldn't find its name in Joseph Conrad, or Alan Villiers or A.J. Liebling or Jack Kerouac, nor in the poems of Basil Bunting or Gary Snyder. There are good reasons for this. With its towering gantries and acres of baking concrete, set below a bleak hill and ringed by a concrete flyover, Gioia Tauro was impressive and depressing.

'I can't work with this,' Nadia murmured at my side, as we tied up. She was looking up at the industrial infrastructure, the gantries marching off into the distance in a dusty golden light. 'When are we getting to Beirut?'

There are docks and docks, Joseph Conrad wrote, and the ugliness of some docks was appalling. It had always been the way.

The town itself looked cheerfully run-down. In bars and at the chemist you could buy postcards produced by a local printer, almost all of which showed the commercial docks from various angles and in different hues of poetic evening light.

We found Dominic's pizza place and shared a table with two men from an American container ship also in port. Doug was a huge retiree from Chicago with a flat mouth and a chin that merged into his neck with no discernible break. He was seventy-seven and good company. Nino was a Romanian engineer with fluffy Benny-from-ABBA hair and a sparse seventies beard. They had just arrived directly from Boston. Doug looked like he was still in shock. 'Gioia is your first stop?' Nadia asked in sympathy. 'That's terrible.'

Doug shrugged politely. 'It's not so bad,' he said, glancing out across the drab square where gangs of teenagers loitered on their mopeds. 'Well, it's a change from the ship, anyway.' He was the only passenger and he had spent twelve days solid doing crosswords and vomiting over the rails. 'Yup, we had some weather all right,' he said.

'How's your food?' Nadia wanted to know.

Doug glanced at Nino and shrugged. 'Well, you gotta say, there's plenty of it. I ain't going hungry.'

There was no pizza available until eight o'clock and the place didn't serve anything else, so we watched the local news service for an hour. A Concorde had crashed in Paris, killing everyone on board.

The following day Nadia and I took the train to Scilla, which was held to be the prettiest town on this stretch of coast. I felt as though I should know this town already, considering how long I'd been staring at its sprawling shape through Mr Fernandes' binoculars.

The day was suffocatingly hot, especially by the time Nadia and I climbed up to the top of the escarpment to which the village clung and found a table at the aptly named Vertigine café bar which overlooked a neat wedge of beach. Despite the heat, we managed to eat several courses each. Nadia wolfed her tortellini as if she was preparing for a nuclear winter. We watched a submarine grinding across the bay, its hull as black and glossy as a seal pelt. A pair of windsurfers were tacking across the outer edges of the bay. They saw it, realised there was a nuclear submarine between them and safety, panicked and fell in. The sub was probably American – Borgman had been complaining to me a few days earlier about the rough sea manners of US battleships on manoeuvres off the Amalfi coast. 'They think they own the fucking sea,' he fumed, eavesdropping on an altercation on the radio. 'But of course, you get out of their way.'

Nadia said, 'This is probably how a war starts. You're standing on the beach admiring the beautiful warships and wondering why they're so close to shore.'

Two big, fat-bellied prop aircraft repeatedly skimmed the bay, shovelling up water. It wouldn't have surprised me if the entire peninsula was on fire.

That night we returned to Gioia and ate at a restaurant called Il Vecchia Trove, recommended to us by the port's doctor, who'd given us a lift to the station that morning. By ten o'clock, when we had stuffed ourselves to capacity, Gioia's single taxi driver was fast asleep. So Nadia went into the kitchens and smiled at everyone, and within seconds one of the pizza chefs agreed to drive us back to port.

The pizza chef took to us like family, despite the fact that we couldn't speak one another's language. Were we married? he wanted to know. No, we said; well, yes, but not to one another. He shook his head. We should be, he said, because babies were *molto bene*. We talked about Gioia. We gave him to understand that although, yes, the south was obviously poorer than the north – his gesture for 'poorer' was to poke his fat cheek with his forefinger and grind it in, like a French Pierrot weeping – the people were much more *simpatico*. No! he protested too much, clearly delighted. Oh yes, we insisted. Very *simpatico*. He'd been born in Gioia Tauro and he had lived there all his life. Nadia described to him some of the dishes Cookie had astonished us with over the past week; our new buddy chuckled at this little joke at the expense of German cuisine, but refused to speak ill of another chef. It is not easy if the chef is not properly trained in the cuisine, he signed laboriously, nearly driving us into a ditch in the process. We arrived back in port that night suffused with the inexhaustible goodwill of our fellow humans. It was amazing what alcohol could do after a week of sobriety.

I offered to pay him when we arrived at the docks, but he wasn't having any of that. He folded his huge palms over the wallet and my hands. There were tears in his eyes. He slapped a skillet-sized hand across one steaky breast, declared that it had been an honour to meet us, he would pray for us and hoped we would have many children.

The docks were an astonishing sight. A desolate plateau of dusty concrete during the day, the wharf at night looked like a

John Wyndham dystopia, an out-of-date vision of the future. Dwarfed by the scale of it, we scuttled back to the safety of the ship among towering cranes, fifteen-metre forklifts and charging shadows thrown by the eerie halogen glare of the floodlights.

The next day I decided to walk into San Fernandino, the small township just north of the port, actually closer than Gioia Tauro but accessible only by way of a long, circumlocutory route via both the *polizia* and *dogana* checkpoints and then over a series of flyovers and overpasses. A crow would have to fly about a kilometre and a half, I guess; by foot, it was at least six. But I wasn't worried, because Nadia and I had had no difficulty hitching rides so far in Gioia Tauro.

Or so I thought. As I walked with growing bitterness the full six kilometres to San Fernandino, I began to realise how crucial Nadia had been to attracting the attention of drivers. I caught curious stares and shrugging looks – the infuriating and *non possibile* of Italian fatalism – from drivers who cruised slowly by in their air-conditioned cars. Some of them actually slowed down as if to get a better look at the idiot navvy who'd decided to walk the whole way from the port to town.

When my shadow finally darkened the dusty main drag of San Fernandino, I felt as if I had crossed a border post into a different dimension. Most of the inhabited houses are made of concrete bricks or timber and stone salvaged from the hundreds of derelict dwellings lining the back streets. There were very few trees. More than half of the buildings in the town were abandoned. Some derelict buildings had caved in on themselves; many others were mere shells built of concrete bricks and gappy mortar which had apparently been abandoned half-finished when money ran out. It was siesta time: the only shop I saw open was a place selling lotto tickets and a few pieces of exhausted fruit. This was not a place where a stranger dying of thirst would be offered water. As in Gioia Tauro, the main activity in San Fernandino seemed to be sitting on a folding chair outside your house, with the doors open front and back to catch the occasional zephyr, and staring at whoever walked by.

I collapsed on a bench beneath the long awning of a beachside pizzeria. The proprietor, an amiable man of about fifty-five remarked that the day was *molto caldo*, as if I, sweating like a fat man in a sauna, had somehow suggested that it was merely warm. He went into a rattling explanation in rapid Italian about how a nun had collapsed on the beach from the heat – or at least that's what he seemed to be saying, judging from his hand gestures – and was expected to collapse again tomorrow. I expressed my dismay at this. He asked if I was working on a ship. I nodded, unwilling to admit that I was a mere passenger. It seemed a sissy kind of role in the macho Italian waterfront, considering that I'd left the Filipino guys sweating over hectares of the ship's airless metal decks, dressed in aptly named boiler suits. He grinned and pointed up to a dusty sign hanging over the footpath: The Seaman's Bar. The first seaman's bar of my journey. Tristan and I had never found a sailors' bar in our tour of the central Mediterranean. I wanted to haul out one of my ridiculous Gioia Tauro postcards and dash off a line to him about my triumph.

But it was too hot.

We arrived at Piraeus, Athens' commercial port, early on Saturday afternoon. I'd just woken up from a long sleep, cradled in my narrow bunk by the steady side-to-side rolling of the ship. Again, I was struck by the torpid stillness of the sea. The humidity shrank the horizon to just a few kilometres.

Piraeus had easily the most striking setting of the ports I'd seen so far. Hills rose sharply behind the stick-figure cranes, hills the colour of well-worn suede, scattered with thousands of salt-white cubes. The port agent, a muscular young guy with an intelligent face, drove us into central Piraeus in his hatchback. He was moving that day and didn't have time to drive us to the Internet café Nadia was demanding. We found a different Internet café, right in town. I checked my messages. Ada had booked a passage for me on a Dutch ship sailing from Tilbury to Cape Town via Rotterdam, Lisbon and the Canary Islands and needed me to pay up to secure my cabin. I was still hoping, perhaps unrealistically, that I might be able to make my own way from Alexandria. I sent back a message putting her off for a few more days.

The languor of siesta hung over the city. I searched in vain for port culture all day long. The first bay I came to had some yachts, a few of them quite large, and several small, derelict craft. A couple of boats were actually half-sunk; the tip of a rotting prow was the only thing still above the surface. In the late afternoon I found the Greek Yacht Club and, a little further on, a cosy little bay edged with candle-lit tavernas in which a flotilla of mid-size yachts were bobbing in a faint swell, their masts like twitching needles against the sky.

I lingered around the first group of yachts, trying to look chesty and fit. I even tried to look suggestible, as though an ouzo-fuelled orgy wasn't entirely out of the question for a happy-go-lucky sailor like me. But there was no-one there to notice any of this. No-one to offer me passage to Gibraltar on their svelte seventy-footer. There were no svelte seventy-footers. The yachts in the bay looked like the dregs of the Piraeus pleasure fleet. On a day like this any self-respecting Athenian boat-owner would be out on the glittering Aegean with a boatful of expensive young things and a case of Krug chilling in the walk-in coolstore, ready for sunset. I knew it wasn't going to happen. Not here. You can't set out looking for adventure, Conrad wrote. 'You just end up with Dead Sea Fruits', by which he meant, I take it, a mouthful of dust.

I met up with Dominic in the evening. We had dinner in a trattoria at the marina. A tableful of tourists was singing 'Waltzing Matilda'.

It was a surprisingly middle-Mediterranean scene. Except for the cheesy bouzouki music being piped through a pair of speakers mounted to a palm, we could have been in Santa Teresa or Golfo Aranci. I was struck by the sameness of these Mediterranean waterfronts, with their weekender yachts bobbing in the marina beyond the café tables, the same Eminem tracks booming out of cruising cars.

I had expected the Eastern influence to grow stronger as we pushed further east, but we seemed to have gone backwards since Venice. 'We could be in Sardinia right now,' I said. 'They're all the same, these sea towns. They're all more like one another than they are like their own country.'

'I'd prefer to be in Sardinia,' Dominic said. 'I prefer Italy. I prefer the television shows. The dancing and singing.'

Dominic's favourite Italian show was the game show 'In Boca Al Lupo' in which most of the dancing and singing was done by fantastically leggy young women wearing as close to nothing as you could get in a family program. Even the band was all-female and virtually nude. The only good thing about our hold-up in Gioia was that he'd been able to watch it every night for a week.

I pumped Dominic for stories. Dominic, I knew, liked to talk. Talking was one of the great pleasures of life, he said. To talk, to drink some of that semi-sweet home-made Romanian white wine, to talk some more, to open more bottles, to pass out at the table. What he hated most about the ship was the lack of conversation. During the painful silences the officers' mess he would cover his ears and shout 'Please! Not too much noise, my ears are hurting!' And so, shamed, we'd all try to have a conversation, usually about the lack of conversation. 'In France,' Nadia said once, 'when there is a silence at the dinner table, they say "an angel is passing by".' This somehow made it worse – it was hard to imagine anything as lovely as an airborne angel at a table like the one in the officers' mess, with its plastic mats, condiment pots with their rime of congealed mustard, and UHT packs.

But Dominic wasn't playing along, not tonight. 'What can I tell you? I don't know nothing about this place. If you go ashore, you see a movie, maybe having some drinks, some food. Then back to the ship. You are always thinking it's an exciting life at sea,' he smiled. 'But we're just the same as you. Ordinary guys.'

'That's not going to help with my book,' I told him.

'I know,' he grinned, looking pleased. He ordered another bottle of retsina. 'I am sorry this wine is so shit,' he said. 'Come to Romania and I show you some *real* wine.'

THE GIRLS IN BRAZIL

When I returned to the ship I passed Nadia's cabin on the way to the passenger deck where I intended to smoke for a while and plan my escape. She was gazing desolately out of her porthole.

We talked for a while. She hadn't had much more success ashore than I, though she'd found the fast film she needed and had been presented with another cigarette lighter by the man running the Internet café where she'd spent most of the afternoon.

'What did he say?' I asked.

She shrugged. '"Please, beautiful lady, for you." Or something like that. It's quite nice, isn't it. You can have it if you want.' It was quite nice. It had a blue-and-white beaded case. 'What about you?' she asked. I told her about my hapless attempts to find my way to the porty heart of Piraeus, how no grizzled mariners or porn film producers had offered me passage on their yachts in Piraeus.

'I thought Dominic was going to show you the sailors' town. Didn't he take you to some places? What did you do?'

'We ate calamari.'

'You're so lucky,' Nadia sighed. 'You're a man. The guys will go to brothels with you and you'll be able to see what they're really up to.'

Both of us were intrigued by what the seamen got up to on their shore leave; the better we got to know the crew the more curious we became. Nadia was torn between the hope that one aspect of traditional life at sea might have survived containerisation, and her distaste for the idea of prostitution. She was convinced that none of the Filipino guys went to brothels because most of them were married. She didn't think Johnny went either. 'Why?' I asked. To me, he seemed like one of the most likely patrons of the pleasure palaces waiting for us in the Levant. 'He's too sweet! You need to get friendly with Sally,' Nadia said, using our code-name for Mr Kuerten. 'I bet he goes. You could go along and smuggle my camera in.'

Frankly, I thought Nadia's faith in the chastity of the Filipino crew was a little naïve. I'd shown her the relevant passage in *Notes from a Sea Diary: Hemingway All the Way*, the book Nelson Algren wrote about a trip on a freighter across the Pacific to India and the Philippines. 'According to the script, [sailors] got homesick in every port. But I'd never seen one hit the beach, with money in his pockets, whose thoughts weren't cutting in closer to the closest whorehouse than to home. Nobody goes for a life on the roving deep whom life on the beach hasn't first made seasick.'

Nadia wasn't persuaded. 'So? That was a long time ago. And he's talking about Americans. These guys are so sweet.'

We didn't have to wait long to find out. The following night, churning our way to Beirut on a starless, humid evening, we settled in for a chat on the passenger deck with Cookie and Johnny. Cookie looked about twenty-five, but was actually forty-six. He was very short and had an overlarge set of false teeth that gave him the appearance of a permanently beaming clown. He was a funny, laugh-a-minute guy, so the falsies suited him. He had been at sea since he was seventeen, and there was nothing about going ashore he didn't know. In fact, far from scrupling to discuss a long and memorable career in whoring in front of Nadia, Cookie seemed to relish an audience.

'You interested in pretty girls?' he asked me. 'Go to South America. Ah, Brazil!' he said passionately, lifting his nose into the sea breeze as if savouring a distant scent of Bacardi and cheap perfume. 'Lovely girls. Very nice. But pretty expensive because of all the American sailors they get there. Sometime you pay even forty dollar.' Worse, Brazilian girls were renowned – and feared – for their jealousy. You chose a girl when you first arrived in a particular port and you were stuck with her for as long as you kept going back. If you decided to change later on, the rejected girl might slash your face with a razor or a knife, or, as Cookie had heard happened, the other girl's face. Either way, you played around in dockside bars there and someone would get cut, and the cutter cuts with complete impunity, protected by whatever code of law operates on Brazilian docks.

None of these complications come up in Venezuela, Cookie pointed out as he settled himself into a pleasant cruise through his memories of the South American coast. 'There are also some very nice girls there. Much cheaper. Very friendly. Not bossy!' Cookie suggested to me that I might like to bear that in mind when booking my next voyage.

'Colombia?' asked Johnny, who was sitting at Cookie's feet a little like a disciple collecting crumbs of wisdom as they were tossed from the table.

'Very good story about Colombia,' Cookie hooted. 'Also very nice girls. But in Colombia there is too much Mafia. One time I go to the place and I see a girl I like very much. So I say, how much? And they tell me the price. And I agree. Then the girl goes to the bedroom upstairs and I pay at the cashier in the bar. Then when I get upstairs, there's a guy standing outside the door. He says, "No, no – first you pay, then you get the girl." "But I paid already at the cashier!" "I say you didn't pay!" "But I did pay!"'

He giggled happily at the memory. For this high-seas chef, South America seemed to live in the memory like a pungent gumbo of girls, gambling and grass. I thought of Philip Roth's Sabbath, who went to sea in 1946 on a quest to find the 'world-wide world of whoredom, the tens of thousands of whores who worked the docks and the portside saloons wherever ships made anchor, flesh of every pigmentation to furnish every conceivable pleasure . . .' Here at last – in the unlikely guise of a boy-faced old salt in a chef's hat – was the incarnation of that mythic lustiness of sailors.

Cookie was off again. 'Then there was the time in Thailand . . . Oh, Thailand!' he cried. 'Oh my ladies . . . !'

Nadia cleared her throat. 'How young was the youngest?'

'Thirteen,' Cookie said. 'Sometimes fourteen, but thirteen too.'

He had just told us with great pride that he had three daughters himself: twenty, sixteen and ten. His wife worked in a bank in Manila. Nadia was beginning to look ill.

'But,' he continued, 'one time I had terrible bad luck in Bangkok. We are in a place and I see one I like very much. So I say, "How much?" "Forty dollars." I say: "Maybe thirty?" And they say, okay. So I am thinking this is very good luck. Not expensive for good times.

'Then we go to the room and get already in the bed. And I take my clothes off. And she is in the bed already. And then I undo the clothes, and I can't find the hole. I am thinking, "Where is the hole?" Then I see . . . It's a boy! I can't believe it! That's why it is so cheap! But he looks so much like a girl! I run out of there as fast as I can go . . . But the worst bit is that I don't even get my money back!'

He laughed and laughed. His face crumpled with delight.

This rotation wasn't renowned for the girls to be had ashore; besides, there wasn't enough time in port. Except, perhaps, in Mersin, where there was a popular sailors' bar and brothel fondly known as the 'Piggery'. Johnny told us that he had once volunteered to accompany a friend from another ship who wanted to see the fabled Piggery. Three of them set out in the middle of the day. When they arrived though, the bar was quiet and the girls perched on the stools weren't up to the standard said to be available at night. The girls they'd expected were instead middle-aged women: 'old girls and big girls . . . They have been in the job too long . . . Some of them have already six or seven children . . .' The *mama-san* didn't like her clients' attitude. Johnny and his pals were chased out of the place by several screaming women old enough to be their mothers. It seemed to me that these guys spent a lot of time running out of brothels.

Eintopf peas. I'd never heard of it but the steward claimed, on Cookie's behalf, that it was a classic German dish. It looked like split pea soup, just like my mother made, but with thick, leathery sausages humorously inserted on the vertical.

Cookie seemed to be waging a private war with the captain in the form of terrible food. I couldn't tell whether he was deliberately cooking up a parody of German cuisine, or whether these dishes were sincerely meant. Nadia asked if she could try some Filipino food. Cookie was thrilled. Of course she could!

The next night he served a pile of pasta covered with partly frozen vegetables swimming in a pale fluid. 'What is it?' Nadia asked in a small voice.

'Chop suey vegetable!' Cookie beamed, proud as punch.

Dominic slurped some gravy off his pork chop. 'What's the matter? You don't like meat? You need to build yourself up!' Nadia gave him a pinched smile and picked bravely at her meal. Two days later, she found sores in her mouth. 'It's the fucking terrible food.'

'What do you think was in it?' I wondered.

'I don't know. But if he makes it again, I will vomit all over the table.'

The captain was not greatly beloved of his crew. In a tone of great wistfulness, Cookie told us that on his last ship he would go ashore with the master and the chief engineer for 'good times', which involved drinking and whoring, all on the captain's tab. 'Ah, he was the best captain. Captain of good times!' Next to that, Mr Borgman simply didn't make the grade.

It turned out that the captain lived in Costa Rica. 'Probably some kind of tax arrangement,' Johnny guessed. 'It's creepy, isn't it?' said Nadia, whose unease with the captain had recently matured into full-blown dislike. 'Overtones of something really sinister, you know?'

Nadia and Johnny were becoming quite close. When he wasn't working, Johnny accompanied Nadia on photographic assignments around the ship, holding reflector boards for her, offering his opinion on what was worth shooting and what wasn't. He also seemed to enjoy airing the ship's secrets within her earshot, and she passed some of them on to me. She warned me not to trust one of the oilers, a hot table-tennis player called Phillipe, to whom I had lent my copy of John Irving's *A Prayer for Owen Meany.*

'Do you mean I shouldn't have lent him my book?'

'I'm just saying that you shouldn't say anything to him about the captain, or anything else. Johnny just said to be careful, that's all.'

Beirut started badly for me when Nadia asked, in a question that was really a statement, whether she could sit in the front seat of the taxi so that she could take photographs. I was getting sick of the photographs and the camera. I stewed in the back seat, muttering to myself. The taxi driver had seemed to know English during our negotiations for a few hours' driving around the city, but it turned out that he didn't know any phrases other than 'I speak you' – which meant, variously, 'Here, I will show you', or 'You will see that', or 'Look over here!' – and 'kaput', which encapsulated the pathos of all the ruined and blasted building shells he showed us.

We motored from one smashed building to the next. It wasn't clear whether the ruins were ancient or modern. The taxi driver didn't care: Roman ruins were not more or less kaput than the various buildings caught in the crossfire of the last twenty-five years. At one devastated apartment building he stopped and got out, kicking the walls with angry excitement. He rolled up the sleeve of his shirt and showed us a tattoo, a wreath of Arabic script skewered by a sword. Could he translate it? 'We will slay all the enemies of God,' he replied, in surprisingly clear English.

Nadia and I had fundamentally different ideas of what we wanted to see. Nadia wanted to conduct a breezy tour of war ruins. I didn't know what I wanted to do, but it wasn't that. 'We want to see where the war was,' she instructed the driver loudly, making confusing gestures with her hands. 'We want to see beautiful things, too, but mostly we want to see places destroyed in the war.'

I cringed at this, thinking of my own forays into war tourism: remembering the old man at the port in Eritrea who had wept with helpless anger to see foreigners come to his country only to spend

103

their time photographing derelict hulks in the ship graveyard at Massawa. But I didn't have any better ideas. In my pocket was the phone number of a friend of a friend who had promised to take me to a nightclub set up in what she described as a former torture chamber, which struck me as perhaps a little bit too authentically decadent. It was a moot point anyway. We had to be back on board well before nightfall.

The driver got the hang of Nadia's needs pretty quickly. He drove us past several buildings with concrete walls sieved by bullet holes. 'I speak you – kaput!' he shouted, pointing excitedly.

We asked where he lived; where the border lines were now; how long ago the rubble along the roads had been buildings. 'I speak you,' he said, and drove us to a golf course, before Nadia, almost wrenching the wheel out of his hands, insisted that he show us some more ruined buildings.

During a long hold-up in a traffic jam on the main coast road, I watched kids working the lines of backed-up cars, selling water, fruit, foil sunguards and even wooden ship models made out of pieces of chipboard and balsa. Their tiny cloth sails were wilting in the moist heat. The models looked like they'd been slapped together in a back shed somewhere, but were obviously supposed to look like the kinds of ships Venetian traders had loaded with spices and silks when Beirut, under Mamluk rule in the fourteenth and fifteenth centuries, was the main trading station between the Arab world and Europe. Lebanon had experienced a much more recent heyday than that, though none of these kids was old enough to remember the days when Beirut's 'free zone' seaport and its thriving financial services sector made the city the hub of the Arab Middle East in the 1950s and 1960s. That all finished in 1975.

I eventually left Nadia with the taxi so that she could take all the photographs she wanted. I rested for a while in the hot shade of some dusty olive trees, then returned to the harbour to soak up the ambience of the waterfront. It turned out later that the taxi driver's poor English was actually pretty useful on the subject of fucking and whether or not Nadia was interested in a quick back-seat screw while her 'husband' was out of the way making a phone call. 'What did he think I was going to say?' she asked me pleadingly. '"Oh yes please, you hairy-arsed ugly bastard, I've been waiting for you to ask?" What's wrong with men?'

Poor Nadia. Even when she made it off the ship she was surrounded by us.

Of all the ships to be on! There were much more romantic boats that mine in the harbour at Beirut. There were ten or fifteen midsize freighters, compact enough to be useful for smuggling, big enough to smuggle something substantial. Some guys fished silently under the iron haunches of their massive ships. As I walked past on the way back to the *Anneke Schliemann* one of them looked up and hawked a gob of spit into the water. He smiled sourly.

These ships looked like they'd crept into the harbour from another dimension. Ships with grimy superstructures, paint jobs peeling, dicky engines and discounted cargo. Ships that had been places. Dodgy, very dodgy-looking sailors, most with giant guts and expressionless dark eyes, none in any kind of boiler suit or uniform, inhabited the decks rather than worked on them; they subsisted on the decks. And you could see pellets of wood, piles of white boxes and sacks of flour and cement being loaded into the hold. This was the way all ships used to be loaded before the containerisation revolution. Now it's just the cut-rate ships that load like this, piecemeal into the hollow guts of the hold.

From a distance, these sailors looked like the real thing. They stared with an envy that had long ago soured into contempt at modern container ships like ours, with our freshly painted decks, our businesslike regimen, the round-and-round, the profitable tick of the clock. These guys looked like they had had plenty of time to chase vice and sedition ashore. Perhaps too much time. They looked like they'd found it sometime around the 1950s and hadn't looked back. If I had found a bar in Beirut that contained more than one or two of these guys, I would have been too afraid to speak, let alone sit in a corner and soak up the sweaty smell of violence.

We unhooked ourselves from the cranes and cables, our propeller began to stir up the murk, making bottles and pieces of string jerk in the water, and then the ship eased away from the dock. The pilot jumped off onto a tug after we'd travelled only a few hundred metres. Darkness fell quickly and the thick haze over the hills of Lebanon absorbed the dregs of daylight. A sprinkling of houselights began to glow in the dusk. This is the time to be going ashore, I thought. A more habitable temperature. A nightclub in a converted torture chamber. Softly lit cosmopolitan avenues lined with swaying date palms.

I felt the irritation and disappointment that had been building up inside me for the past week. These twelve-hour stopovers were hopeless. I knew that superficial contact was in the nature of sea voyages, but this was ridiculous. Apart from the withering heat, the problem with walking around these port cities during the day was that the forensic sunlight flattened out the city so that the idea of adventure seemed ludicrous.

Dominic leant heavily on the rails, narrowing his eyes in the smoke from his cigarette. 'Beirut, eh. It's all fucked up. A pity.'

'Did you ever see it before the war?'

'No. I am not a hundred years old. There is always a war on here.'

'Have you ever been ashore?'

Dominic squashed his nose with his thumb, a gesture that seemed to help his memory to function. 'Well . . . I had to go ashore to go to a dentist once. I had an abscess. The dentist was very pretty. She didn't speak much English good, but she was nice to look at.'

So someone had good memories of their time ashore. 'But don't the guys every go ashore here? Get into some fights in bars? See some women?'

Dominic snorted. 'You're not going to be happy until you've seen a punch-up, are you? I tell you, when is there time to go ashore? It's all different now. You came twenty years too late.'

I didn't know whether he was referring to Beirut before the war, or seafaring before the profession had its marrow sucked out of it by containers and efficiency.

I could only imagine what it once looked like. Even today, from a distance, with the lights coming on across the amphitheatre of hills, it looked entirely different from how it had seemed up close. I watched the glowing blue sparks from a bit of repair welding on the ship berthed next to us scattering into the sea.

Dominic gave me an amused look. 'I have heard of this thing,' he said, 'that when someone sees something nice it's nice, but when that same someone drinks some beers and makes him all happy, then suddenly it's very beautiful.'

'I bet there's a lot about the world that looks good after a few glasses of that Romanian schnapps you make.'

'Well it sure looks fuzzier, anyway.'

The bridge of the *Anneke Schliemann* was eight flights of stairs above the main deck. Whenever someone came up at night, the rubber doorframe sighed shut, there was the muffled click of the latch and then the heavy breathing of whoever had just arrived. If it was Mr Kuerten it was a healthy, deep-breathing sound; if it was one of the more elderly Filipino sailors on night watch, it was a smoker's cough; if it was the captain, his belly teetering on spindly legs, his knuckles white as he gripped the chart table for support, it was a painful groan, muttered curses and a damp wheeze that went on for several minutes.

I sat at the chart table one night, going through the ship's maps. Mr Kuerten was playing solitaire on the master's laptop at the other end of the bridge. From where I sat I could see the radar screen. Smudges of green light caught on the arm as it swept lazily through 360 degrees, picking up disturbances which gradually resolved themselves into ships or coastline, or – if they were wave echoes, the white noise of radar at sea – vanished on the next sweep. I pored over charts of the eastern Mediterranean seaboard. I was fascinated by these charts. There was something lyrical about the way they took the inscrutable emptiness of the sea and filled it with a fabulous world of peaks and ravines, wrecks and currents, sketching out a place full of unknowable depths and slow-moving shadows. Humans have seen less than one hundredth of one per cent of the deep ocean floor. Who knew what was down there? Maybe that's where the sea monkeys lived: on underwater islands deep below sober hydrographic data and safe from any attempt to prove that they didn't exist.

But the charts were also telling me something practical. Somewhere between planning and execution, my voyage had drifted off course. I had come a long way from the Fleet Street Starbucks, but was no closer to Massawa or to anything like it. I'd taken the *Anneke Schliemann* because it would take me east to the Levant; from Alexandria I had hoped to negotiate a passage down the Red Sea, to Port Sudan and Jeddah. But in the harsh light provided by the chart table's plastic lamp, it was suddenly clear that wasn't going to happen. Young Marco had wandered out of range of my radar and, for the time being, off the charts altogether. It looked like I'd be on Ada's Dutch ship.

Over dinner, Dominic and Nadia argued about movies. Nadia had made the mistake of suggesting that Disney animations were lobotomised rubbish.

'Blah blah! I suppose you think the best film in the world is *Casablanca*,' Dominic ragged her. 'Or – don't tell me please – Orson Welles.'

'No, I don't. Actually, my favourite director is Mohsen Makhmalbaf.'

Blank faces all round.

'He's Iranian. I really want to go to Iran sometime,' she continued, prompting a sharp intake of breath from Andrej. 'It's a fascinating country. Really it is. You should see these films.'

Dominic couldn't believe his ears. 'But tell me, have you actually seen *Pocahontas*? Tell me the truth. Or *The Lion King*?'

Nadia had to admit that she hadn't.

'Ha!' Dominic crowed, turning to Andrej. 'She hasn't seen it so she wants to go to Iran instead.'

'What for you want to go there?' Andrej demanded. 'They chop off your hands there for picking your nose exactly!'

'And your nose as well!' Dominic added.

'Have you actually been to Iran?'

'Why I go to Iran?' Andrej giggled. 'I know exactly it is Africa there also!'

Laughing despite herself, Nadia turned to me for help. 'What's *your* favourite film?'

'Er . . . *The Usual Suspects*?'

She rolled her eyes.

'See?' Dominic crowed. 'Forget about Iran!'

They both adored her. The next couple of weeks were going to be complicated.

SHOPPING WITH PIRATES

After a couple of weeks at sea, I'd begun to get a grip on the mariners' globe.

> Best place for 'ladies': Brazil
>
> Cheapest 'ladies': Kenya, Vietnam, Thailand
>
> Best clothes shopping: Syria and Turkey
>
> Best place to buy mobile phones: Mersin, in Turkey
>
> Cheapest computer equipment: Lattakia, in Syria
>
> Place not to get off the boat if you can help it: Lattakia
>
> Best place to sign off at: Gioia Tauro, because the company will pay for business-class flights home from there
>
> Place where you are most likely to get beaten up: West Africa, closely followed by East and Southern Africa
>
> Best place to retire: for Andrej, it's Australia. Why? Good climate. And because no-one gets upset about anything there. I think he just said that for my benefit.

We spent two days in the Syrian port of Lattakia.

Nadia, whom the captain had begun to refer to as 'Lady Passenger', asked the captain whether she should wear something to cover her head while she was ashore. The captain went red in the face, as if she'd asked whether a bra was necessary. 'Don't ask me!' he said, but then added, 'I don't zeenk you will have some problems. The last lady passenger went ashore in Lattakia and had no problems.'

'Great,' Nadia whispered to me. 'She was also seventy-five years old.'

We went ashore with Phillipe, the guy who'd borrowed my copy of *A Prayer for Owen Meany*. He was on a mission to buy copies of Windows 2000 and the *Encyclopaedia Britannica* for the chief officer and the chief engineer. But before he did that, he said, he had a couple of things to attend to. We agreed to meet him at a café a little later in the day.

Lattakia felt a lot friendlier and more prosperous than Andrej had led us to expect. It was busy, lots of people everywhere, plenty of women as well as men in the streets and narrow covered markets, everyone scrupulously polite to strangers. The buildings were dusty concrete cubes, but were lively with people's colourful washing, and television antennae that sprouted haphazardly on the roofs. The men were dressed in the standard Arab uniform of simple button-up shirts, with slacks and sandals; the women were not as severely covered as we'd expected. Maybe it was the liberalising influence of the port? Whatever the reason, the spirit of trade and cultural exchange seemed to be alive and well. A grinning boy who looked about fourteen offered me forty camels for my 'beautiful wife'. I think he was just trying out his English. I told him I'd consider it. Nadia told him he'd never be able to handle her. The boy grinned at her, delighted.

Lattakia's civilisation is unimaginably ancient. It was a thriving port in the third and second centuries BC during the Seleucid period. Just north of present-day Lattakia lie the ruins of Ugarit, a palace and royal town, discovered in 1928 when a farmer bent a ploughshare on some buried stone. Clay tablets inscribed with the earliest known alphabet were unearthed there in subsequent excavations. They turned out to be 5000 years old.

We wandered in the markets for a while, where we saw heaped sacks of spices and nuts, lentils, beans, pistachios and chickpeas.

Some streets were shaded with cloth and were busy with people shopping, drinking tea and running errands. Most of the offices seemed to be closed. There were model boats on sale, rough hand-carved versions of the usual chocolate box of famous ships: the *Mary Rose*, the *Constitution*, the *Bounty*. 'If I had a ship,' Nadia noted, 'I think I'd call it the *Lady Passenger*.'

At one point, we turned a corner and saw a sheep slumped on its side on the footpath. It was a sheep dying a slow halal death. Its head and ears were black with dried blood. A man stood over the sheep, one flip-flopped foot on the animal's neck. Two little girls sat on the footpath next to the sheep, watching us watching it die. Its kicks were regular, but weakening. Bright red blood was squirting in a thin stream onto the concrete and a boy with a squeegee was scraping the blood into the gutter. The flies seemed to be keeping a respectful distance.

For the sailors, Lattakia was the place to buy software. Phillipe returned in the early afternoon and we joined him on his quest to find the pirated software he was after. We tried three different places, all of them specialising in ripped-off software. At the third, the proprietor, a friendly fat man with a terrible limp, copied the software we needed from licensed originals while we browsed his shelves. Each disk cost US$3. He wrote the serial numbers or passwords required to run the software in black felt-tip pen on each disk. Nadia bought some image libraries; I bought a golf game. I couldn't play golf, I just thought it might help to kill some time on board.

When we left Lattakia, the crew conducted a stowaway check. Dominic stood next to me at the railing. Not for the first time, Dominic had contrived to be the only crew-member not actually working.

Like everything else in a sailor's life, procedures for dealing with stowaways had become more bureaucratised and complicated by international law, insurance requirements and the relative civility of the late twentieth century. Like all maritime officers, Dominic had been required to watch a video on the subject, but his grasp of the proper procedure seemed hazy. 'You have to ask them questions, take down all their details and make a dossier to give to authorities at the next place. Because it can be dangerous on board, these people. They might do crazy or dangerous things. If they throw themselves overboard, someone could say that he was thrown overboard, and the master could be in trouble for killing him.' He told me what sounded like an apocryphal yarn about a German captain who had tested his carbon dioxide fire extinguishing system in the hold soon after leaving a port in West Africa, only to discover afterwards, to his enormous – some might say unconvincing – surprise, that three stowaways had been hiding in the hold and were now conveniently dead.

Dominic described how in Africa, stowaways wait in canoes outside the port. As the ship passes by, they use a grappling hook on the end of a long pole to climb aboard. Once they're aboard, they're the ship's problem. According to Mr Borgman, the main problem with stowaways is that once they get aboard, they're very hard to get rid of. No other country wants to accept responsibility for repatriating them, so the ship is stuck with them until it returns to the port where they got on. If it's a tramp route, the master pointed out, you may never return to the port. Stowaways have been known to remain on ships for several years.

The crew rattled around the decks, banging containers with wrenches like beaters on a hunt trying to scare game into the open. Bursts of radio static came through the darkness as each deck was reported clear. There was something faintly sinister about it all.

'I know it looks bad,' Dominic said, 'but they're luckier if we find them than if we don't. Sometimes stowaways get into containers and of course they die of cold or exposure. And if we don't find them until we're at sea, they'll be looked after until we get to the next port. They're lucky. Everyone knows what happens to stowaways on Chinese ships.'

I thought I could detect the telltale odour of a red herring among the diesel fumes. 'Why? What happens to stowaways on Chinese ships?'

Dominic smiled grimly and made a jerking motion with his

thumb over the side of the rail. 'And not just Chinese ships.' Dominic smiled at my expression and shrugged. 'It's not so bad. Usually they're shot first.'

Leaving Lattakia was even better than Beirut. We passed a row of anchored cargo ships. A few had their deck lights on, but some of them were just empty hulls. One seemed to be being dragged very slowly under the water by its anchor. Empty ships, pointing out to sea. We were going to Mersin, in Turkey; these ships were going nowhere ever again.

That night I was back on the bridge with Mr Kuerten. He was writing emails to his girlfriend in Hamburg. It was almost completely dark on the bridge, just the luminous green from the two radar screens and the desk lamp lighting the chart on which Mr Kuerten marked in pencil at regular intervals the speed and direction of our drift. Below us, the cargo bay was brightly lit by floodlights mounted on the ship's cranes. Now and again the radio crackled to life and Mr Kuerten adjusted the volume so that the yachties chatting to one another on the ship's band didn't upset him too much. 'They're idiots. It's supposed to be used only for emergencies. One day they will have an emergency but no-one will come because everyone has turned off the radio. It's like the boy who shouted at the wolf.' Occasionally the dot matrix printer in the chart room hummed into life and rattled out two more lines of weather reports.

Mr Kuerten was an unknown quantity to me. I knew he wasn't popular with the crew. I suspected he was just shy and tried to compensate for it with a blustery manner. He was a good choice for health and safety officer. He took very seriously his duty of distributing condoms to the Filipino crew, some of whom were twice his age. His severity and underaged paternalism probably strengthened the prophylactic effect of the rubbers.

'Don't sailors ever go ashore to the pub?'

'When do we have time?' he asked. He told me about a friend of his, a Croatian boatswain, who had spent a lot of time on bulk freighters between the United States and South America.

Brawling was one of his favourite pastimes. He had developed a technique for getting into the bar fights he was so fond of. The idea was to fill the pockets of the greenest and youngest crew-member with change and send him over to the bar's jukebox with instructions to program in the same song over and over. Invariably this would irritate other seamen in the bar, particularly the ones who hated Michael Bolton, and sooner or later someone would approach the hapless kid and start pushing him around. Which, of course, was the trigger for the hardened sea dogs to step forward in the boy's defence and enjoy the brawl which they'd been priming themselves for with whiskey shots.

I could only assume that he was talking about a very different kind of crew to the one on this ship. What I know about brawling would fit on an eye-patch, but I would have guessed that a reasonably fit group of nuns would have had the crew of the *Anneke Schliemann* bloodied and double-nelsoned in minutes.

'But,' Mr Kuerten finished, 'those are the good days. They are mostly gone for container ships like this. Only a couple of days in port at the most and everyone has to work all the time.'

The phone was ringing when I got back to my cabin.

'I thought you must have jumped ship in Lattakia,' Nadia said.

'Just shooting the breeze with Sally.'

'Can you come down? I need to talk.'

'It's two in the morning.'

'Please? I've got cold beer.' Unlike mine, Nadia's cabin was equipped with a fridge.

Romance had finally appeared in my journey on the sea – in the form of Johnny's passion for Nadia. He was contriving to bump into her, as if it was by innocent chance that he happened to be loitering most of the night in her corridor. He followed her whenever she went to take photographs. He was gallant, but heartbroken. He would dial her up on the intramural phone line just so that he could feel nearer to her. 'I am in love,' he told her nightly. 'You must help me. Please help me!' She kept telling him that it was normal for a young man who hadn't seen a woman for

115

months to feel attracted to the first one he saw. Johnny denied this. 'You don't understand! I'm dying! Help me, Nadia!'

For me, romance on board meant kissing the photograph of my beloved before going to bed, wiping off the smudge marks which resulted and keeping an eye on the steward, who I thought had begun to fancy me a little. He had begun giving me a special, mysterious smile sometimes when we encountered one another smoking on the main deck in the evening. He used to call me 'My Man'; lately he had begun calling me 'Big Man'. I quite liked that.

I awoke to the shudder of a full container being placed into the hold. I peered out through my porthole, trying to remember which part of the world was supposed to have arrived overnight. Like the magic faraway tree, a working ship on a busy route is a place which is magically visited by a succession of lands, whose surface similarity, their spidery cranes and rail tracks, somehow conceals the fact that the world's variety is being served up to you on a giant lazy Susan.

I went down to breakfast, passing the conference room where the captain was entertaining some Turkish port officials, oiling the cogs of port diplomacy with cans of Sprite. Breakfast was boiled sausage again. When it was over, the captain presented me with my shore pass for Mersin, as if by way of apology.

If the crew were to be believed, this shore pass was the equivalent of Charlie's ticket to the chocolate factory. For the crew, Mersin was the promised land. Not because of the Piggery; you could find a brothel anywhere. No, it was the best stop on the route because you could get a mobile phone cheaper in Mersin than anywhere else in the Mediterranean.

I stood at the railing and contemplated what I could see of Mersin – more acres of sun-drenched concrete and stacked containers with flaking paint and baking contents. I felt tired and lacklustre. I watched a shore party leave the ship, striding purposefully past a couple of taxis parked beyond the customs checkpoint and on towards the town and its market stalls where serried rows of discounted Ericsson and Nokia phones were waiting for them.

Nadia and I spent the day wandering the town. Nadia hated it almost at once. I was indifferent. We shopped around for a while looking for a battery she needed for her camera. I bought some more dated newspapers and some Turkish delight. If anything, Mersin seemed more deadeningly sensible than Gioia Tauro and mildly more prosperous. Nadia didn't bother to take any photographs. 'I mean, where is the culture in this place? It's all just crappy clothes stores and depressing cafés.'

In fact, it was a perfectly pleasant working town. Office workers were eating their lunch out of paper bags in the park between the town and the shore. There were several other tourists here, all of them Turkish. We stood out. A couple of small boys carrying shoe polish boxes hassled us relentlessly, one of them trying to paint my faded brown walking boots with his liquid black polish. They chased us out of the park and we escaped to a shady café further along the waterfront.

Touching in at the shores of the world here and there, I began to get a strange sense that the world around me was accelerating, that it had begun to move at the speed history usually moves at. In the pages of the *Economist*, the world seemed to be teetering from one epochal disaster to the next. Bill Clinton seemed to be flashing around the world from peace conference to disarmament talks at cartoon speed; troubles in Palestine seemed to be escalating at a remarkable pace.

Dinner that night was a couple of oven-blasted capsicums artfully stuffed with grey mince. Mr Kuerten asked me whether I had enjoyed my time ashore.

I told him that I thought Lattakia was more interesting.

'You like Lattakia better?'

'I think so. Something about the energy of the place.'

His eyebrows twitched with disbelief. 'Of course, Lattakia is better for computer software. But Mersin is best for mobile phones. Much cheaper in Mersin than in Lattakia. You should have gone with Johnny and the others.'

✳

One thing that hadn't changed in the merchant marine was sailors' complaints about change. Sailors have been complaining about change for at least a hundred years. As Dominic became more expansive over our evening beers, I heard more and more about how much life at sea had deteriorated in the past twenty years. But Jack Kerouac saw the same thing fifty years ago when he was working on a cargo ship out of San Francisco: sailors then were never as violent, as romantically minded or as drunk as he would have liked. And Kerouac was merely echoing Joseph Conrad who, fifty years before that, was convinced that everything worthwhile about life at sea was about to disappear forever, the glory of sail crushed by the implacable 'plodding sound' of the screw propellers of steamships driving on into a future made safe, but dull, by engines and iron.

As we left Mersin, Dominic used the several ships anchored outside the harbour to illustrate his point about freighter design. He picked out a creaky-looking general carrier. 'Panama,' he said. 'At least twenty years old. You can tell from the superstructure. See how it sprawls out? Because when it was built, they needed a much large crew. They never build ships like that now.' He pointed at another one, a mid-size freighter, that seemed to be listing somewhat at the stern. It looked like a browbeaten camel that refused to stand up properly. 'A coaster,' Dominic said confidently. 'Probably forty years old. Full of asbestos I bet. Probably has a crew of ten, but when she started out there was enough room for thirty.' When Dominic first went to sea in the late 1970s, there were plenty of ports in the world where you could be held up for weeks. Sailors loved it. 'At least on a bulk ship you still get to spend a week or so in port. Of course, you work during the day, but after that you can live like a normal person. Hang out in some bars, maybe meet some nice girls.'

He lit a cigarette for himself, then one for me. No-one could light a cigarette in adverse conditions like Dominic. He cradled his hand around the lighter, making a safe harbour against the breeze. He claimed to have once lit a cigarette on deck in a force eight gale with a soggy match. He claimed to have done a lot of things.

Bad news filtered down from the bridge that evening. Our last scheduled stop in the Middle East, Alexandria, had been cancelled by the charterers. Which left only Tartus, another Syrian port. Ninety-four nautical miles from Mersin; six hours' sailing.

Nadia wasn't perturbed by this setback. She was excited with other news. Johnny, the love-struck Filipino cadet who had been trying to persuade Nadia to marry him for the past week, had abruptly lost interest. He had met another girl in Mersin.

'You're kidding. A prostitute?'

'No, he met her in McDonald's. I think she was working there. Anyway, when her shift was over they went to her house.'

This seemed like an amazing turnaround in Johnny's fortunes: this was the guy who had once been ignominiously chased out of the Piggery by a mob of veteran prostitutes. It sounded unlikely to me. Taking a sailor home for hot sex didn't seem like the kind of thing a nice Turkish girl who worked at McDonald's would do.

Nadia smiled crossly. 'I said he's in love, I didn't say he'd had sex. They *talked*. They talked for three hours.' Johnny had made the announcement to Nadia as soon as he'd arrived back from the mobile phone emporium. You have to understand, he'd told Nadia gently, there had been an instant *sympatico* between him and the girl whose job it was to do the fries. Nadia would have to try to forget everything Johnny had said.

'Did he really say *sympatico*?

Nadia grinned broadly. 'They're fickle, aren't they, these seamen?'

Breakfast the next day was described on the blackboard as 'Excramble Mexico'. Scrambled eggs with tomato. At least Cookie's sense of humour remained constant.

I was very excited about Tartus. Only an hour's drive inland were the remains of the magnificent Crusader fortress Krak des Chevaliers (in Arabic, Qala'at al-Hosn), which T.E. Lawrence described in 1909 as 'the best preserved and most wholly admirable castle in the world'. It was built in the twelfth century and overrun by Beybars, Sultan of Egypt, in 1271. Depending on how much time we had, I knew I mightn't get to Krak des Chevaliers, but at the very least, I would get to see the twelfth century fort built by the Knights of St John.

I visited Nadia in her cabin. She was trying to rig up her curtains so that she could take photographs from her porthole without being observed. Photography was strictly forbidden here. Dominic claimed to have known a Filipino sailor who'd ended up in jail for two months for taking a snap here of his pals on the deck with a disposable camera.

I never got ashore at Tartus: the immigration officials wouldn't allow it. The captain was at pains for me to understand that it wasn't his fault; that for some reason unbeknown to him, the officials here were much more leery of foreigners than their colleagues in Lattakia. 'Don't ask me,' shrugged the captain. For once it seemed that he was genuinely sorry that he couldn't help. 'They never tell us why it is not possible. They don't even give the Filipinos an application form. I can't tell you why.'

In the evening I stood at the railing, passing time. The docks were almost deserted. I heard somebody whistling, then saw a wiry old man in a battered fez ride past on a bicycle. When he looked up curiously at our aft decks I recognised him – I'd seen him in the morning, vainly trying to sell a metre-long swordfish in his basket to one of the Filipinos. There had been no takers. Now he made a few lazy circles in the gloom, apparently taking an idle interest in the ships. Then he turned suddenly and rode towards a stack of timber that had been unloaded earlier in the day from a bulk carrier at the berth opposite us. He got off his bike and casually scratched his armpit. He looked around. Then he snapped into action. Working quickly, he dragged four or five short lengths of timber off the pile. He pulled some twine out of his pocket and glanced around accusingly. No-one watching. He tied the wood to the back of his bike, climbed on, and then ground down on the pedals as hard as he could, sprinting away towards the port gates, his head low over the handlebars and his load of contraband wobbling on the back. I was glad to see that someone was getting something out of Tartus' docks.

We left a few hours later, passing within forty-five metres of the two submarines Dominic had told me to look out for. They were both sagging at their moorings, the second one, in particular, barely above water. On the dock behind them was a row of thirty tiny prefab cabins. Groups of soldiers sat around tables in front, playing cards and looking up as the tugboat nosed us out to sea.

We had a boat drill the next day. The crew stood around solemnly while Mr Kuerten shouted out their names. No-one seemed to be able to recognise their name from the list. Mr Kuerten grew irritated. The captain was nowhere to be seen: presumably he intended to go down with the ship if we sank. Eventually we all climbed into the fibreglass boat. We sat there for a while. Then we climbed out again. Mr Kuerten delivered a lecture on speedy deployment of the boat.

Dominic wandered over. 'And so we are all saved by the quick thinking of Mr Kuerten,' he smiled.

'You wanna play some table tennis later?'

'You and me? I'm too good for you.'

'You could play left-handed?'

He shook his head. 'Forget about it.'

For a while I'd been back on the table tennis table with Johnny and Phillipe, the guy who was still reading my John Irving. 'It's very long,' he told me. 'But it's good. I don't think I will finish by the time we get back to Venice.' I told him he could keep it, partly hoping that he would go easy on me in table tennis. It didn't work: he had an unusual grip and electric reflexes, and an infuriating ability to win points while yawning and picking wax out of his ear. I was more evenly matched with Johnny who was vulnerable to my deep back-handed serve, especially when he was playing up the end with the valve tap that stuck into your back. Affairs of the heart had weakened his game. Whenever I passed him on the deck he'd ask, 'Have you seen Nadia? Where is Nadia?' I suspected he was only playing table tennis with me in the hope that I would volunteer some insider information about his loved one.

Nadia was mostly hiding in her cabin with the phone that

connected her to every other cabin in the ship off its hook. 'He never stops calling. He says I've broken his heart.'

'What happened to his sweetheart at the Mersin McDonald's?'

'I guess it didn't last.'

According to Dominic, it was now well known throughout the ship that Nadia and Johnny were having an affair. The captain was giving her strange looks in the corridor, she said. 'I can't believe that's what Johnny would tell people,' she wailed. 'Now even the master thinks I'm fucking the cadets.'

Three days later we were back in familiar waters. It was like a homecoming, seeing Stromboli again, watching it drift in and out of vision, as if we and it were connected by a long but determined piece of elastic. We were due to go alongside that night, but I didn't like my chances. The ship was supposed to be in Trieste by now. I was supposed to be in Rotterdam – having missed the ship in Tilbury – and boarding my next ship to Lisbon, the Canary Islands and Cape Town. I wasn't. Unless I managed to get to shore sometime and thence to Naples airport, I wouldn't be going anywhere. Except back to the pizza restaurant in Gioia maybe.

Stromboli was still there in the morning. I felt like banging my head against the railing.

I spent the day watching the volcano, hoping for a violent eruption that might force us to head inshore. In my head I could hear Billy Bragg's version of the Woody Guthrie song 'Ingrid Bergman', about the filming of the Roberto Rossellini film called, simply, *Stromboli*. In 1949 Rossellini and Bergman, fresh from her triumph in *Casablanca*, began work on a film about a Latvian refugee who married a man from Stromboli and struggled to cope with her new life there. Despite Rossellini's eccentric methods, which included writing the dialogue moments before shooting a scene, and forcing Bergman to walk around the volcano's crater in bare feet and deliver her lines in clouds of hot ash and smoke, the actress was besotted.

Their affair quickly became an international *cause célèbre*.

122

Eventually Bergman's husband and manager, the brain surgeon Petter Lindstrom, flew to Stromboli to get his wife back. It didn't work, not least because Rossellini threatened to kill himself – perhaps by throwing himself into the volcano, as Bergman's character planned to do in the film – if Bergman went back to Lindstrom. Both Bergman and Rossellini had their first marriages annulled so that they could marry the following year. Amazingly this romance, forged in the heat and the hysterical atmosphere of the island, survived until 1958, when Rossellini went to India, fell in love with an Indian actress and made a film which he called, surprising no-one, *India*.

I found out months afterwards that while we were drifting between the island and the coast, Tristan was holidaying in Stromboli with his own leading lady. Since we'd parted in Genoa, he had been making better use of his time than I had. While I was taking notes on the tedium of not travelling while at sea, my actor buddy was wooing Emily – also an actress – on Stromboli's smouldering slopes. Must have been too far away for Mr Fernandes' binoculars to pick them out.

In the hope that we would finally go ashore the next morning, Dominic and Andrej that night invited me down to the television room for a farewell beer. Nadia was there too. Andrej showed us photos of his twin daughters, his son and grandson, and lots of photographs of the various ships he'd worked on and the shore leaves he'd taken with various workmates, almost all of them people he'd never seen again. The photos were all from the early 1990s, but could easily have been taken twenty years earlier. I marvelled at the fantastic capacity of seafarers to drag back the clock. Was it just the dumpy Eastern-European clothes the men wore? The Polish sailors out on the town in 1995 looked like they had arrived in Vegas in 1981 during the reign of Cindy Lauper and *The Breakfast Club*, with their yellow short-sleeved shirts, T-shirts with sailboat print patterns and orange-tinted sunglasses.

There were a few pictures of Melbourne from 1997: Andrej standing on Swanston Street in front of my old haunt The Lounge

Bar, in front of the gunmetal cone of Melbourne Central, with the green leaves of plane trees fuzzy in the background; and in front of Crown Casino. Most of the photographs seemed to have been taken from a very low angle, as if by someone lying in a gutter. I half expected to spot my own furtive figure in the background, guiltily smuggling a polystyrene lunch box of lemon chicken out of the food court.

'Melbourne is very nice city,' Andrej said respectfully. 'Very nice.'

'Do you really think so?' I asked, suddenly shy and proud. 'Most people from overseas seem to prefer Sydney.'

'Of course, Sydney is the best place. Very beautiful. Lots of parties. But Melbourne is good too.' He seemed to be dredging his memory for something more flattering. 'Nice girls,' he said, flashing his radiant gap-toothed smile. He patted me on the back.

Dominic presented me with a gift: it was a pirated copy of the *Encyclopaedia Britannica* on CD. 'I had a spare one. It's so you can check all your facts and remember Dominic,' he said.

I was touched. It was the perfect present to give a port-hopper: a defence against all the sailors' fictions I would be hearing over the coming months, and pirated goods to boot.

When I returned to my cabin I paused in the corridor to slip off my shoes. From behind the captain's cabin door, I could hear Serge Gainsborough turned up loud. Usually I heard the muffled sound of European football matches. In the morning once, I was leaving my cabin when the steward was entering the captain's suite with his bucket, disinfectant and toilet rolls, and I had glimpsed its sad acreage of synthetic carpet, an expensive television mounted on the wall and a computer on the desk. The captain himself had just emerged from the head. His jellied bosoms and belly tumbled over the band of his boxer shorts. Our eyes met briefly as the door closed behind the steward.

As I stood outside his door on what I hoped would be the last night, I realised that there hadn't been a barbecue for us. Did he hate me? Did he hate Nadia? I never found out. I never got *Owen Meany* back from the table tennis champ either.

THE FLYING DUTCHMEN

The delays off Calabria meant that not only had I missed the ship in Tilbury, I'd also missed it in Rotterdam and Lisbon. Never mind, Ada said. The rest of the route was falling into place. From Gran Canaria, it was ships all the way to India. So now, here I was making my way from Gioia Tauro in southern Italy to Las Palmas in Gran Canaria, Canary Islands, not on a ship, or even a yacht, but on a 737.

I tried to shut out the rows of block-booked holiday-makers and the irritable excitement of their bleary-eyed children and focus on my mission.

I opened my badly worn copy of Warren Miller's *All Around the Mediterranean*, which was published in 1924. I'd found Miller in a second-hand bookshop in Robin Hood Bay, on England's North Sea coast where decades of unfashionable titles had washed up on the shelves. If his prose sometimes read as though he'd dictated it to his secretary over a third Martini, it was also steeped in sun, gin and cigar smoke. Miller was every bit as cheerful as you'd expect someone to be – a journalist, of all people – who seemed to be able to take a four-month holiday every year. I liked his breezy remarks. I liked the way that his jazzy sentences were hammered into the pages like cattle brands, slightly misaligned, as if the impact of the press had jangled the surrounding letters.

The Las Palmas of Miller's story was an eccentric but thoroughly satisfying stopover for cruise passengers. More Spanish than Spain, he declared with approval:

Palm gardens, ablaze with tropical flowers in full
bloom, where the señors and señoritas take their
airings . . . One such square was a dream of tropical outdoors. . . Banks of purple Bougainvillaea
and scarlet poinsettia bordered it. And, in the cen-
ter, a fountain with a long reflection pool running
both ways the length of the square, and every inch
of it blue and red tile. . . It was a heavenly place to
sit and imbibe something cool and cheering.

I dumped my bags in my room on the fifth floor of a plainly fur-
nished hotel in Las Palmas de Gran Canaria and headed straight
back out again. The streets had a tired, grimy smell, like the sour
aftermath of a giant party. The beach was deserted, but the cafés
and bars lining the boardwalk above it were still full of people
swaying on stools and laughing hard into one another's faces. I
eventually perched myself on a barstool a few streets in from the
beach, in a place where an old oil storm lamp hung from what
might have been a beam recovered from some drowned ship.

I shook a cigarette out onto the bar and ordered a beer. I took my
bearings. Nautical lamp notwithstanding, it was a fairly nondescript
place, though authentically dingy for a seamen's bar and, with beer
on tap, bottom-shelf liquor in bulk and a dinted cigarette machine.
On a wall behind the bar was a brass barometer mounted on a paddle of distressed oak, more likely distressed in the back room of a
chichi craft shop than on the bridge of a salt-encrusted schooner.

I smoked the cigarette, if only to feel less like a blow-in, and
immediately began to feel ill. The loneliness was back, refreshed
by a couple of days at home. No-one spoke to me except a guy
in a Chicago Bulls shirt who wanted a cigarette. In three days'
time I'd be boarding another freighter, this time for ten days of
solid sailing.

That night, I received a message from the gods. *The Poseidon
Adventure* was showing on cable television. Less optimistic souls
might have taken this as an ill omen; I couldn't believe my luck.

I hadn't seen this classic since the late 1970s. With nostalgic fascination I watched, groggy but unable to switch off, as Gene Hackman, Shelley Winters and the rest of the cast succumbed, one by one, to the remorseless calculus of the disaster movie. I was particularly pleased to see Shelley Winters expire after her heroic underwater dive, just as I remembered from childhood. Comforted, I drifted off into a deep sleep.

Two days passed while I tried to soak in the maritime heritage of Gran Canaria. For lack of a better place to start, I headed to the Museo de Colón in the old historic centre, which was once thought to have been Christopher Columbus' house. Locals now concede that Columbus may never have even come ashore here, but this hasn't deterred the museum curators from dedicating rooms of maps to the Spanish voyages to America.

The best thing in the museum was its collection of antique maps. There were diagrams showing how the Canary Islands, and Las Palmas in particular, had provided crucial staging posts for the westward voyages of exploration which were looking for an alternative route to the East. These were fascinating, if disconcerting: the Spanish managed to discover the islands of Maluku, formerly the Moluccas spice islands, in the western Pacific. By the time they reached America, the cartographers were seeing the world in surreal terms. One confidently drew a map of the voyage showing China fused to the North American land mass, a wishful conclusion which conveniently eliminated the world's largest ocean – the Pacific – from the problem of a route to the Indies.

The *Catalan Atlas* of 1375 was an extraordinarily beautiful, blue-and-bone-coloured map in twelve panels attributed to Abraham Cresques. Portolan charts like it began appearing after the development of the magnetic compass in the late twelfth century. It showed the Mediterranean littoral packed thick with place names. As is usual on portolans, the interior areas were less accurately depicted, and the yawning white spaces were filled with sketches of sultans, desert tents, elephants, camels and castles – all the things, in other words, mariners might have to reckon with if they were unlucky enough to find themselves separated from the sea. The carefully plotted names clinging to the sea's edge were the product of the aggregated maritime wisdom of hundreds of years of seafaring; the cartoons in the interior were the product of hundreds of years of sailors' whoppers and inventions.

This exquisite object was, I realised, a diagram of the inside of Andrej's head. Dear Andrej, the Polish electrician who had travelled the globe and never penetrated more than a couple of kilometres inland; who skipped around the rim of the world like a pebble skimming across water, confidently dismissing anything south of Kraków as Africa, and sketching in the great gaps of the inland world with trolls and monsters and other mariner hearsay.

The *Van Riebeeck* was berthed at the very tip of the longest of the docks in Las Palmas port. The ship was so big it blotted out the afternoon light. In fact the word 'ship' did not immediately come to mind. The *Van Riebeeck* loomed over the docks like a warehouse, at least eight storeys high and nearly 300 metres long. There wasn't an elegant curve to her stern, no ship-like rake to her bow, just a sheer cliff-face of iron sheets welded in grids and all of it painted black. A long chute of collapsible stairs scraped on the concrete with each faint shift of the hull. Several men in grimy white boiler suits watched as I struggled up.

I was left in the office off the main deck corridor while someone tracked down an officer. With its creaky swivel chairs and bare fluorescent globe in the low ceiling, the room had the feel of a factory foreman's office. The walls were covered with maps of the ship's decks, safety instructions, risk assessment tables, loading schedules and shelves packed with binders, all dated and numbered. I swivelled coolly on my squeaking chair, trying to appear relaxed and amused; the kind of guy any sailor would be glad to have along as a passenger. I knew how all this worked.

The man who appeared in the doorway introduced himself as the chief cook. The whites of his eyes looked like they'd been soaked overnight in cold tea. He had a straggling beard and was wearing a fake Lacoste T-shirt with a soft collar and horizontal stripes, probably picked up during a shore-raid in Singapore or Kuwait.

I followed him down a wide corridor with grey linoleum to an elevator. 'There is a party on,' he explained. 'In zee officers' mess. On Friday nights we always make a party.' Well, that explained the state of his eyes. We got out on the fifth deck. Again, a spacious corridor with glossy linoleum, wide enough for hospital gurneys. He fumbled with his keys and opened several doors into empty passenger cabins. They were identical. 'You choose,' he said. 'Zay are all zee same.'

I picked a corner cabin.

'Whatever,' he said, working the latch of the door.

'But the other passengers . . . ?' I wasn't sure if the cook had heard me. He smiled to himself, revealing slimy teeth which had weathered into sinister brown points.

'Where are the other passengers sleeping?'

'There are no other passengers.'

'No other passengers.'

'We never have any passengers on this ship. Just you. And wife of the second engineer, but she's not really a passenger.' He burped fulsomely, then grimaced and rubbed his belly. 'You want to see the ship?'

We took the stairs this time, down to the galley deck. He showed me the kitchen, which was industrial, a blur of aluminium and sterilised white-tile acreage, then the officers' messroom. The room contained two fake pot plants, some mounted photographs of the ship and several others like her, and three tables: two large round ones at either end and a small square table in the middle with one place setting. 'Zee passengers usually sit zair,' the cook said, pointing to the small table.

I laughed lightly. 'But this time there's only one passenger . . . That's what you said, right?'

He nodded. 'And zat's vair he sits.'

He gave me an ironic little smile, with perhaps a touch more warmth in it this time. 'Come on,' he said. 'Come und haff a drrrink.'

Entering the officers' bar on the *Van Riebeeck* was a scene straight

129

out of a John Ford film. Everything happened in slow-motion. As I stepped inside, the last words of a joke died in the throat of the barman. I saw perhaps ten men, all but two or three under thirty years in age, all in crisply starched uniforms. I registered a low-ceilinged room wallpapered to mimic the grain of some dark wood, with a bar up one end – complete with racks of liquor, a blackboard for scoring drinking games and barfly swivel stools – and at the other end, two sets of lounge suites arranged around coffee tables. There were ships in bottles, maritime paintings, a miniature brass rudder wheel and several plaques on the walls by the bar engraved with drinkers' saws. Every eye in the room, emboldened by Dutch beer, was on me as I stood silhouetted in the fluorescent corridor light. There was a deep silence. I inhaled bitter cigarette smoke as I waited for it to finish.

'Meet the passenger,' drawled the cook, with a camp bow. 'Mr Passenger, meet everyone.'

I offered the room a pathetic little wave. The officers kept staring. One or two may have grunted a greeting. Then they returned to their beers. As my eyes focused, I saw that in front of me, at a card table, sat a middle-aged woman with large, yellow horn-rimmed spectacles. She was waving brightly for my attention. 'I'm Carol,' she said. 'I'm the second engineer's wife.' She nodded to a thin, crinkled man sunken into a lounge chair at the other end of the room, who was also wearing yellow-tinted reading glasses, and was clutching a can of Amstel. She was South African married to a Dutchman, she explained. She offered me slices of melon and Swiss cheese. I accepted a beer from the cook and sat down, the worst of it over, to be filled in at length by Carol.

I sat alone at breakfast on day one, with my personal passenger steward in crisp whites standing to attention by the toaster only three metres away. The steward was a good-looking man in his mid-twenties, who looked so startled when I introduced myself that I was myself startled and failed to catch his name. Since then he'd been looking very pleased with himself and I was afraid of having to admit that I had missed it.

We were the only people in the room. He watched closely as

I spooned cornflakes into my mouth, both of us conscious that the only sound in the mess was the sound of my spoon scraping the bowl and nervously clicking on my teeth. I found swallowing difficult.

'Don't the officers eat breakfast?' I asked.

'Yes, but not now.'

I spilt half a litre of milk down my chin and the steward watched, unmoved but interested, while I cleaned myself up with several paper towels. Then he inquired as to whether I would be taking toast this morning. He had a row of bread slices lined up on the sideboard. It was an ordinary domestic two-slice toaster, but my steward handled it like a maestro, inserting each slice of bread not once, but three times at three different angles and intensities of heat, so that every last millimetre of the bread was evenly toasted. The result was a giant golden crouton, its surface so crisp and brittle that it was impervious to the softening influence of butter or jam. It probably only took me ten minutes to chew through both slices. I escaped with relief past the bowing steward.

I was back at eight the next morning. The room was deserted again. The steward watched me impassively through the cornflakes, then two slices of chipboard toast. I asked him how long he had been on the ship and whether he enjoyed his work. I asked where he was from.

'Indonesia,' he said.

'Where in Indonesia?'

He looked surprised – pleased, but wary. 'You have been to Indonesia?'

'Oh yes. Well no. No, no I've never actually been there. But I've read a lot about the area.'

His face fell. 'Sarawak,' he said, in a tone which suggested that of course I would have no idea where that was. But I *did* know where that was. '*Really*?' I said, with too much force. 'I've always wanted to go there.' I racked my brains. 'Orang-utangs,' I nearly shouted. 'You have orang-utangs in Sarawak, don't you?'

He stared at the floor and shook his head faintly, whether at my general knowledge or my desperation I couldn't tell. 'You want more toast?'

'Ah . . . no. No, I won't.'

Captain Bisset dropped around in the evening. He was an attractive man in his early fifties with dark skin and a clever face. He had neat, amused features and an effortless air of authority. He was born in Surinam and went to study for his certificate in Holland when he was eighteen. Some time in the past the bridge of his nose had been broken in a perfect horizontal line. Somehow, his crenellated profile added an attractive edge of danger to his suave demeanour.

He invited me up to the bridge any time, and said if I wanted to see the engine, something could easily be arranged. 'I'm worried that you're going to be bored with us dull bunch. What are you doing all day, Neil?'

My name had been listed on the ship's manifest with my middle name first (and I'd given up trying to explain).

I told him about my book. He examined my computer, ran an eye across the spines of the library I'd brought aboard. 'Why did you choose a freighter instead of a passenger ship?'

'Cheaper,' I said. 'And because it's real life.'

'You know Mr Neil, there is a library on board? You haven't seen it? Oh yes, quite a large one. And not all in Dutch. There is a wide range: fiction, informative books, magazines. I'll get someone to show you.'

Stepping into the officers' bar each night at six-fifteen for the customary pre-dinner drink was a harrowing experience. On the first night, no-one looked at me. After dinner the officers retired to the bar where, by custom, they took their coffee. I sat at a separate table for as long as I could bear it and then escaped to my cabin.

All this was repeated on the second night until we got to the coffee stage. The junior officers all sat around a table with no spare chairs, laughing and smoking, a couple of them reading the print-outs of the Dutch news emailed by the shipping company every morning. I lit up and settled myself at the next table, alone, looking as relaxed and approachable as I could, with a two-week old copy of the London *Daily Mail* open on the table in front of me. Then my luck changed. There was a silence, and then I heard someone speaking English. It was one of the junior officers. He was asking why I was on the ship.

I explained that I was hoping to write a book about ports.

He frowned. 'But we don't go to any interesting ports,' he said. He was tall and had pocked skin and a raw Adam's apple that hitched when he laughed. His name, I later learned, was Henrik.

I told him that I'd meant to join the ship in time to make a thorough study of Rotterdam and Lisbon. The officers seemed dubious about this. 'It seems like a strange idea for a book,' one of the others said. 'I read mysteries myself.'

'It's mostly Cape Town I'm interested in anyway,' I explained.

'That's ten days away.'

This was perfectly true.

'Why Cape Town?'

'Well . . . it's very historic.'

'Not as interesting as Durban,' Henrik yawned. 'Are you going to Durban?'

'I'm not planning to,' I admitted.

'Durban's much better,' said Henrik. 'Big sharks there.'

If the ship's public spaces looked like they were going to be a challenge, then my cabin was a luxurious hideout at the top of the ship's superstructure. Together with the passenger lounge which opened onto the corridor directly opposite my door, I commanded an area the size of a generous London apartment. I had a video, television, two beds, a coffee table, a few chairs and a bathroom. Like all the passenger cabins, this one was recently fitted as a part of a new company business plan to reintroduce passengers to intercontinental rotations. The cabin smelt of sawdust. The rivets in the fibro sheeting on the walls sparkled with newness. Slices of discarded carpet kept turning up in drawers and under mats.

The rest of my deck felt uncannily deserted, with its impersonal fittings and the strong ammonia smell from the daily round of mopping. At particularly paranoid moments, I wondered if the place mightn't be haunted. At night, when the wind came up and the ship rolled gently from side to side, the empty corridor reminded me of Kubrick's Overlook Hotel. Even in daylight hours, the wide stairwell echoed with the distant rustlings of people I never saw.

Wandering listlessly around the main deck on day three, I found a door with a sign addressed to passengers. There is something daunting about a public sign which is addressed to only one person. This one read: 'Out of respecting the crew's privacy, please not entering during mealtimes and after hours.' What was this? A giant crew privvy? I waited for a slow afternoon when I was convinced I couldn't hear any noises coming from the other side. I tried the latch and entered a small antechamber with clothes hooks and a boot scraper; beyond the next door I found the crew's bar. Here was the bar I'd been looking for ashore and completely failed to find: with its garish furnishings and complete banishment of natural light it was almost a Rabelaisian parody of the officers' version. I saw a completely enclosed bar in faux teak vinyl, packed with bottles of brandy, a collectors' rack of Taiwanese and Chinese beer cans and a ninety-centimetre saffron-coloured Buddha with a Fourex Bitter eyeshade strapped to its domed forehead. Soft-focus Indian and Singaporean girlie pin-ups lined the walls. There was a powerful smell of stale cigarette smoke. Yellow lampshades in the corners produced a pale, iniquitous glow. In one corner was a derelict table-soccer board. Someone had left a karaoke microphone coiled between the rows of players. There was the unnatural quiet of a room used to noise.

I was admiring the Buddha's paste-jewellery anklet when I heard the outer door slam. The boatswain appeared in the doorway, hard hat in hand, grinning at me like a gamekeeper who'd caught a poacher. 'Mr Neil! Has anyone showed you around yet?'

I put the Buddha back down. 'Not yet, no. Just checking out the weights.'

He shook his head. 'Someone should show you around. Has

someone given you safety drill yet?' I shook my head. 'Unbelievable,' he grinned. 'I'm busy now, but maybe later.' He waved and left.

I kept track of the days with the aid of the printed menu which changed every day. It was a professionally printed menu. From this I deduced that our food had been planned at a distance of several thousand miles and at least a month. These were seriously premeditated meals.

During the days I wandered around the ship, stepping over abandoned ladders and carefully avoiding welding equipment and fresh paint. The *Van Riebeeck* had been built only twenty-five years previously, but in container ships that was another age, when twice as many mechanics and oilers were needed to keep the ship's massive engines running. All over the decks were rust pockets and discarded scrap heaped in corners. The lifeboats seemed permanently grafted by rust to the steel hawsers which lashed them to the deck.

From the ship's high prow it was possible to look down and see, far below, flying fish snap up through the water's surface and skim along with the ship for five or ten seconds at a time, like green sparks gleaming in the shadows, then vanish back into the water. Carol spent hours each day watching them. Some days we watched them together.

But the heart of this ship, the place where I hoped to siphon all the seafaring tales out of its officers, was the officers' bar.

I came down late one night and found the second officer, Martin, sitting alone watching *Starship Troopers* on the video. He invited me to join him. During the battle scenes Martin was transfixed, but between the battle scenes he told me a bit about himself. He'd been at sea for nine years; he was thirty-five, though his shock of straight blonde hair and fleshy pink cheeks make him look ten years younger. He was due to be married to his Malagasy girlfriend later in the year; since he'd met her he had spent three months of most years living with her and her family in Madagascar. 'Is the ship helping for your book?'

'I don't know,' I answered truthfully. I glanced around the room. 'I think this is the closest I've come to an old-fashioned sailors' bar. I haven't found anything like this on land yet.'

He snorted, but not unkindly. 'Then you haven't gone far enough. This is nothing.'

The only other passenger Martin had ever seen on the *Van Riebeeck* was a retired English army major who had fought in World War II in Asia and was travelling to South Africa the slow way to visit an old army buddy. 'He spent all day in the bar mixing himself drinks,' Martin remembered. 'He'd have weird cocktails lined up for us when we came down for dinner. He was a very funny guy.'

Mostly though, we watched *Starship Troopers*. Martin loved the bits where the alien bugs exploded in showers of green gunk.

My main source of conversation at that point was a slight, earnest young man called Paul, who was doing the eight-to-twelve shift on the bridge, morning and night. He proudly showed me around the bridge. The radar system was the same toxic-green display used on the *Anneke Schliemann*, but the rest of the equipment was clearly designed around the time the 'Blake's 7' sets were built and the influence was unmistakable. The ship's ten-metre dashboard looked like it had been recycled from an obsolete spaceship: grey steel cabinets and consoles with rows of unsophisticated-looking Bakelite buttons and warning lights. The wheel was the same tiny handset you might use to steer a go-kart.

Paul was thrilled to have the chance to work on a piece of living history before it was scrapped in a few years' time. Days spent in the 45-degree heat of the engine room, monitoring the vital signs of the ancient 53,000 horsepower engines, were particularly prized.

I quickly took to Paul. He told me that he sometimes went forward and, when no-one was looking, did Leonardo di Caprio's 'I'm the king of the world' line balancing on the prow. 'It feels quite nice, with the wind rushing past.' He smiled sheepishly.

'Actually it feels pretty silly. But I think it would be very nice if you had Kate Winslet there.'

We spent long hours on the darkened bridge discussing facts, the world and conspiracy theories, to several of which Paul wholeheartedly subscribed. He was reading a history of the spice trade, he said, a book which contained conclusive evidence that the Portuguese behaved even worse than the Dutch during the European age of discovery. He had strong opinions on the danger of mobile phones, the origins of the English language and childhood learning patterns. He was also interested in theories connecting the builders of Angkor Wat temple in Cambodia with the builders of the Egyptian pyramids and urged me to read *Fingerprints of the Gods* by Graham Hancock. Before he'd read it, he too had been sceptical, but you had to admit the arguments relating ancient geometry to star formations were pretty interesting.

Paul had plenty of time to look at the stars.

On day five, I took my books up to the monkey's island. The monkey's island was not as well designed as the one on the *Anneke Schliemann*. For some reason, the top deck attracted fierce winds, no matter how still the air seemed on the lower decks. There wasn't a great deal to see apart from the sea, oily flat and zinc in colour, and the oppressive emptiness of the horizon. The further we sailed down the coast of Africa, the fewer ships I saw. Africa itself was way out of sight. It lay somewhere on the other side of the curved horizon. I was truly elsewhere this time, elsewhere to every other place I could think of. 'The ship, a fragment detached from the earth, went on lonely and swift like a small planet . . . A great circular solitude moved with her, ever changing and always the same,' Joseph Conrad wrote in *The Nigger of the* Narcissus. Personally, I was struggling to comprehend idleness on the scale I was now experiencing it. I found a couple of broken deck chairs folded away under some roped canvas and discovered that if I laid very low, I could keep below the slipstream. Thus I was able to research sea monsters and get out of my cabin at the same time.

Considering how long most European mariners on sailing ships had been at sea by the time they reached this part of the globe, and taking into account the traditional ale rations of the nineteenth century, it was hardly a surprise that these southern Atlantic waters had been unusually fertile for sightings of bizarre and monstrous sea creatures. In 1848 the British warship *Daedalus* reported a sighting of an 'enormous serpent', estimated at over thirty metres in length and apparently bearing a remarkable likeness to the Loch Ness monster as depicted in, say, 'The Goodies'. The creature remained in sight for twenty minutes, during which time it was witnessed by all of the ship's officers. It approached the ship with its head and shoulders 'kept about four feet constantly above the surface of the sea', nearly shaving the ship's bow as it passed through the wake, not deviating 'in the slightest degree from its course to the SW, which it held on at the pace of from 12 to 15 miles per hour, apparently on some determined purpose'. In 1875 Captain Drevar of the barque *Pauline*, loaded with coal and headed for Zanzibar, saw three very large sperm whales, one of which was being strangulated by what appeared to be a huge snake. 'Its girth was about eight feet,' the Reverend E.L. Penny, a Navy chaplain, wrote to the *Cape Argus* newspaper. 'Using its extremities as levers, the serpent whirled its victim round and round for about 15 minutes, and then suddenly dragged the whale down to the bottom, head first. The other two whales, after attempting to release their companion, swam away upon its descent, exhibiting signs of the greatest terror.' The same ship twice sighted the same monster five days later. On one of these occasions it was seen to stand perpendicular almost twenty metres out of the water.

No sign of these marvellous things from where I crouched below the wind. Just an emptiness of steely grey sea: swells covered with fading nets of white foam and between them, inscrutable depths.

Back on the monkey's island, day six. We were probably three or four hundred kilometres off Liberia now, heading out to the gap in the sea left by Africa's giant armpit. Still no other ships in evidence. Rain began to spit onto the pages of my book, so I climbed down the ladder and entered the bridge. It smelt strongly of bathroom cleaner.

The chief officer was on duty. He was a huge, happy, ham of a man, with a lolling tongue, bug eyes and not enough room in his shorts for the tail of his shirt. He seemed permanently amused by everything. He rolled an unlit cigar around his mouth, winked at me and passed me his binoculars, pointing away to an unremarkable segment of the empty horizon. After a few moments I found a fishing boat at the limit of the binoculars' range. Po-faced, Chief asked if they were pirates. I knew this routine. 'Friendlies,' I said. Nodding seriously, he asked me to keep him informed of any hostile developments. I promised that I would.

Captain Bisset joined us soon after. 'What are you looking for, Neil? You lost something?'

The chief officer roared with laughter. 'Just pirates. He thinks the pirates are coming to get him.'

'Neil, Neil, Neil,' the captain shook his head. He flicked on the kettle. 'Coffee before you walk the plank, Neil?'

'Actually, I was hoping to spot a whale,' I said. 'Do you ever see them around here?'

'It's too hot for whales up here,' the chief officer said.

'It's not,' said the captain. 'I've seen whales this far north.'

'Global warming,' the chief informed me. 'They get too hot and sweaty.' Chief looked a bit like a sweaty whale himself.

'Anyway, you don't really want whales wandering around, Neil. They're very dangerous.'

'Oh yes?' I asked.

'Hitting a whale is a disaster. Of course, it's not so good for the whale either.' Sometimes whales bounced off, he said; sometimes they would be killed instantly. But either way, a collision with a whale in certain waters could be a real hassle. 'The forms! And the explanations! Everybody is a greenie these days. The whale should apologise for the trouble!'

'They should make the whale fill out the insurance forms,' the chief officer giggled.

Captain Bisset said he'd give a standing order for the officer on watch to call me in my cabin if dolphins or whales were spotted, but warned that I'd have to get up to the bridge fast. Apparently the dolphins soon get exhausted trying to hop the bow wave.

Carol took it upon herself to organise me. Carol's family lived in Paarl, sixty kilometres north of Cape Town, and she was going to visit them while the ship headed up to Durban before returning again to Cape Town. Carol was very proud of the Cape, but felt it necessary to warn me about the rising tide of crime. She told me not to drive at night and to watch out for gangs of eleven- and twelve-year-old boys who haunted tourist precincts day and night. It was terrible, she said, but the Cape was changing. People were coming out of Pretoria and Northern Province and bringing their violent ways to the lovely Cape. 'If you stop for a red light in Cape Town at night-time,' she explained, 'you're taking a big risk. You see, if you stop completely, the car-jackers can get you. You stop, and next thing you know, there's a man tapping on your window with a gun in his hand.'

I gradually worked out that Carol's obsession with crime was fed by the excellent television reception she enjoyed in her home in the Netherlands: with her remote control she was able to switch between the dismal newscasts of France, Germany, Belgium, Luxembourg and England, hovering over the world like a one-woman crime watch.

'England!' she cried at pre-dinner drinks one night. 'I ask myself what is going on with the people there? Whenever you turn on the television, this person's been robbed, this little girl has been kidnapped, this person has been poisoned. It's really terrible.' She seemed genuinely distraught. 'And Australia? Is it bad, too?'

I had to admit that it wasn't any better than London, but then she seemed to view London as a Blakean swamp of industrialised deprivation, pollution and crime. She shuddered. 'It's the same all over the world! Drugs and crime are out of control. One thing you can say about crime,' she said grimly. 'It's not getting any better, anywhere in the world. It's always getting worse.'

'And the world is getting hotter and hotter,' added the chief officer, with a completely straight face. 'Global warming.'

Carol had been at sea for twenty-nine years. Her favourite places were South America and the Far East which, of course, were nicer in the old days when you could go ashore for dinner and dancing in the officers' club in Buenos Aires or Rio de Janeiro, and buy cigars in Havana. Really, her favourite place was the old days. In the old days life aboard was much more lively. Children used to travel with their parents in the 1970s, she said; back then, when most women didn't work outside the home, there were lots of wives aboard ships like this one. In school holidays, she said, the officers' bar would be a riot of children running around, bits of puzzle sprayed across the floor, toys on the stairs. On warm nights the officers would set up a sixteen-millimetre projector on the boat deck and show films on the funnel. Sometimes there was music and dancing.

You can't go to that place any more.

In the officers' saloon the next night, Henrik was dominating the conversation from a stool behind the bar. He hadn't bothered to change out of his boiler suit, which was unzipped to the navel, revealing his hollowed-out chest. Dolly Parton was playing on the stereo. As usual I'd perched on the walnut cabinet behind the bar, picking at a tray of deep-fried nibblies, drinking my beer too fast and reading for the twentieth time the 'Rules for Successful Drinking' poster tacked to the wall.

Then there was a breakthrough. As I shook one of my last cigarettes out of the packet and lit up with that air of practised diffidence I'd acquired, Paul shifted on his stool and turned to me.

He nodded at Henrik. 'They're saying that in the old days the girls would come aboard and clean your cabin and do your washing.'

'You pay a girl to come aboard and do your washing?'

'And other things, of course,' Paul smirked. 'Mostly the other things, if you know what I mean.'

Henrik had sunken eyes that looked as if they'd seen much to be cynical about in their thirty-odd years on earth. 'That was more in the old days,' he said. 'Back then, you see, there were lots more sailors. The bulk ships had bigger crews, so the port was the best place for the girls to find customers. Now, they don't want to come aboard. You have to go to them now. Too many other tourists with more money.'

Brazil, again, loomed as a distant paradise. '*You* should have gone to Brazil,' Martin said.

Another beer was opened in front of me. 'But I'm going to Madagascar and Zanzibar,' I said hopefully. 'And then India.'

That was the right thing to say. It triggered several long reveries about the attractions of East African ports.

'When I first went to Madagascar I stopped in Toamasina,' Martin said. 'Is that where you're going? It's fantastic. I liked it so much I went back there for my holidays and spent three months. I met my girlfriend there and I've been back five times. You will love it there. It's an amazing place. Like no other place in the world.'

Henrik preferred Zanzibar. 'Every night at eight o'clock the lights go out. I'm serious. Maybe they have to change the filter on the generator or something. Anyway, the first time you're there, you're sitting around in the bar and they start passing out kerosene lamps and you think: "this is very nice, very cosy", and then the lights go out completely! It's incredible. And then the power comes back on a couple of hours later.'

'Does the beer get cold?'

'No,' Henrik said seriously. 'No, they must use ice or something.'

'It's a very strange place,' Martin said. 'It's good because they're very slow in the port. I've been on duty before and watched them unloading one container in twenty-four hours.' He shook his finger. '*One*. I'm serious. I love those guys. When the dock gets full of containers, they throw up their hands: "What do we do now?" And they wait sometimes for days for someone else to organise a fork-lift truck. Not like Réunion, which is run by the French and is very efficient.'

'Too efficient,' Henrik said sadly.

'Ya, too efficient. But Zanzibar is very nice. Except you're not allowed to smoke in the bars.'

'But the girls are also very nice,' Henrik said. 'When you go there don't be a stiff. Some guys you see there don't want to spend any money, they just sit there drinking, looking, drinking. When we go there we are surrounded by girls all the time. Why? Not because we are better looking than them or having bigger dicks. It's because we are prepared to spend money and have a good time.'

'Although,' Paul piped up, 'we probably do have bigger dicks.'

'Probably,' Henrik admitted.

Martin rolled his eyes. 'But the thing to understand is it's not about money there. In Brazil, it's always about money. It's not like that in Madagascar or in Zanzibar. Back before I was with my girlfriend, I'd be able to arrive in port, have some nice dinner, maybe go dancing. Then you'd go to a hotel to do the wild thing and then I'd leave some money in the morning. No questions asked. Plenty of money, you know, more than they would ask for. Thirty dollars. Perhaps more sometimes.'

Henrik poked me with his cigarette hand. 'Here's a bit of advice. Make sure you carry a torch with you when you go out at night. Because just recently a guy from the company went ashore and he fell down a hole in the middle of the street because it was so dark. He broke his wrist and two ribs.'

'Was he drunk?' I asked.

'No! This was *on the way* to the bar.'

Everyone agreed that was terrible luck, getting injured before and not after you'd been to the bar.

Talk of injuries was Henrik's cue to tell horror stories for a while. He told us one particularly splendid medical case study he'd had the chance to observe on a ship operating out of Singapore. A sailor had arranged for a tattoo parlour in Taiwan to sew a pair of small metal balls into the underside of his penis. 'It's supposed to double the pleasure,' he explained, using an unlit cigarette and two peanuts to demonstrate. 'They were stuck under the skin along here. Unfortunately, his cock had become infected and swollen to an enormous size. I've never seen anything like it. It was like a football. Of course, he was in agony, he could hardly walk.

'On that trip we happened to have aboard a real doctor. The

doctor looked at him and was very excited because it was a text-book example of a particular kind of venereal infection. He gave the guy some injections but he took photos first for his students. They had to go up on deck to get enough light for the camera. He was very embarrassed.'

'I'll bet,' I agreed.

'Yes. It was very cold outside and it made his balls disappear.'

On wet or misty nights, when visibility was poor, one of the crew would be brought up to give the officer on watch another pair of eyes. There were a few night-watch specialists on this crew; one of them was an Indonesian man in his mid-twenties. I sat up next to him one night on one of the stools on the bridge. He introduced himself as Said but was widely known on the ship as the 'electric eel' for his uncanny ability to produce static electricity. 'He is a human battery,' Martin had told me. 'You could start a car with just his fingers. No-one can explain it.' Said seemed to enjoy the attention but when the conversation moved on he always seemed to end up quiet and alone, like the kid in the playground who was too strange to make any friends.

Said was leaning forward, staring through the angled glass. I half expected him to glow in the dark. 'Your eyes adjust,' he told me in excellent English, clearly pleased that I was interested in his spotting ability. 'And also it takes experience. After a few weeks you start to learn to pick up lights and shapes. You learn how to see things in the dark. It's not magic.'

I asked him if he'd ever seen a sea serpent. He didn't know what this was, so I tried to describe the beast reported by the *Daedalus* in 1848.

He seemed to give this subject serious consideration. 'Thirty metres long? No, never,' he said. 'I have never seen this. Have you seen?'

'Er, no.'

Sometimes you could see containers that had washed over-board, he said; once he'd seen a crashed weather balloon and a few times he'd seen giant squid floating dead on the surface. 'And – ,' he glanced warily across the bridge where one of the junior officers was intent on his Game Boy and lowered his voice, 'I have seen the *Flying Dutchman*.' He watched my face closely. 'Some people don't believe, but it's real. I have seen it twice. Once on this ship just off Cape Town. And once in Durban.'

For a sentimentalist like me, this should have been the highlight of my trip so far. Mariners are supposed to be superstitious, but until now there hadn't been much evidence of it: the age-old crossing-the-line ceremony hadn't even been mentioned when we hit the equator – the only trace of it so far was Paul's interest in crank astrology. So to be sitting on the darkened bridge of a huge freighter with a high-wattage seaman who had witnessed the fabled spectre of the southern oceans should have been a moment of triumph. But being a sceptic, I felt a bit like I would have if Said had claimed to have been inseminated by alien sheep.

He was waiting for me to say something. 'Isn't that a sign of terrible luck when you see the *Flying Dutchman*?' I asked lightly.

Said burst out laughing and slapped his thigh. 'Ooh-hoo! Thas funny! It just a ghos' story,' he laughed, looking around at the officer on watch. 'Don' believe everything you hear on ship.'

I laughed sheepishly. On the other side of the bridge, the officer with the Game Boy grinned at me. His face looked like a skull in the green light of the radar screen. I felt stupid. 'So you didn't see the *Flying Dutchman* at all?'

Said stopped laughing. He blinked. 'Yes, I see it. I tell you I see it two times. But it not bad luck. It is very beautiful.'

I killed an afternoon grazing over the shelves in the ship's library. 'Library' was a grand word for the stacks of battered paperbacks in the passenger-deck broom cupboard, but it served my needs. Most freighters maintained the quaint tradition of a ship's library, often stocked by seamen's missions en route. This one was a time capsule of passengers' holiday reading. Among about three hundred volumes, I picked out *Jaws*, which I read for the first time, then Alistair Maclean's *Bear Island*, sporting a fiercely ugly paperback cover, which had cost someone ninety-five cents in 1974. The edges of the pages had turned honeycomb yellow. There was a copy of C.S. Forester's wartime propaganda piece, *The Ship*; a Patrick O'Brien; and a well-worn copy of Erich von Daniken's *Chariots of the Gods*. There was also lots of soft-core pulp that was so popular in the 1970s, including, to my delight, that classic of the swinging, key-party scene, Luke Rhinehart's *The Dice Man*.

You could read too much into peoples' bookshelves, I knew, but I couldn't shake the suspicion that when this ship was younger, it must have been a floating ark of middle-class vice and sedition. 'In the old days', as Carol put it, when officers' families often travelled on these big Dutch ships, people took all their photographs ashore on slide film because it was cheaper. In those days everyone would retire to the officers' lounge after dinner and show slides of their shore expeditions. I wanted to know more about those days, about the sexual mores of life on cargo ships in the swinging seventies, but I was afraid to ask Carol any more in case she thought I was abetting the moral disintegration of our times with my sleazy questions.

'What's wrong with the people in England?' she demanded at lunch. Nazeem, the only Englishman aboard, kept his eyes on his soup. 'Another murder in Birmingham today I heard on the radio!' When she wasn't watching the flying fish on the prow, Carol spent her afternoons huddled over a short-wave radio in her cabin, fiddling between frequencies, trying to extract as much bad news out of the planet's airwaves as she possibly could.

Two nights out from Cape Town, Captain Bisset ordered a barbecue. A rusty, coal-fired barbecue was dragged out of a storeroom and dusted off. The crew cleared the fourth deck of chairs and debris, erected a long trestle table between the two massive funnels and laid out bowls of nuts and dried fruit, platters of salad and stacks of tenderised steaks. The swimming pool was filled with crystal water. There were a CD player and speakers. Someone suggested that Said might be used to power the stereo, but an extension cord was found instead. Several large buckets which had once held paint were filled with ice and cans of beer.

The crew sat apart, their backs to the funnel, joking among themselves. The captain, Carol and the senior officers gathered around a moulded plastic table and smoked cigars. Something about the fun-by-decree atmosphere made the junior officers solicitous. Paul made sure my plate was full and the others treated me like a new in-law at a family barbecue, filling me in.

At Henrik's insistence, several toasts were offered to one of the Filipino sailors, a very fat and thoughtful-looking man called Juan. According to some unexplained joke, Juan was worshipped by the rest of the crew as a minor deity, perhaps because he looked so much like Buddha. He said nothing but smiled indulgently and lowered his eyelids in acknowledgement.

The chief cook was enjoying his night off. At one point he fell onto a plastic foldaway chair next to mine and surveyed the scene through wet eyes. 'Everybody drinks too much,' he slurred. 'These guys,' and here he waved his bottle in the general direction of a group of crewmen picking at bits of roasted fish on their paper plates, 'are great guys. Indonesians, they are best. You see, Filipino sailors like to drink too much beer.' He took a long swig on his whiskey, then wiped his mouth with the back of his hand. 'Everyone knows this in our business. Have you noticed this? You will see. But the problem is Filipinos are cheaper, so what do you do?' He wandered off to mock someone's steak-grilling technique.

Later the party moved to the officers' bar. By now, I was beginning to feel at home in there. It was just a pity that it had come so late in the voyage. It was also a pity that there was no piano. I might have been able to lead the lads in a few verses of 'Boogie Woogie Bugle Boy' or 'Eye of the Tiger', both of which my fingers still remembered from that faraway country of piano lessons.

I ended up sitting with Martin while the others played cards. Martin launched into a mariner's appraisal of Australian cities. He loved Australia, he said, partly because the docks were so inefficient. What would take twelve hours in Singapore took three days in Melbourne, he explained, which was bad for the ship but great for the sailors, who got to go ashore. He particularly liked Sydney, where he spent millennium eve, but also Hobart, where

147

he had lovely memories of an arrest on a drunk and disorderly charge. 'You wouldn't believe it,' he said. 'I was just pissing on the street, minding my own business and these cops pulled over and said that I wasn't allowed to do that. So I said: "Okay, arrest me, but do you mind if I finish?" They said that was okay.

'But then they handcuffed me and threw me in the van. I was going mental, shouting and calling them fucking bastards. I was very angry because we were supposed to have seen a nice strip show but it was closed and we had to bang on the door for a while before they let us in to drink but still no strip show. So they locked me up. I demanded to see the Dutch ambassador. They just laughed. In the morning they drove me to the ship and didn't even give me a fine. I like Hobart.' He paused while the details came back to him. 'Great oysters there as well.'

I gazed at the pictures of the old sailing ships on the walls and thought of Joseph Conrad lamenting the end of the great days in *The Mirror of the Sea*. For him, the transition from sail to steam signalled the end of a phase of human evolution and with it, the end of a whole culture of seamanship.

> The seamen of three hundred years hence will probably be neither touched nor moved to derision, affection, or admiration. They will glance at the photogravures of our nearly defunct sailing-ships with a cold, inquisitive, and indifferent eye. Our ships of yesterday will stand to their ships as no lineal ancestors, but as mere predecessors whose course will have been run and the race extinct. Whatever craft he handles with skill, the seaman of the future shall be not our descendant, but only our successor.

There were 'photogravures' in the bar of the *Van Riebeeck*, scattered among the drinking jokes and a scroll printed with a bawdy sea shanty, but I'd never seen anyone looking at them, not with inquiry, not even with indifference.

We were due to arrive in Cape Town the following morning. Up on the bridge, Africa's gigantic outline had nudged back onto the right-hand side of the charts. The straight line of smudged pencil lead tracking our progress was slicing in towards the very bottom of the continent; at two-hourly intervals our position was recorded in delicate squares drawn along the line.

When I arrived on the bridge at seven forty-five, a huge black mass, slumped above a rim of fog, loomed directly ahead of the orange bugs' feelers on our prow. The captain was sitting in his high chair, peering at the view over the top of his glasses. He must have heard my sneakers squeaking on the linoleum, and swivelled around.

'Neil! What do you think of Table Mountain, eh?'

I grabbed some binoculars. Nothing of Cape Town itself was visible yet, but the sheer face of the mountain was clear on the horizon, sharply etched by the low sun. Suddenly my sails were full of enthusiasm again. I was sailing into Cape Town! One of the most beautiful port cities in the world! On a perfect day!

'You can't say I don't look after you, Neil. You wanted to see Table Mountain on a clear morning,' he spread out his hands like a game-show hostess showing the prizes. 'Now you see it.'

'But what happened to the 35-knot wind you promised me?' I asked. 'You couldn't fly a kite in this.'

He shrugged, a smile crinkling his eyes. 'You're right. I'll have to talk to the agent about this. And no fog, either. He said also there was going to be fog.'

Within an hour we'd cruised northwards to the edge of the bay and Cape Town opened itself before us, glinting in the sun. Behind us, long lines of surf unfurled on the rocky edge of Robben Island, where pilgrims went to see the cell where Nelson Mandela was imprisoned for so many years. It was a miraculously pretty scene, with picture-perfect sailboats tacking to and fro in the bay trying to catch a murmur of breeze, and ramshackle fishing boats chugging past us at low speed. But the most sublime thing was the city itself – a beard of glittering roofs and windows clinging to the mountain's lower slopes and the long waterfront.

The captain slipped off his high chair, pointing and shouting: 'Whale! A whale, Neil! Do you see?'

I couldn't see anything. He came so close that I could sight down his pointing arm. I could smell his aftershave. And then I caught a faint puff of spume drifting across the surface.

I grabbed the binoculars and scrambled out onto the bridge deck. 'What service!' Mr Bisset crowed behind me. 'A perfect view of Cape Town and now a whale! You got everything you wished for, Neil! I think you should give me a tip!'

The whale was about a hundred metres off our port side. I tracked its delicate little plumes of spray for about five minutes and then glimpsed the whale itself when it poked its nose into the air for a moment and then rolled slowly back under and out of sight.

We remained off shore for several hours, watching the light slowly picking out the city's buildings, one by one. Carol pointed out various places of interest, managing to identify from where we stood a kilometre and a half out no fewer than three hospitals, a university, a police station, at least seven suburbs and a number of separate restaurants on the Victoria and Alfred Waterfront which was laid out in front of us. All of these areas were danger-ous, she emphasised. 'Always take a taxi. *Always.*' She pointed to Groote Schuur Hospital and the green lower slopes of Devil's Peak. 'That is where District Six used to be. You have heard of District Six of course? You haven't? I can't believe that. It was very famous. Cape Town is not the same without it now. It wasn't beautiful but it was a part of the city, you know? Indians, coloured people, blacks, everyone mixed in together. They bulldozed it during apartheid.'

The pilot came aboard in the early afternoon, also in a white uniform which glowed in the steady afternoon sun. As we crept into the docks, the pilot kept up a running commentary on the var-ious disasters which had beset ships entering and leaving the port over the past fifty years. The engine mount was all that was left of one tanker victim; it was still visible just below the lighthouse on Green Point. 'We still don't really know happened,' the pilot said cheerfully. 'He was cleared to leave but I think a fishing boat cut in across his bows and he had to pull away to the port side to avoid him. He crashed onto the rocks.' Then there were several other vessels which had simply been smashed by heavy weather into the rocks along the edges of Table Bay.

The captain tut-tutted and winked at me over the pilot's shoulder.

As we crept inside the Ben Schoeman Dock – the port's largest, outermost dock, built in the mid 1930s – the pilot pointed out one sad rust-bucket of a tanker which had been impounded by the South African authorities. 'Leaking like a sieve, it was,' he said. 'Our people couldn't believe it when they went aboard. They've arrested the captain.'

Our captain clucked his tongue. 'Look, a seal, Neil,' he said, pointing. A mid-size sea-lion was rolling around in the brown water between our hull and the dock.

'You can't say I don't show you everything, Neil,' the captain said, beaming. 'Now I've shown you whales and Cape Town in the sunshine and a sea-lion.'

'That's true. But you still haven't shown me a dolphin.'

'You can see dolphins at the aquarium,' the pilot said.

'But Neil, a sea-lion is rarer.'

'And it's a very nice one, too,' I said.

The pilot said, 'Of course, where there are sea-lions there are always great white sharks.'

He pointed to the sky above where two helicopters were beating their way around Signal Hill. 'Shark spotters,' he told us grimly. 'Since we had a windsurfer attacked two weeks ago here – ,' he waved in the general direction of Sea Point as he said this, 'they've stepped up the flights again. Fucking sharks everywhere. You should see Durban. You going to Durban? Don't. In summer the air's thick with choppers watching out for sharks.'

Then the pilot's attention turned back to the business of bringing the *Van Riebeeck* alongside. The entrance to the Ben Schoeman dock was very narrow and we were barely moving ourselves, just being dragged a few metres at a time by the tugs.

Carol had returned to the bridge with a business card. She gave it to me.

'When you go ashore you must call this taxi company. They're very good. Always ask what is the number of the taxi, because taxis can be very dangerous in Cape Town now.'

'It can't be that bad.'

'Oh, yes. It's terrible. One boy on this ship last year, an engineer he was, was going ashore. I said to call the taxi from the ship, just to be safe. But he said, "Oh, it'll be all right, it'll be all right."' Carol fixed me with a baleful stare. 'So he walked out to the gate and when he got there a man in a taxi said, "I'm your taxi. You called for a taxi, didn't you? It's me." So the boy thought the agent must have called a taxi for him and he didn't think anything of it. He got inside and, of course, they drove him away to the Flats and they took all of his money and they cut his throat.'

'They cut his *throat*?'

'They took all his money as well. Oh, it was terrible. Terrible.'

'He died?'

'No. No, he didn't die.' But the way she said it conveyed an impression that he wished he had. 'So, do you want the card?'

I certainly did. The card gave the number of the taxi company and suggested that I call Errol. Errol would be my personal pilot guiding me safely through the treacherous shallows of this benighted city.

As I got off the ship, Carol blessed me. 'You must be so very careful. Promise me?'

'I promise.'

'Don't carry money in your pockets. Don't look up at the buildings. Always look straight ahead.'

'Right.'

'Never use an ATM machine after dark.'

'It's going to be okay, Carol.'

'I hope.'

Odd that Carol never said anything about the bombs.

THE SEA AND THE QUEER THINGS THAT COME OUT OF IT

> The whole Town may be considere'd as one great
> Inn fitted up for the reception of all comers and
> goers. Upon the whole there is perhaps not a place
> in the known World that can equal this in affording
> refreshments of all kinds to Shipping.
>
> Captain James Cook, writing on Cape Town,
> *Journal,* April 1771

From the decks of the *Van Riebeeck*, Cape Town looked like a city that belonged more to the sea than to Africa. It looked like a great metallic anemone in fact; one that had hauled itself out of the sea, slumped on the shore, taken a quick look at the deserts, mountains and jungles of all of Africa rolling away into the north-east and made a snap decision to face the sea for good. The centre of the city huddled in the lee of a natural stockade formed by Table Mountain, the Lion's Head to the west and Devil's Peak to the east. Despite the sprawl of slums on the Cape Flats to the south-east, the city centre and adjoining docklands still look like a foothold on a far-flung shore.

Pleasure boats made restless curves out on the water, trying to get the best view of the shimmering buildings and the famous profile. On the Victoria and Alfred Waterfront, the great shining mall occupied by cinemas, souvenir shops and brasseries, land-lubbers watched the water. The whole scene seemed very pleased with itself.

The downtown area was denser than you'd guess from the bridge of the *Van Riebeeck*. Below the banks and offices I found myself in a cold, shadowy grid. It felt like a stubby Gotham of office blocks and insurance buildings. Cool wind sluiced down the streets. It was difficult to find the Metropole Hotel with my eyes neurotically focused on the pavement, but I managed it eventually. With its slightly tatty colonial feel, the Metropole looked like it would suit my escapist purposes nicely.

I was prepared to love Cape Town. For starters, I was terribly glad just to have arrived. I couldn't help feeling like a lost sailor grateful for any kind of shelter after the gruelling conditions in the *Van Riebeeck*'s officers' bar. Cape Town is *the* port in a storm, and there's almost always a storm brewing on the Cape where the meeting of the hot and cold waters of two oceans on the Algulhas Banks provide a constant backdrop of turbulent weather. In the middle of the nineteenth century, the shipwreck survivor's tale became a staple of melodramatic Cape journalism, a genre which typically featured an ominous sighting of the *Flying Dutchman* in the days leading up to the disaster.

Long Street was overhung by iron latticework balconies and shaded by colonial-style verandahs which reminded me of the hotels in Australian country towns. But it was a disorienting kind of homecoming. I felt as though I'd stepped ashore from a fable and found myself dumped back onto the tourist route; out of the *Van Riebeeck*'s alternate reality and back to daily life. I felt like I should glow or smell strange. But if I looked like a refugee from another dimension, none of the waitresses or taxi drivers remarked on it. They gave me my rooibos tea and pizza like I was just another of the backpackers who congregated in the bars and hostels at this slightly seedy end of the city, just another punter, a few more rand.

The next morning I staggered down the stairs to the coffee shop below the hotel and scanned the menu for something, anything, that wasn't a giant golden crouton of baked toast. The breakfast menu was a pageant of eggs, fried toast and a variety of fatty meats. I ordered a 'Double Nelson', which might have been a reference to the English Admiral Nelson, Nelson Mandela or perhaps to the impact of the breakfast on your system.

Over the next few days I savoured the town's frontier feel. If Table Bay's imposing geography was meant to protect Cape Town's see-no-evil sea-facing aspect, it wasn't doing a very good job – at least judging by the news reports I saw on television that week. Small car bombs were going off almost daily in the city centre. The concierge at the reception desk handed me my keys each day with another vitriolic serve at the expense of these would-be terrorists. 'Cowards, that's all they are. Couldn't hurt a fly.' Thankfully the minor splinter-group terrorists that the papers blamed for the bombings weren't terribly serious about carnage, couldn't afford much TNT or didn't know how to make a decent bomb.

Of more concern to my concierge was the increasing incidence of car-jacking and murder on the N2 motorway between the airport and the city. Now that I had arrived and safely signed in, she felt at liberty to tell me that I was taking a big risk just being there. 'If people knew what went on out there on the N2, people would stop coming.' She thought that I'd made a good decision arriving by sea which meant that I didn't have to run the gauntlet of car-jackers and thieves who lurked behind the levees of the motorway waiting for motorists to break down, or pull over to take a mobile phone call. She was a friendly person, but clearly was just a couple of decades short of becoming another Carol.

My business was at the waterfront and that's where I began. It was immediately obvious that I wasn't going to have to look at Cape Town's waterfront through seawater goggles. The modern city's foreshore was literally built on its maritime history: the biggest concentration of wrecks on the southern African coast lay buried beneath the reclaimed land of the foreshore, which was built from sand excavated in the 1930s during the construction of the modern cargo terminals – the Ben Schoeman and Duncan docks. After the Suez Canal opened in 1869, Cape Town was no longer a necessary port of call for ships on runs from Europe to the Far East. Despite this, Cape Town remained a major port, a hub for feeder services to Namibia and other West African countries. From there fresh fruit, steel and fish were shipped to Europe and Asia. More than six million tonnes of goods passed through Cape Town's port each year, and it looked like it.

Cape Town's waterfront blended function and pleasure better than any other place I'd seen. A continuous seafront ran from the giant modern docks to the smaller nineteenth-century wharves and dry docks which were now straddled by the giant malls of the Victoria and Alfred Waterfront. At the café tables on Quay Four, outside Victoria Wharf, you could sip your beer and listen to the industrious blatter of pneumatic paint guns and electric rivetters working on the trawlers in the Alfred Basin around the corner.

The waterfront was not only sea-facing; it was also past-facing. As well as peddling jeans, ebony rhinoceros and milkshakes, the Victoria and Alfred Waterfront was in the business of nautical nostalgia. The Cape Town of 'The Tavern of the Seas' was alive and well there. You could buy Union-Castle Line pens, piratical fridge magnets and miniature ships. My quick survey of the model ships on offer revealed the universal preference for disaster nostalgia: there were *Mayflower*s and plenty of *Sao Rafael*s, but the miniature *Titanic*s, *Bounty*s and *Lusitania*s were the hot items.

But it's not all anodyne commerce, or tat, as Tristan would have said. When seated at one of the waterfront's cheerful cafés, the eye is drawn first to the deep blue of the bay, and the yachts and powerboats cutting white lines across it, and then to Robben island, which was the home of some of the first slaves brought from Malaysia and Zanzibar. It was then used as a leper colony and finally it became the notorious prison where murderers rubbed shoulders with the ANC leadership for thirty years.

The waterfront, like the rest of the city, was full of overseas visitors flocking to the *idea* of this place. They shuffled in a religious hush through the cells on Robben Island, then returned on the ferry to sit on the waterfront and gaze with contentment upon the busy port and the work-in-progress that was the new South Africa. But I suspect that Cape Town's multicultural character hadn't much to do with the waterfront. The crowds enjoying the amenities at the

Victoria and Alfred Waterfront were overwhelmingly white. Most of the trawlers in the docks there were foreign-flagged, yet few of the grizzled Korean and Taiwanese fishermen you could see hosing fish blood off the decks of their boats turned up in the oyster bars. Perhaps they couldn't afford to; maybe they hadn't the time.

Historically, Cape Towners had participated in the sea mostly from the shore, providing waystation services to the ships that called there. Most of the argosies that called there were dreaming of places and profits further afield. Apart from Huguenot refugees and mariners desperate for fresh meat and vegetables, not many of Table Bay's early visitors stayed any longer than it took to revictual on the cheap. One Portuguese merchant who landed nearby at Plettenberg Bay in 1506 was pleased to find that the native Khoikhoi people would happily barter their cattle for mere trinkets: 'There are many animals and there is much fish in this country and for this reason these people will not take any money.' But that wasn't a reason to stay, just a good reason to drop in now and again. England's Elizabethan spice fleets headed for the East Indies broke their voyages there only out of strict necessity. 'The world doth not yield a more heathenish peoples,' wrote one unsatisfied tourist in the early seventeenth century. 'When we threw away their beasts' entrails, they would eat them half raw, the blood lothsomely slavering.' What the Khoikoi made of these shiploads of scurvied navvies is not recorded. The Dutch only became interested in establishing a permanent settlement there after the *Haerlem* was wrecked in Table Bay in 1647, and the sixty survivors were forced to live for nearly a year on their wits alone. By the time the next company ship had arrived, the castaways had built rudimentary fortifications and gotten used to the place.

Whatever troubles still bedevilled Cape Town, they didn't come off boats. A few days later, flicking through a women's magazine at the British Airways Travel Clinic in Adderley Street – the site of another half-hearted car-bombing two days earlier – I came across an article which claimed that crime gangs could arrange for child prostitutes to be delivered to the door, like pizza, to sex tourists in Bo-Kaap. I doubt that many of the sex tourists were mariners. They probably couldn't afford it. The guys on the *Van Riebeeck* would be too frightened to go that far into town. I'd guess they didn't get much farther than the shopping at the Victoria and Alfred Waterfront or the strip of girlie bars on Riebeeck Street. It's true that the Planet Hollywood café on the waterfront had been bombed two years earlier, in August 1998, but the historic edge of danger and desperation associated with ports had entirely vanished from Cape Town's prosperous seafront. In certain hotel rooms in Manila, they say, you could arrange to have an entire ship stolen for a mere US$350,000. To its credit, Cape Town couldn't compete with that.

When I checked my email I found that Ada had confirmed my passage on the *Anna Böhme*, a British-owned ship on a rotation from Singapore through East Africa – including Dar es Salaam, Mombasa, Zanzibar and Mahé in the Seychelles – and Kochi (Cochin), in southern India. I collected the copy of the ticket she had forwarded to the shipping agent's office in Cape Town. That wasn't the only good news. Sarah was arriving in a week's time for a fortnight's holiday. By plane. I'd have to organise an armoured car to pick her up.

At the Crew Bar on Waterkant Street in the city there were no ship's crews, but a slightly less family-oriented atmosphere than anything I'd found at the waterfront and – more importantly – a working television. The news was astonishingly bad. I began to feel like Carol witnessing the implosion of the world. Apart from a litany of local beatings, murders and one satanic killing, the planet at large seemed to have become a more dangerous place since I left London. A Concorde had crashed; there had been a ferry disaster in the Aegean; now the world's sharks had embarked on a killing spree. In one weekend, two surfers were reported killed by great white sharks off South Australia and a swimmer was reported eaten off Dar es Salaam. To put this news bite in context, the network took the opportunity to dig out a video of a shark attack on the beach at Port Elizabeth the previous summer. The footage was so matter-of-fact in its fearfulness it was almost funny: a shark the size of a nightmare reared out of the water like a surfacing submarine, a heaving mass of vicious bulk and racks of insane teeth. Somehow its quivering maw missed the young surfer and clamped around the surfboard instead. Incredibly, the surfer escaped with only a few souvenir cuts.

To keep in a seagoing mood, I made a point of seeing *A Perfect Storm* while I was in Cape Town. Sitting with a couple of truant schoolkids in the virtually empty Labia Cinema in the afternoon, I was struck by the deep pleasure of contemplating disaster from the safe cosiness of a cinema. I particularly enjoyed the bit where a huge freighter was shown crashing over Himalayan swells, its containers smashing into the water. I began to think I wouldn't mind a taste of heavy seas myself before this was all over. There was hope yet; my next and last ship would be sailing through the hurricane-prone seas around Mauritius and Madagascar.

Gratifyingly, my study tour of Cape Town's seedier bars threw up a few of the characters I'd hoped to find in dockside hangouts. My favourite was Henry, a cockney born in London's East End, who sailed out to Rhodesia in 1969 and had bummed around the shores of south-east Africa for the last thirty years. He was like a jukebox that played yarns. I got the feeling that you could feed Henry drinks all night and the stories would keep coming.

He was delighted to hear that I had worked as a subeditor. As a young man just out of national service, Henry had worked as a sub on the London *News Chronicle*, 'the paper started by Charles Dickens'. Any literary pretensions the paper may have had under Dickens' editorship were in decline by the time Henry did his cadetship. Henry recalled how he was often given 'fudge', perhaps six lines from a news wire on a story out of 'somewhere like Abyssinia', and told to file a full column for page two. 'Oh, the amazing things we made up!' he remembered fondly. Young Henry created entire wars, ended famines with biblical rains, enthroned new chieftains and sank ships, all from his desk in Fleet Street. 'You couldn't even call it being creative with the truth, since there was hardly any truth in it! We had to. The terrible stories we told!' When my beer money dried up, Henry lurched into the smoke whence he had come, vanishing like a balding djinn.

Cape Town's nostalgia merchants give London's a real run for their money. It didn't take long snuffling around the dusty corners of a second-hand bookshop to dig some treasure out of Cape Town's silted-up maritime past. The treasure took the form of a tattered first printing of W.L. Speight's *Swept by Wind and Wave* from 1955, a book-length act of shameless *schadenfreude*, in which a long history of maritime disasters was recalled in loving detail. Among the shattered timbers and gargled screams of drowning men, Speight finds room in his preface for a wistful note about the decline of the sea's importance to South Africa. 'The sea and the queer things that came out of it were very much matters of daily converse to the forebears of South Africans now living so far inland that perhaps it is difficult for them to realise how vital the sea once was to the support and nourishment of their ancestors.' And to their entertainment, apparently. I couldn't decide whether Speight would have enjoyed the Victoria and Alfred Waterfront or not.

At another place on Long Street, I dug out from behind a wedge of Hammond Innes paperbacks a volume by one T.V. Bulpin called *Islands in a Forgotten Sea*. The sea in question was the Sea of Zanj, the Arab name for the East African waters sailed by Sinbad: the Bahr-el-Zanj, or Sea of the Blacks.

'T.V. Bulpin!' exhaled the store's proprietor, slapping some dust off the spine. 'A classic. You've heard of him, of course? No?' He looked indignant. 'Then you're in for a treat, boy. A real gem, this. Tom Bulpin's works are considered collector's items now.'

'Really?'

'Yes indeedy. He died last year, see. And most of his books are out of print now, so they're only going to get more and more valuable.'

Despite the inflationary effect of Tom Bulpin's passing, I doubted I would ever recoup a big profit from reselling *Islands in a Forgotten Sea*. But I didn't regret buying it. An engrossing historian, Bulpin had a passionate disgust for ports and the kind of colourful life that clings to them. He was going to be good company in East Africa.

I headed down the coast for a couple of days of shipwreck voyeurism with Speight as my guide. There was probably no better coast in the world for that kind of thing. The Cape of Good Hope had been a busy shipping route for hundreds of years. In pitifully small ships, slaves, soldiers, convicts and missionaries went east; cotton, silk, tea and spices came back. As Europe's looting of the Far East went on, unwieldy ships built to carry more and more booty increasingly came to grief on the reefs. Speight's taste for vicariously experienced doom was not new. A collection of terrible shipwreck stories was published in Lisbon in the seventeenth century under the title *The Tragic History of the Sea* and reprinted many times for the delectation of generations of Portuguese readers.

I understood the attraction. It was amazing how a stretch of desolate coast came alive when you knew how many ships had smashed themselves on its rocks and reefs. 'Beside the spouting rocks, along the whispering beaches stand memorials to bitter disasters of an earlier, less fortunate age,' Speight wrote. He was particularly ghoulish on the wreck of the transport *Arniston*, which fetched up on a desolate stretch of coast forty kilometres north-east of Cape Algulhas in 1815. Three hundred and sixty people were drowned when the ship was driven onto rocks by a gale. Six survived. They were discovered weeks afterwards by a local farmer and his shepherd who were looking for lost cattle. 'The unbearable stench from the beach set their stomachs reeling in protest, but something compelled them to investigate. Mounting a dune, they saw the beach below horrible with strewn corpses, beyond which reared the bows of a ship hard upon the sands.'

After a quick tour through the shipwreck highlights of

Hermanus and Plettenberg Bay I made the mistake of stopping at the Cape Agulhas lighthouse. I didn't blame Algulhas for this, I blamed my sentimental luggage. Anyone who grew up with 'Doctor Who' will always struggle to appreciate the qualities of any lighthouse which doesn't bear a close likeness to the magnificent sets built for the classic episode 'Horror of Fang Rock'. That lighthouse, some readers will recall, soared above the rocks. A series of cosy little rooms was packed into its tapered trunk. The lighthouse at Cape Algulhas, built in 1846 to prevent more disasters like the *Arniston,* didn't look like that at all. It looked like a stubby tower stuck on a shed. The tower droned in the wind like a doleful cello. The building had become a dedicated lighthouse museum and the only thing of interest in an ugly and oddly desolate seaside town. Apart from the water, which was a frigid emerald, the town was a ghetto of bad-taste beach houses stuck on a wind-blasted heath. This was how I imagined Blackpool might have felt in the winter of a Depression year.

Waiting for Sarah to arrive, I passed an evening in the bar at the Mount Nelson Hotel. In Cape Town, the Mount Nelson Hotel represents the apotheosis of retro travel luxury. Less a hotel than a gated suburb, its buildings were set in its own opulent parklands above my low-life haunts in Bo-Kaap. It wasn't a place for sealovers travelling steerage. Oak-panelled corridors and broad staircases were decorated with prints and furnishings that oozed expensive colonial nostalgia.

The walls of the clubby Lord Nelson bar were hung with a series of etchings depicting the progress of the Battle of Trafalgar, 200 years and half a world distant. As I followed the story told in the etchings, I noticed that things got steadily better and better for the bar's eponymous hero as my eyes circumnavigated the room from the liquor shelves around to the plush leather chairs. Then, with the epic battle all but won in an etching on the far wall, and with a third Campari and soda in my hand, things suddenly went pear-shaped. The great admiral was felled by a sniper's musket ball, just next to the service door to the kitchen.

A LITTLE DEN OF INIQUITY

Two weeks later I arrived at Mauritius' international airport. A pan flute was warbling dolefully through 'Feelings' on the immigration hall's PA system. After two weeks in South Africa with Sarah, I was on my own again. I watched my fellow passengers drain away through the passport controls towards their holidays, leaving just me, a few late-night cleaners polishing the floor and two passport officials. Things got steadily worse after that.

I was suffering from recurring document failure. My problem wasn't the fact that I only had a photocopy of my ship ticket out of Mauritius, and not the ticket itself. The problem was that my immigration officer required written proof that my ship was due to arrive. In a small room to one side of the hall, my official carefully searched a large ring folder full of faxes for any mention of my ship, the *Anna Böhme*. I showed him my ticket which indicated that the ship was due in five days' time, my itinerary and every other piece of paper in my wallet, including a picture of Sarah. 'Very nice,' he said politely. On the public address system, the pan flute moved on to 'I Just Called to Say I Love You'.

All immigration officials are equipped with distress sonar, and soon the cubby office was crammed with uniformed worthies eager to have a piece of the trouble. After much discussion, lots of chin-scratching, searching stares at me and my footwear, and what appeared to be a game of gin rummy, it was decided that my passport would be impounded until concrete proof of my ship's existence could be provided to the Ministry of Immigration in

Port Louis. Still amiable as ever, my official gave me instructions on how I could find my passport again, drawing me a map in red pen on the back of my ticket stub. If everything went according to plan, he assured me, I should be able to get it within the next few days, possibly even before my ship sailed. He asked me to pass on his compliments to my wife.

'Ebony and Ivory' was playing as I collected my lonely backpack from the abandoned luggage department. Outside, in thick night air, I fell into the passenger seat of a taxi.

It rained steadily all the way to Port Louis on the other side of the island. It was too dark to see anything. For all I knew of the island's interior, I may as well have arrived by boat.

In Port Louis, the taxi driver and I acted our respective parts with grim determination. The driver began by expressing his horror when he learnt which hotel I had booked for the night. He told me that my hotel was known to be the worst hotel in all of Mauritius. 'In fact,' he mused, 'I think it has been condemned by the authorities? Yes, I think it has.'

We were crawling down a narrow, deserted street. In the darkness I could just make out some wooden balconies looming above. The city seemed to have been evacuated. 'This hotel would be a terrible mistake,' the driver continued chattily. 'On the other hand, luckily I know a very nice hotel – '

'No thanks.'

'It has hot water. And pretty girls . . .'

'Just take me to my hotel or no tip.'

I insisted on my original choice, but the driver was right. My hotel room was an afterthought at the end of a family's corridor above the street. The shower unit in the bathroom down the hall was strapped to the tiles with a web of masking tape. Someone had written in Texta on the wall: *Please turn on the tap and THEN flick the electrical switch. If not, you may be electrocuted. Thank you.*

I really liked that 'thank you'.

I dragged the plastic garden chair – my room's single amenity – out onto the creaking boards of the balcony and lit up a cigarette. I was in the middle of Port Louis, but it was almost totally silent. The only other person on the premises, a friendly and good-looking young Indian guy, had explained that the public holiday called for the election had closed down all the shops and anywhere I could possibly hope to buy a drink. On the balcony it was just me and the mosquitoes. I respected these mosquitoes. These were mosquitoes with form. In 1887 their ancestors helped a plague of malaria wipe out half the population of Port Louis.

I took my breakfast with the proprietor, a round Indian gentleman called Mr Bathiswani. Mr Bathiswani scrutinised the election results in his paper, then gave me a quick translation of a few items that caught his eye in the international news. He knew I was from Melbourne so he translated aloud an item which described, inaccurately as it turned out, police beating protestors into a critical state in Melbourne during a rally against the World Trade Organisation meeting being held there. I didn't believe it, so he showed me the picture that accompanied the story. I recognised Crown Casino in the background. Around us the women of the house worked in silence, mopping floors, wiping down surfaces and wringing out clothes.

Mr Bathiswani was interested to hear that I was travelling between port cities. 'You should have been here thirty years ago,' he said. 'There were many more ships then. Lots of Muslims.'

By which, I assumed, he meant Arabs. 'What were they doing here?'

He lowered his paper. 'Everything: fish, sugar, scrap, whatever. Not so much now. It's all bulk and containers now.' He wrote out the telephone number of a friend of his who had worked in customs at the port. 'Retired now. But he'll be able to tell you everything you need to know about shipping.' Mr Bathiswani also urged me to visit Curepipe. 'You haven't heard of Curepipe's ships? Beautiful model ships. Thai teak. All made by hand. Any ship you like. Very nice. Everyone gets one.'

By the late eighteenth century, Port Louis was a true cesspit of frontier dissipation, populated by the usual demimonde of demobilised sailors, bankrupts, con artists, traders, prostitutes

165

and missionaries. As the principal revictualling port of the French fleets doing battle with the English over the treasures of India's Malabar Coast, Port Louis was crawling with the un- desirables of two empires.

The real business of settling Port Louis began with the French in 1721. They arrived on Christmas Eve at the spot in Port Louis that is now occupied by the Company Gardens. At first the French followed the lead of the Dutch, preferring the port in the island's south-east – now Mahébourg – for the capital because it was closer to good farmland. But Port Louis' advantages as a port became obvious, and in 1729 it was declared the island's capital.

Most of what I knew about Port Louis I'd read in Tom Bulpin's *Islands in a Forgotten Sea.* He was at the top of his outraged form when describing the state of Port Louis after the 1763 Treaty of Paris temporarily suspended ongoing Anglo-French hostilities in the Sea of Zanj: 'As usual in such circumstances, an upper scum of war profiteers and racketeers had formed to exploit the situ- ation,' he noted. 'Port Louis had become a little den of iniquity, with practically the entire sugar crop of the island used to produce arrack for the 125 taverns which infested the place for the edifica- tion of the military.'

Slavery kept Port Louis in business for the next 150 years. In the mid-nineteenth century, up to sixty ships could be seen anchored in the beautiful natural harbour dropping off a human cargo or waiting to fill their holds with sugar.

Port Louis may once have been a grand sinkhole of colonial opportunism, but a quick glance at Port Louis' modern waterfront revealed that any hope of catching a whiff of that venal heritage was long gone. Of course, local residents were probably relieved about that. There were no more than five or six 'taverns' left, and most of them seemed to be patronised by freshly showered students and dive instructors on the way to and from the airport. The old cus- toms house had been hollowed out and refilled with arcades of leisure wear outlets. A wistful little sign near the waterfront reminded passersby that before the advent of commercial air travel in the 1960s most people arrived in Mauritius via Port Louis' small passenger pier. The pier now hosted part of the waterfront complex and only small ferries were allowed to tie alongside, but if you narrowed your eyes at sunset, you could almost imagine families of French tourists surging down the pier, trying to keep an eye on the coolie servant racing ahead with the luggage.

I'd never seen a place as closed as Port Louis after dark. The ritzy waterfront development remained open in spirit into the evening, but only á scattering of tourists survived past nine o'clock. At five o'clock when I wandered through the market, the place was a riot of activity. Shop-owners were cheerfully emptying into the gutter their paper rubbish and octopus dregs and torn sacks of lentils and salt; yet by eight o'clock, the gutters had been sluiced clean and the streets deserted. The downtown grid was tightly shuttered, gates chained, windows latched and bolted. It felt like the streets were bracing themselves to weather a cyclone of petty crime. Only the city's population of howling canines remained, dusty bundles of dog curled up on the footpath like the fossilised turds of a prehistoric monster.

The agent returned my call the next morning to apologise for the stuff-up at the airport. He assured me that my representatives at the agency would be collecting my passport personally. I thanked him. Then I called Mr Bathiswani's friend and got no answer. I went to Mahébourg instead.

Though modern Mahébourg was only settled at the beginning of the nineteenth century, the town today is on the site of the first Dutch settlement on the island. The land there is so flat that the wide, affable bay simply seems to continue right where the land stops. I'd simply never seen water as clear, nor in such an idyllic peppermint tint. As a kid I drank lime spiders that were the same colour. I had a coffee at a beach restaurant. It was the consistency of chicken broth. I had to spark up a smoke to smother the taste.

Within eyeshot of this spot in 1810 was fought the gruesome battle of Vieux Grand Port. Despite the poetic accounts you find in C.S. Forester and Patrick O'Brian, most sea battles fought

167

between ships of the line in the late eighteenth and early nineteenth century were essentially slug-it-out affairs, with ships squaring up to pound out deafening broadsides designed to shred the enemy's rigging and kill as many sailors as possible. Grand Vieux Port was even less balletic than usual. The battle was fought around the coral reefs just north of Mahébourg harbour, and the pugilists' boots were strapped to the canvas within minutes of joining the battle as heavy seas impaled most of the ships on the reef. The French came off better than their opposition. Of the 281 crew who'd had breakfast that day aboard the *Néréide*, the British flagship, 92 were dead by dinner time and 169 were wounded.

The building where both wounded commodores were treated afterwards was a small, but affecting museum to the history of the island. It felt strangely like the kind of plantation house you could tour in Louisiana or Alabama, with its window boxes offering views of penitentiary bric-a-brac and slave paraphernalia tacked to the walls of airy staircases. There were few pieces of interest there, other than some Chinese porcelain salvaged from local wrecks, but a gripping horror story was told in the upstairs picture galleries describing the history of slavery in Mauritius. At least 800,000 slaves were imported to Mauritius before the practice was outlawed by its British governors in 1835. Drawings depicted slaves dragging their shackles across the dirt quay of Port Louis as they were disgorged from nightmarish holds.

There was also a display of historic lithographs and photographs of the island, the recurring theme of which appeared to be natural devastation. Port Louis after the terrible cyclone of 1847 and after the fire of 1873. In these pictures, Port Louis was a city of terraced sepia bungalows clustered around the timber needles of the clippers in port, and in most of them, a pall of disaster – fire, smoke, cyclonic disturbance, disease – hung over it all like a miasma. Or maybe they'd just faded with age.

People were encouraged to record their thoughts in a visitors' book by the door. Not surprisingly, some of these thoughts were fairly banal, considering that a lot of visitors seemed to have come inside only to escape a sudden downpour. Many of them ('Fab!',

'Amazing!', 'A lovely day out') were smudged by perspiration. But one French visitor had written something like: 'Oh, nostalgia for ages past!', which struck me as an odd thing to say about a museum describing the history of an island founded on slavery and vicious piracy, which had been continually devastated by hurricanes, and where the so-called *marrons*, or 'wild men' who roamed the interior, were, for many years, hunted for sport.

I stopped in Curepipe on the way back to Port Louis. Perched on the lower slopes of an extinct volcano, it was a pleasant town, built in the island's cool centre for relief from the monsoonal heat. Around the volcano, the foliage is so lushly verdant you could almost hear it growing. Walking along the street I passed through a sequence of smell zones: biryani, petrol exhaust, licorice and air-conditioned air.

But I wasn't there to enjoy Curepipe. I was there for a model ship. The question was: which one? Unless you wanted a *Mayflower* or an America's Cup-winning yacht, choosing was a matter of weighing up the virtues of various Indian Ocean pirates. I settled on the *Confiance*, a three-masted corsair built in Bordeaux in the late eighteenth century. Its captain was the French pirate Robert Surcouf, a gentleman murderer who spent ten years gaily plundering British and Dutch ships throughout the Indian Ocean, waging a private extension of the Napoleonic wars for his own enormous profit. In 1800 his small ship famously captured the heavily armed British East Indiaman, the *Kent*, in the Bay of Bengal. Like a bushranger, Surcouf could be soft-hearted: he once boarded a Dutch ship, the *Bato*, and found its crew in a terrible state, sick with scurvy and half-starved. The *Bato* was easy pickings, but instead of ransacking its cargo and inviting its sailors to walk the plank, Surcouf re-provisioned it and sent it on its way. In those days criminals could retire in style. When he returned to France, Napoleon made him a Count of the Empire.

My *Confiance* came wrapped in a vulnerable-looking wedge of butcher's paper and masking tape. Amount of boyish pleasure I'm going to get from watching its sails – each one carefully dyed in Indian tea – gather dust on the bookshelf at home? Enormous. Likelihood of me getting it to London without dismasting? Almost zero. My bonsai *Confiance* would, I feared, limp into the ship-breakers' at Heathrow, only to be savaged by the x-ray machine and perhaps also by a mighty tax from one of my old pals at customs.

Back in Port Louis, I tried to call Mr Bathiswani's friend again, but was told that he hadn't lived there for years. My proprietor had stopped appearing in the mornings – his ferocious mother was collecting my daily rent payments now – so I wasn't able to check the number. I spent my last days in Port Louis wandering around the markets and the suburbs. I felt a bit insubstantial in Port Louis, a little ghostly. No-one spoke to me unless I was trying to buy something, which wasn't often.

The opening ceremony of the Olympic Games in Sydney began as I was standing in front of the reconstituted dodo in Port Louis' Natural History Museum. I could hear it beginning. Following my ears, I stepped past the case which contained the giant egg of an extinct giant bird, passed into the next room and ducked beneath a massive papier-mâché cod. And there, at last, beneath a pickled giant octopus stuffed into a specimen jar, was a black-and-white television set.

I watched the ceremony for a while. Sydney is one of the world's great port cities. Unlike Melbourne, which fattened itself on gold and wool in the mid-nineteenth century, Sydney prospered like a giant polyp, feeding off the detritus and driftwood of the great ocean it overlooks. It suffered a brief bout of bubonic plague in 1903. Nineteenth-century Sydney was an opportunistic and contingent place; a lively, radical society built on pilferage and swagger. Modern Sydney still has swagger, but is now a very different place to what it was, one which seemed impossibly far from where I stood among the stuffed fauna of Mauritius.

I'd had enough of Port Louis. The Sea of Zanj beckoned.

Getting aboard wasn't easy. My taxi arrived just as the agent had promised it would, at nine o'clock, but instead of whisking me off to the ship, I was taken to the agent's office. Several calls were made by a harried-looking secretary, who informed me that I would, after all, be required to go to the immigration department to rescue my passport in person.

The taxi driver didn't like this any more than I did. He walked back to the taxi sighing through his nose, then drove the two blocks to the government building at a peevish dawdle, then made two agonised circumnavigations of the block. Finally, sighing heavily, he told me to get out of the car and walk. 'But when you are *fini*, monsieur, you will find me right here.'

I zoomed eight floors to the immigration and passport area, where I was rebuffed. Go to the mezzanine floor, I was told. From there, a process of elimination took me through five different offices, one typing pool and an abandoned toilet, until I found a glass door with some immigration officers sitting behind it.

The man sniffed my fear like a stink on my clothes. With lordly slowness he invited me to sit in front of his chipped pine desk. Then he ignored me. He did this very thoroughly. First, he doodled on a piece of paper. Next, he sighed thoughtfully over a message someone had written on a piece of scrap paper. He held it up to the light. He traced the ink of the letters with the tip of his finger. He tapped his desk with a fountain pen.

Nicely warmed up, be began his lecture. He harangued me on the stupidity of arriving in a country where the shipping agency had failed to inform the airport immigration people about their ship and its potential for carrying passengers. Didn't I realise this was plain idiocy? He felt bound to inform me that my application to enter could have been disallowed. I could have been put back on a plane. On a *plane*. Perhaps to help me picture this nightmare, his own right hand took off like a passenger jet full of disbarred miscreants, away from the island paradise of his desk.

Watching his neatly clipped fingernails and knuckles soar away over his ink pot, I wondered where people like this came from. I could have found this man in London or Melbourne. People like him are the inhabitants of a strange country I keep accidentally wandering into, no matter how far from home I travel.

I was about to meet another one at the helm of the pea-green *Anna Böhme*.

RAIDING TOAMASINA

Sooner or later, every ship carries a doomed man.
Nelson Algren

Captain Chatterji was a smirking little man with an overlarge head which, I found out later, he considered necessary to house his overlarge IQ. He had intensely black eyes and fleshy lips the colour of chicken livers. He looked like someone who might have won a beautiful baby contest fifty years ago and had never grown out of his fat cheeks and roly-poly neck. I didn't like the way he was looking at me.

It would be hard to say how Captain Chatterji and I went so wrong so quickly. True, I failed to provide him with the starched sheets of documentation he was clearly anticipating but then, he failed to provide me with any evidence of a sense of humour. He was outwardly horrified – but, I sensed, secretly delighted – that I didn't have my ticket for the voyage on my person. The original was still in Ada's office back in London. In lieu of that, I had several photocopies of the ticket, signed, unsigned, stamped and blessed. Mr Chatterji had several copies himself, which had been forwarded to the shipping company by my booking agent.

The captain instructed the steward to show me to my cabin and then to bring me upstairs to his cabin where I could sign a photo-copy of the ticket, presumably for his personal satisfaction. He pinched each morsel of my documentation – vaccination forms, doctor's certificate, insurance – between thumb and forefinger as if he was savouring premium snuff.

He was still lecturing me when we met in the officers' mess for dinner a few hours later. 'We have hardly any passengers on this route here,' he said, spooning some chutney onto a microwaved chapatti. 'It is a lot of extra work for everyone. You see, the first priority is the cargo.'

I was feeling right at home already. His eyes had a mineral hardness to them. If I wanted to go onto the bridge, he told me, I would require his permission. This was ominous: the bridge was my main form of entertainment on these cargo ships. He couldn't be serious, surely. 'I am the captain,' Chatterji reminded me. 'You must always ask me.'

The label on my cabin door said *Supercargo*, the title traditionally given to the officer responsible for the ship's commercial transactions. But it'd been a long time since this ship conducted negotiations on the run.

I gazed at the label for a moment. In the light of Chatterji's brusque welcome I couldn't help reading some significance into this echo of a long-gone epoch. Sure, it had a super-hero ring to it, but I wasn't feeling like super goods just yet. Superfluous perhaps? Maybe I was paranoid, but I couldn't help feeling that Chatterji had given me the cabin he thought I deserved.

I got talking to one of the junior officers at the railing before we left Mauritius. Rakesh was, I'd guess, close to two metres tall. The third engineer, a sleepy-eyed man called Moses, was standing further along the taffrail with a couple of crew-members in boiler suits. He limply offered his cigarette packet. 'Don't accept!' Rakesh grinned. 'He smokes medicinal cigarettes. For his liver, you see.' Rakesh shook two Marlboros out and lit them both.

'You're our first passenger on this rotation,' he said, exhaling smoke with relish. 'We were expecting someone older.'

Rakesh asked what I was doing and listened with interest as I explained it. He was himself reading *Men are From Mars, Women are From Venus*.

'How is it?'

'It makes a lot of sense.'

'My book's more of a travelogue.'

Rakesh nodded into his smoke. The apron lights were switched on as we watched. It was a softly lit prairie of concrete. Several football fields could fit into those docks. Forklifts and people carriers sped across the open space. A Russian bulk carrier with a black hull was loading something in giant hessian bales at the far end. 'What did you think of Port Louis?'

I said I thought it was fine, but quiet.

'The girls aren't much, but usually you can get a card game at the seamen's mission. Or at a bar. Do you play cards?'

'I can play Spite and Malice. And Five Hundred.' I could see from his face that these weren't the games he had in mind. We smoked quietly for a while.

'Have you been to South America?'

Oh God.

'What?' he asked, seeing my face.

'Nothing.'

He slapped my back. 'Never mind, eh? We'll find something for you to write about. Maybe in Madagascar. Very nice girls there, very clean and cheap as chips.'

The night was utterly still. The ship, probably ten years old at the most, swivelled slowly then angled away from the harbour, imperceptibly gathering speed. The lights on the shore transformed the grim slick of the industrial harbour behind the breakwater into a shimmering bay of light. Buoys twitched green-blue and red in the middle distance. It was so still that spume from the smokestacks of a factory behind the docks rose perfectly straight up into the night sky, the columns of smoke back-lit by the full moon.

First stop on the rotation was Réunion, only ten hours away. The captain bailed me up at breakfast, his face glowing with the pleasure of delivering bad news. 'Of course you realise that Saint-Denis is two hours' drive,' he said as, in my mind, I launched myself on the café-lined boulevards of Réunion's chic capital.

'Two hours!'

'More or less, that is correct.'

'But it's only fifteen kilometres!' I waved my map in his face. 'It says on the itinerary that we go to Le Port.'

'You'll have to speak to your agent about that,' he murmured, looking more pleased all the time. 'Oh,' he added, 'it is also very expensive for getting a taxi. Around US$60. But you can negotiate with the seamen's mission.'

Chatterji inhaled luxuriously. My irritation was working on him like a tonic. 'Of course, we will only be here for perhaps eight hours. It could be more, but I cannot be sure, so you must be back here in six hours.'

Mr Mahmood, the chief engineer, advised me to wait for the emissary from the seamen's mission, who usually came aboard to sell phone cards, collect mail and give sailors a ride into Le Port. Mr Mahmood was known universally as Mr M, or the Divine Mr M. He was in his late fifties, amiable and comfortably rounded. When he spoke in English, with the soft dental plosives of the Indian accent, he moved the top of his head from side to side as if his neck was mounted on a loose spring. I'd taken to him straight away.

The van eventually arrived in the late morning. It was driven by a man with the fatalistic air of a priest resigned to a life of managing sin, rather than preventing it. 'I told you he was coming!' ejaculated Mr M, pleased. 'He will take you wherever you want to go.' Sadly, there was nowhere in Le Port I wanted to see: I'd been anticipating a civilised day or two wandering the boulevards of Saint-Denis, soaking up the eccentric chic of a French capital that orbited Paris at a distance of thirteen thousand kilometres and several years. Le Port didn't quite cut it.

Crew-members filed into the officers' messroom and purchased phone cards from the priest. The phone cards were all US$20. For that, the lowest-paid members of the crew, from Myanmar and the Philippines, got around fourteen minutes of phone time to Yangon or Manila. The officers could expect around twenty-seven minutes of phone time to India for their money. And I – the only non-working member of the ship's company, the supernumerary – could get ninety minutes if I decided to phone home to the UK. The sailors trooped out onto the dock to the nearest phone where they would speak, in the precisely allotted fourteen minutes provided by the card, to their wives, mothers and children; carefully saving most of their spare cash, Rakesh explained, for visits to the pleasure palaces of the East African waterfronts.

I was getting keen to go by now. But the seamen's mission priest gladly accepted a cup of tea from the steward, despite the fact that it was at least thirty-five degrees inside the ship and probably forty out of it. He'd reached that stage of life that hits most people in their sixties: when he was thirsty he drank tea.

When we finally climbed into his van on the dock, my saviour realised that he'd left his hard hat somewhere. So we turned around and drove along the docks, parking in the shadow of the *CGM CMA La Bourdonnais*, the only other big ship in port. He climbed the gangway nervously, grabbing at the wire handrails when he staggered.

I studied the ship with interest. *La Bourdonnais* was named in honour of that great French imperialist of the Indian Ocean Bertrand François Mahé de La Bourdonnais who, as governor of Île de France, as Mauritius was then known, oversaw massive growth in population and productivity in the 1730s. Later he famously captured Madras from the English with a fleet of merchant ships refitted for battle. I'd had the chance to take *La Bourdonnais* to the Far East via the Red Sea but the schedule hadn't worked out, so I was on the *Anna Böhme* instead. Ada had urged the French ship on me on the grounds that French freighters carry excellent chefs. I glanced at my watch: one o'clock in the afternoon. Somewhere in that freshly painted, innocuous-looking superstructure was a table groaning with sweetmeats and a crisp Sancerre; probably some *duck à l'orange*, nicoise salad, bread fresh from the oven and an oven-load of soufflés rising sweetly up to the oven lights, like sunflowers craning towards the sun.

The priest returned without his hard hat. He drove me out of the port and dropped me off in the middle of town about five kilometres distant, setting me on my way with a photocopied, hand-drawn map which showed all the sites of interest to a seaman: the bank, the post office, the chemist and the hairdresser.

I chose the hairdresser. The girl who washed my hair extracted without comment burrs, shreds of prawn shell and whatever else was there, gradually working up a lather despite my corona of diesel exhaust. She passed me on to the chief cutter, a thin, lean French boy with a motley moustache. We grinned at each other. We didn't speak one another's languages terribly well. 'I've never had a sailor before,' he confessed at once, in English.

In French I tried to explain that I wasn't actually a sailor, but I think I must have ended up saying that I liked to read detective novels. 'Usually they just shave the head,' he said in English. 'They should let the hair be itself!' He told me that he had done 'hair fashion' in salons in Paris and Nice and thought London would be next, though he had heard that living there was *terrible* expensive. Doing hair, he said, was fairly interesting but probably not as interesting as my job, sailing around the world on ships. 'Australians are good swimmers,' he noted.

'The French are good cyclists,' I replied, returning the compliment.

'But how can you make a cycling on ships?' he asked, amazed.

'I'm not a sailor,' I replied. But he shaved my head as though I was. We exchanged pleased grins again, then he charged me at London salon prices.

Conversation was constipated at dinner in the officers' mess that night. Much to my surprise, the young wife of the third officer – Mr Patel, an amiable boy scout with an Errol Flynn moustache – materialised from the mysterious heights of the ship's superstructure wearing a magnificent sari in the green of unripe lemons. She didn't say a word during dinner, though she giggled in a maidenly fashion a couple of times at a few things the captain said in Hindi.

The Indian officers were served chapatti and curry. 'You too can have curry,' Captain Chatterji said in my direction. He sat at the head of the table, propped up on a cushion like a pasha. 'You should try different food.'

I hadn't been offered curry, of course. Instead, I was eating a couple of stiff pork chops floating in what appeared to be mushroom-flavoured instant soup. 'Maybe tomorrow,' I said, trying to making eye contact with the steward. I wasn't successful.

I was unsuccessful with the steward in most respects. From the moment he saw me, grabbing the luggage out of my hands and clumsily bashing my beautiful model *Confiance* against the door jamb, Nyem went to work on me as a source of free cash, telling me constantly and completely out of context – when we bumped in the corridor, for instance – how hard he worked and how poor he was. He had the face of a battered Roman senator, a fleshy, flattened nose and pinched cheeks. Service of any kind was only going to be had at a price.

Tense silence radiated from the head of the table, where Mr Chatterji peered at us over the rim of his curry bowl. I felt like an intruder at a family gathering who was being gently savaged by excruciating politeness. The second officer, universally known simply as 'Second', was watching me with a look of suppressed hilarity. Perhaps hoping to trigger a flow of *bon mots* from their passenger, he asked me what I thought of the food aboard. I stared at him. He gazed back innocently. It wasn't an innocent question. But with the chef in earshot, there seemed little to be gained from stating the obvious. 'Fine,' I lied. Someone sniggered.

The problem for me was that the Indian officers spoke so many languages each that they actually had two shared ones: Hindi and English. Since they were more comfortable in Hindi, they used it to talk among themselves.

At afternoon tea time, the usual gang was sitting around the second table with its plastic gingham tablecloth. Moses, the guy with the medicinal cigarettes and drowsy eyelids, was leading a discussion in animated Hindi. I tried to work out what they were talking about. I deduced from the gestures and body language – Mr M, in particular, seemed extremely indignant about something and Chatterji kept drawing his finger around his forehead –

that they were talking about the odious practice of eating monkey's brains from the skull. Or maybe they were discussing the brain-eating scene from *Hannibal*? Possibly, I conjectured, they were talking about the use of boiled charcoal as a thickening agent for the hair, a subject Thomas the electrician had already spoken to me about in relation to his own lush mop. Chatterji noticed me.

'You know what we are talking about Mr Neil?' (Once again, my middle name was listed first on the ship's manifest.)

'Eating monkey's brains?'

He blinked. 'No.' He nodded at Moses. 'We are talking about if you peel an onion it makes you cry, nuh? And third engineer is saying that if you place half an onion on your head first, it stops the tears coming.'

'You put the onion on your *head*?'

'I don't see how it can work,' Mr M said, not pleased.

'It does,' said Moses.

'But I cannot see the science in it.'

'It's actually a well-known method,' Moses added, with a hint of a smirk.

Only twenty-five days to go.

We left Réunion in the late afternoon, rolling towards sunset. I had my T-shirts and undies drying on a hanger in front of the open porthole, silhouetted by the pinkening light behind it. We were not carrying many containers yet, so I had a magnificent view of the cargo bay from my cabin: Genstar, Nedlloyd, CGM. No-one seemed to know what was in them. No-one seemed interested. There was a knock at my cabin door and Rakesh poked his head in. 'Enjoying yourself?' he grinned. 'It's a lonely life, eh?'

'It's not so bad. Plenty of time for reading.'

He nodded at my drying washing. 'The captain wants you to pull your curtain. The light interferes with navigation at night.'

'Okay.'

'By the way, don't mind me telling you, you should keep the

porthole closed tight. The captain won't like it. He hates mosquitoes, and besides, there is air-con.'

I laughed. 'Anything else?'

'There is a card game later on,' Rakesh added. 'Do you want
me to call you?'

'Yeah, sure.'

'It's poker,' he added after a slight pause. 'You don't have to play.'

'Why wouldn't I?'

'Only Nyem said you didn't have much money.'

Rakesh never did call that night and I went to bed with Tom
Bulpin, who was just getting onto the missionaries in Madagascar
and the terrible things that happened to them.

The next evening I sat with a few officers in the saloon after dinner while they watched the Bollywood blockbuster *Fiza*, directed
by Khalid Mohammed. It was on DVD and was turned up very
loud. Captain Chatterji came in later carrying a fine china cup and
saucer he must have kept in his room. His body language made it
plain that I was sitting in his favourite chair.

There was a critique of this film in a copy of the *New Indian
Express* which compared its conservative political message to the
Mehboob Khan's 1957 blockbuster, *Mother India*. According to
the reviewer, 'The film chugs on through glycerine-tears,
Kalashnikov hatred and two sub-plots revolving around love, to
end in a tragedy.' Personally, I was struggling to pick out these
themes in what I was seeing. Most of the tragedy appeared to be
told in big musical numbers featuring a fantastic number of cos-
tume changes. Were we watching the right film?

But Captain Chatterji was transfixed. As the action shifted from
one celebrated Mumbai locale to the next, he bawled out a commentary over the dreadful racket of the television. 'That is a very
expensive restaurant!' he shouted to me. 'Seafood is very expensive in India!'

The captain continued to emit noisy gasps and gargles of pleasure
as the story wound on, particularly during the frequent outbreaks of
highly choreographed singing and dancing. In one scene our hero

attempted to catch a beautiful young woman before her train pulled out of a crowded Mumbai train station, parting the crowd on a horse (where did the horse come from?), riding up the escalator (still on the horse) and galloping in heroic slow motion out onto the platform. Sadly, however, it was clear that he was not going to make it without a supernatural burst of speed from the horse. The lovers were doomed.

Chatterji leant forward in his chair, his tea cup trembling in its saucer. 'But it's too late!' he groaned. 'He will never make it!'

But what was this? A supernatural burst of speed was precisely what the horse came up with next! Our hero in the saddle just managed to pass a folded note through the open window to the outstretched fingertips of his love, and Mr Chatterji subsided with a moan of relief into his chair. 'She got it!' he whooped, with a hand over his agitated heart. 'You see? She got the message.'

The port of Toamasina, Madagascar's biggest, is set at one end of a curving bay of sparkling turquoise water. Among the palms and baobabs that line the shore are a few colonial buildings with sagging porches, a church and a few beachside shacks and bungalows. A beautiful beach frames a small bay of bilgy jade water, kept calm by an offshore sandbank. From my porthole I could see the long beachfront promenade stretching away to the north of the port in the direction of Île Sainte Marie 160 kilometres distant, once the world's most notorious pirate lair.

In the old days, as Tom Bulpin kept reminding his readers, ports were notorious hang-outs for a cosmopolitan range of scoundrels. Brigands, thieves, slave-traders, desperate refugees, corrupt officials, cut-throats and chancers invented globalism in the patois of the docks. Or so I liked to believe. I hadn't seen many of them yet. Then, that afternoon, when the Malagasy immigration officials commandeered the ship's office aboard the *Anna Böhme*, I understood what he meant.

It was clear from the expression on the captain's face that we had trouble. He'd promised me a visa for less than US$20. I was perfectly happy to pay the full US$30 for a formal tourist visa, but somehow beating the authorities down over my shore pass was a matter of pride with Chatterji. He demanded they be reasonable. They didn't want to be reasonable. I sympathised, considering that Madagascar was a desperately poor country; I would have sympathised more if those three hadn't looked so much like the country's only three millionaires.

The captain wheedled, smiled, snarled, banged his fist on the walnut linoleum of the table. He explained to the men in moving detail how I was going to write passionately about their beautiful country. The three money men stared at me sceptically. They refused to budge. After about ten minutes of this, I was called outside where Mr Kadirgamar, the chief officer, was eavesdropping. 'You've got to be hard ball,' he whispered. He demonstrated a bit of ad hoc choreography that would, he said, clinch the deal – I should throw my hands in the air, say I couldn't possibly afford it, and then storm out. 'Quickly!' He pushed me back into the room.

But I didn't get the chance to put his plan into effect. By this time the captain had handed over the standard bribe of three cartons of Marlboros and I was promptly given a shore pass for free. 'But – ,' said the official who had been playing good cop during the negotiations, 'only for one day. Tomorrow.'

'Only one day?' I yelped. 'But you see – '

'Shhh!' This was Mr Kadirgamar behind me.

'The only problem is – '

The captain caught my eye and dismissed me with a brusque nod.

I went out on deck to regain my composure. From the lifeboat deck, I could see Toamasina's waterfront, a white beach curving like a blade around the bay. Below me on the docks, were some local men perched on stacks of iron sheeting or bollards, staring up at the decks of the infrastructure. I waved. After a moment, a couple of them waved back suspiciously.

For me, dinner was a doleful affair of leathery whiting fillets. Thomas the electrician crunched through a large crab at my side, his big, delicate fingers gently deconstructing the animal's shell and legs, piece by piece. 'How's the crab?' I asked, as Nyem was scooting past, his waiter's napkin prim on his forearm. 'Very delicious,'

Thomas replied solemnly. 'You should try some.' He was going ashore, he said, I should also. I told him that I didn't have a pass. 'Don't worry,' Thomas said. 'They won't check your pass. If something goes wrong we can make them see reason.' He winked. 'These guys earn nothing.'

Chatterji arrived late. 'You are very lucky,' he said to me. 'I could hardly believe they gave you a shore pass for free.'

'Thanks very much,' I mumbled.

'You *should* thank me.'

Nyem set a plate of curried vegetables in front of the captain. Chatterji told him to take it away. 'Bring me crab.'

'I'll have a crab too, thanks,' I nodded at Nyem.

He hovered anxiously. 'No crabs extra, sorry. You want curry vegetable?'

'No.'

'You *should* try the crab,' Chatterji said to me, crunching into a stick of celery. He smirked at the ceiling.

Nothing I had read in Larry Nixon's taxonomy of merchant captains had prepared me for Mr Chatterji. I had heard of captains who banished their officers from the dinner table because their manners were insufficiently genteel to share it with passengers; the captain who roamed the decks at night firing at rats and sea birds with an air rifle was well known; stories of captains who stalked the bridge at night stark naked and raving were commonplace. But Chatterji was really one out of the box.

I cleared my throat. 'I'm thinking of going ashore tonight.'

Chatterji's smile vanished. 'But they said you could only go tomorrow.'

'If it's all the same to you, I'll take my chances tonight.' The truth was, I was afraid the ship would have moved on before I'd get another chance to look at Toamasina by night. This was what I'd come to see: a port that hadn't been able to afford to leave history behind yet. Chatterji didn't look happy. 'It'll be fine,' Thomas said, crab juices dripping down his chin. 'We'll look after him.'

Chatterji frowned at Thomas. 'It's not my responsibility,' Chatterji said. 'If you get put in jail, there's nothing I can do.'

He grinned one of his horrid little grins and I grinned back. Frankly, I could have done with a spell in a Malagasy jail. The food would probably have been better.

As I had sat in the officers' bar aboard the *Van Riebeeck*, taking in stories about the good times to be had in Toamasina, I'd imagined something different from what I eventually found. From my stool in the bar, the real world radiated out beyond the rattling bottles of Amstel in garish technicolour. In that hothouse environment I'd hatched a vision of Toamasina as a town out of a tropical spaghetti western, with a sinister main street, lots of quiet men with scars and a rowdy bawd house that turned nasty after midnight.

Rakesh organised a taxi to drive us off the docks. We wound around the bay, then turned off into a series of quiet streets. Wooden houses peeked from behind wet salad-green foliage. Then we arrived outside the Queen's Club.

Within seconds we were sitting at a table inside, surrounded by attractive young women. Moses and Second sat themselves on a couch next to a new television, which was showing equestrian events from the Sydney Olympics. Rakesh sat opposite me, laughing with a girl he seemed to know well. To my left was Teng, a Filipino ordinary seaman who had been on the ship for nearly a year. He was short, with a thin, fibrous body. He lit his cigarettes with a sleek blade of flame fifteen centimetres long.

A tall dark-skinned woman with unfocused eyes slipped into the seat to my right. She tilted her head to one side and gazed at me. 'Hi,' she said.

'Hi.'

She slipped a cigarette out of the packet on the table in front of me and popped it between my lips. 'I'm Florida.'

'I'm Harry.'

'In French it's *Florina*, but in English I say *Florida*.'

'I see.' Florida was wearing a tight halterneck top. She held the lighter so that I had to lean across her compressed décolletage to reach it.

'I think it sounds nice. Harry and Florida. Florida and Harry.

Nice, you think?' A couple more women who had gravitated to our table agreed that it sounded very nice indeed.

'I'm married,' I told her, feeling like a stiff.

Florida examined my wedding band and shook her head reprovingly. Her hoop earrings, at least fifteen centimetres in diameter, flashed in the candlelight. 'Naughty Harree,' she murmured, stroking my arm.

Before long there was about twenty of us crowded around a couple of small tables. Under Thomas' orders, beer and peanuts flowed.

Most of the guys seemed to know the women. Most of them looked delighted. Moses didn't, however. He and Second had left the television to join us; Second was happily cradling a small and bossy woman on his lap; Moses was slumped unhappily next to a handsome woman who was blowing pink bubble-gum bubbles and carefully picking the gum off her painted lips. She showed no interest in Moses.

'Why you no like talking to me, Harree?' Florida pouted.

'How many languages do you speak?'

Florida held up four fingers, then looked away with interest as another unmarked taxi deposited a load of sailors from the Taiwanese ship onto the grass outside.

Thomas caught my eye. 'You must be C-A-R-E-F-U-L with the G-I-R-L-S,' he said to me, across two tables and several other conversations. 'Don't tell about your V-I-S-A. They K-N-O-W-E-V-E-R-Y-T-H-I-N-G going on.'

To my beer-fuzzed mind, which was also stoked on nicotine I didn't need, this spelling-out of words seemed like an exhilaratingly patronising caper. Sure, the girls could speak five languages each, but we could S-P-E-L-L!

'I am just W-A-R-N-I-N-G you. They K-N-O-W everything and they will T-A-L-K to the A-U-T-H-O-R-I-T-I-E-S perhaps.'

I was having trouble keeping up. Was he talking about my lack of visa?

Florida lit another cigarette for me. 'Why you no talk to me, Harree?'

Thomas was still trying to communicate with me through the

smoke. 'The best way is just to R-E-L-A-X and have F-U-N. Take a broad P-E-R-S-P-E-C-T-I-V-E. It's a different life for us.'

There was no reason why he should have spelt out 'perspective', but I was so impressed that he could do it, I didn't notice. I suddenly felt adult and salty with experience. I flashed an experimental grin at Teng, who winked right back. *Okay.*

But Thomas still looked anxious. 'Hey don't W-O-R-R-Y,' I said brightly. 'Life's too . . . ah, S-H-O-R-T.'

Rakesh took control of the party. He proposed that we all decamp to a restaurant down the road. At the restaurant, he demanded the establishment's largest fish. 'We want to share. And don't be buggering me around with small portions,' he warned the *maître d'*. 'I am entertaining my guests.'

The *maître d'* bowed. Unfortunately, he informed Rakesh, there was only one size of fish and it wasn't very big.

'Then give us five fish,' Rakesh scowled. 'And make them the biggest small ones!'

'Don't worry, Rak,' Teng piped up. 'There are no decent fish in Toamasina.'

'Why's that?' I asked.

'Sharks,' Florida said dolefully.

'We never fish here because there are none to catch,' Teng said. 'The only thing worth fishing for in Madagascar is girls. But you don't put bait. Instead of bait, you put dollars on the hook and then you just drag them in!'

The girls laughed hardest at this.

A warm wind blew up, which seemed to add to the surreal fragrance of the evening. People kept arriving and departing on bicycles. More taxis cruised past on the way to the Queen's Club up the street. I tried to imagine Martin from the *Van Riebeeck* here, cruising by on his BMW road bike, with his thinning hair fanning in the slipstream and his girlfriend riding pillion, the pair of them dreaming of escaping from the West to paradise.

When the fish was picked to the bone, an older woman arrived at the table. Rakesh made room for her. She was wearing a zipper bag around her waist. She conferred with Rakesh.

Someone made a joke at Moses' expense and he leapt up, shouting 'Fuck off all of you, I don't even want you. You're all ugly!' and ran off down the street in the direction of the Queen's Club. His girl muttered something in Malagasy and the others shrieked with laughter. The women switched easily between languages, apparently so that they could insult us in Malagasy and then return to English in order to reassure us that they'd never seen a finer bunch of sailors. 'Oh Moses,' purred Second's girl, feigning sexual delight. 'You make me so horny.'

Second sniggered and leant across the table to refill my glass, pouring half the beer onto the salad. 'I hope you are having a good time.'

'Unforgettable,' I assured him.

'Why you no talk to me, Harry?' Florida pouted.

'I *am* talking to you.'

'Why you no talk to her, Hee-yary?' Second's girl demanded.

'You no talking to me,' Florida sighed. 'I talk to you. You no talk to me. It's very sad.' Florida's main conversational move so far had been to make clear to me the fact that she only liked white men from ships. She only came down to the port, she said, when the shipping schedule she kept in her room at home indicated ships likely to be carrying white officers. Holding her long, thin brown arm next to mine, she sighed theatrically. 'I like the colour very much, you see. They look nice together, huh?'

Back in control, Rakesh beamed at me. 'Everything is organised very nicely,' he said. He patted the arm of the woman with the money belt. She was devouring the salad with audible slurps. 'I have spoken to *mama-san*,' said Rakesh. 'The girls are just US$20 each. It is a bargain. Nowhere else in Africa is it so cheap. These are rock-bottom prices.'

As the others disappeared to various places, I simply gave Florida all my money, to make up for the fact that she'd hitched herself to such a duff sailor. I ended up sitting on the porch of the Queen's Club, smoking of course, trying to escape the industrial quantities of smoke inside. My eyes felt like they were going to explode with nicotine.

I doubted this was what the IMF and the World Bank had in mind when they promote globalism as an engine for Third World development. There was certainly an exchange of wealth going on here, but it was fun at fire-sale prices, the sort of fun which concealed the wide opportunity gap dividing the officers from the sailors, and the sailors from the women. For the women working the bars here, ships like ours were a chance to find a man who could be a ticket out. Florida was desperate to move to California, but had never travelled even as far as Antananarivo, the country's capital, 200 kilometres inland. The crew may have been acting like the Rat Pack on a bender here, but the high-roller act was an illusion. Thanks to the globalisation of the ship-manning industry, merchant seamanship was a career that had drifted lower and lower in status over the past three decades. Teng was paid about US\$400 a month. He and his colleagues would carry out a rigid stowaway check when we left to make sure that Florida's brother hadn't crept aboard, but they were only paid gatekeepers to the West. Teng would be no more welcome in California than Florida would be.

Florida found me on the porch. We watched Teng dancing, eyes closed, with Estelle, a startlingly pretty girl whose huge breasts and tiny waist tucked into a corset of yellow lycra.

'She loves him,' Florida sighed. 'She wants to get married, but he is still married in the Philippines. I don't like Asians, though. I have an English boyfriend and a German one. He's very, how you say, long. Very big.'

She examined me with a leisurely, measuring gaze. I gazed back. I was wondering how I could get out of meeting up with her tomorrow. She was probably wondering how she was ever going to get out of Toamasina if the ships kept bringing her married wimps like me.

Rakesh eventually stumbled back down the dark street at around three in the morning, looking decidedly seedy. 'Let's go,' he said. 'I think I am going blind.'

As I got up to leave, Florida grabbed my arm and insisted on meeting me later in the day. 'Not for special massage,' she said.

'Just because I think I love you. I want to show you my city.' I promised to meet her at the port gates at ten o'clock.

I woke in the morning to the crash of a container smashing into the superstructure just below me, followed by shouting and laughter. From my porthole I could see a twenty-foot container swinging gently on its chain cables. The crane operator waved apologetically at the men in the hold who staggered around clutching their hard hats to their heads.

I crept out of the port gates with a thumping hangover, squinting in the harrowing sunshine. The last thing I intended to do was meet Florida again. I wanted to see some of the town. Most of all, I wanted to call Sarah.

Opposite the gate was a row of *pousse-pousse*, Malagasy rickshaws, resting on their arms in the shade. Behind them was a line of young women in make-up and dangling gold earrings, standing with their arms crossed, keeping a close watch on the traffic tumbling out the gates. 'Welcome to Tamatave, sailor man. You like pussy? *Parlez vous* French? *Sprechen Sie Deutsche*? Why not like pussy, mister?'

I couldn't see Florida. I hurried up the street. There were crowds of young men and schoolchildren walking towards the town along Boulevard Ratsimilaho, which followed the curving bay all the way around the waterfront. Whenever I saw a taxi or *pousse-pousse* coming the other way, I tried to lose myself in the crowd or behind one of the palms above the beach.

After a few hundred metres I spotted a newsstand and crossed the street. A car screeched to a halt behind me. I tensed.

'Harreeee!'

I turned and saw Florida perched in the back seat of a dilapidated Renault. She was wearing bug-like sunglasses and a scarf over her head. She looked like an Amazonian version of Jackie Onassis.

I waved sheepishly. She hooked a finger and bade me approach.

I leant down to the open window. 'Hi Florida,' I sighed.

'Tut-tut.' She shook her head.

'What do you mean?'

'What do I *mean*?' she repeated, raising her voice theatrically. 'Where are you going Harree? We are supposed to be having the big date today at the port gates at ten o'clock.'

'I was just getting a newspaper.'

She narrowed her eyes, shook her head and finally broke into a forgiving smile. 'You are a very naughty boy Harree.'

We had an excruciating day. I spent an hour at the bank trying to extract some Malagasy francs from my credit card and then trying to find a hustler who would give me US dollars for them. Florida approved of this. No point having a man without money. Then I waited in line for an hour at a public phone booth to make a call to Sarah, which then lasted for about thirty seconds. Florida endured this with the stoicism of the eternal mistress. Then we walked around the town, every hundred paces or so, Florida sullenly punctuating the silence: 'Why you no speaking to me Harree?' She waved and stopped to chat in French every time one of her friends from the Queen's Club passed by in a *pousse-pousse*. The girls from the club appeared to be the only local people who could afford to use them.

Florida wanted to go to the market to help me buy things. I said I didn't want to buy anything, except a newspaper. When I bought a month-old copy of the *Economist* from a bookseller behind the market, she didn't bother to conceal her disgust. 'Look!' she said to everyone else in the store. 'He spends eight dollar on a piece of paper! I cannot believe it.' I couldn't quite believe it either. But when I suggested she might prefer to spend the day with her friends, she insisted that she was staying with me.

Eventually we ended up sitting above the beach at La Recrea Café like a couple of miserable newlyweds. But our table did have a splendid view of the *Anna Böhme* tied up to the docks across the bay. A couple of ships had arrived during the morning, one of them a large bulk carrier.

'Polish,' Florida said, taking one of my cigarettes. She'd given up lighting mine for me.

'Ours is bigger.'

'They stay for ten days,' she said petulantly.

I paid the bill.

'Where are we going now, Harree?'

'I wanted to look at the museum.'

Florida rolled her eyes. 'Boring boring boring.'

That night in the officers' saloon we watched *Courage Under Fire*, starring Meg Ryan and Denzel Washington. The battle scenes were so loud it felt like the war was taking place in the messroom next door. 'I am cheering for the Iraqis,' Moses announced in English, as Meg Ryan's helicopter gunship came down.

There was a chorus of disapproval. 'How can you say that?' Thomas shouted above the gunfire. 'What is this shit you are talking? Meg Ryan is a wonderful woman. Look at her!'

We watched while Meg Ryan bled, left to die by her comrades on a rocky escarpment somewhere in southern Iraq. Thomas was irate.

'I call it an outrage!' Chatterji ejaculated. 'She has a daughter. She has responsibilities!'

Nadia would have hated this. But I was quite enjoying it. Maybe it was the food aboard, but I was beginning to change my thinking in a number of significant ways. Meg Ryan wasn't such a bad actress after all.

I spent one more day in Toamasina. In the morning I wandered around the docks, looking at the other ships. Then I headed into town with an envelope Thomas had given me to deliver to his friends, missionaries who ran a clinic outside town.

I met Hans and his wife Cherie at a snack bar on Boulevard Joffre. Hans was a big Swiss man in his mid-fifties, with a powerful handshake and a chest like a birdcage; not at all what I was expecting. Cherie was tall, too; an Englishwoman in her forties, with alert green eyes, a long girlish braid of orange hair and a baby daughter on her hip.

Hans thanked me effusively for the envelope and insisted that I have a beer. The café only served juices and milkshakes, but Hans leant across the bar and spoke in French to the owner. Three cans of chilled Heineken appeared.

Hans had just come from the port himself, he said, where he

had been negotiating with customs officials to allow in a shipment of clothing and school equipment. 'It's all a matter of who you know,' he grinned. 'I'd hate to be starting out again now. When I started I had no idea how the port worked.'

'Why,' I asked. 'Because they're hostile to the mission?'

'No, no. Just because they think they're as poor as anyone, and everyone has to be looked after, everyone has to get something out of each transaction. It's the mentality. It actually works pretty well. We never have any trouble now.' Most of the money needed to run the mission's programs, Hans explained, came from reselling scrap cars he imported from Réunion for a few hundred dollars apiece and had repaired at little cost in local garages. He would stuff the car bodies with donated clothing so he didn't have to pay freight separately.

I liked these people; I admired them. But I also experienced the uneasiness I felt in the company of people whose faith was such a large part of their conversation. Disconcertingly, Cherie kept referring to Jesus in a very personal way, as if the Son of God were Himself strolling among the heathens of Toamasina. 'Thankfully, Jesus went with Hans, so I knew they would be safe together . . .' she said at one point. Then later: 'We asked Jesus where he was going, he said . . .'

They had eleven children, the youngest of whom, an angelic little girl sitting on Cherie's knee, kept trying to reach for the beer. Eleven sounded like a lot of children to bring up in Madagascar, I said. 'I don't mind them at this age,' Cherie replied. 'It's when they become teenagers that it gets hard to handle. Jesus, for instance,' she went on. 'Once they get older they think they can go anywhere. I can't count the number of times we've had to drag Jesus out of the Queen's Club.'

I couldn't believe my ears. 'Really?'

'When he comes back from college for the holidays, he goes a bit wild, doesn't he, love?' Hans smiled faintly and crushed his beer can in his fist. 'He can do what he likes here. He's a bit wild.'

I was wondering whether anyone had told the Vatican about this.

'Jesus is our oldest,' explained Hans. 'He's twenty-two. He is studying in the States, but if he had his own way, he'd settle out here. But there's no way that's going to happen.' He gave me a courageous smile. 'Too many distractions.'

They had originally wanted to work in Mauritius, but when they had arrived at Mauritius airport, aglow with their civilising ambitions, the authorities had told them that they weren't wanted. So, right there and then, they had decided that they would come to Madagascar instead. That was fifteen years ago. 'I wouldn't have come if I'd known what it was going to be like,' Cherie admitted. 'I would never be able to cope without the servants. It's been a real shock. But they need us here, which makes it all easier to bear.'

I admired their bravery. In many ways, Madagascar had been an unlucky island for missionaries. The first Christian school was set up in Toamasina in the early 1800s by Welsh missionaries who were massacred in 1828 when the Anglophile King Radama was succeeded by one of his wives, the pagan queen Ranavalona-Manjaka. In 1834 the queen delivered a public ultimatum to 150,000 of her subjects, ordering that they renounce their criminal beliefs or face punishment. Many did; most of the missionaries put discretion before honour and departed immediately. The atrocities continued: there was a massacre of recalcitrant Malagasy Christians in 1837; a year later fourteen Christian leaders were rolled in coconut matting and pushed off a mountain precipice near Tana. In 1845 British and French ships bombarded Toamasina in retribution for a diplomatic incident and the skulls of those British sailors captured during a subsequent shore raid were impaled on spears lining the beach. Eight years later, in 1853, those skulls were still there on their spears; they were the first sight that greeted the eyes of the London Missionary Society's Foreign Secretary, the Reverend W. Ellis, when he arrived in July to investigate new possibilities for proselytising.

All the world would be Christian, were not Christians so unlike their Christ, as Gandhi said. This wasn't a thought I shared with Hans and Cherie.

Hans had brought along a folder containing snaps of God's work being done in their own backyard, a lushly verdant paddock behind their modest house. They clearly lived an extraordinary life there. There were photographs of children lining up to accept clothes donated by the good people of Houston and somehow inveigled by Hans through the Toamasina docks, and shots of Cherie distributing sacks of grain and leading villagers in prayers. They told me how Madagascar's vanillin industry had been almost single-handedly wiped out when a cyclone devastated a town in the north of the island earlier that year. 'Eighty per cent of the crop was wiped out,' Cherie said. 'It's their only source of income in those places.' All telephone links were down, and at that time of year there were no passable roads between Toamasina and the stricken areas. So Hans had set out in a small coaster, trying to beat his way up the coast with a load of donated clothes. But the weather was too bad. 'I thought I was going to drown at one point,' he laughed lightly. 'We were running up against the wind and it was just too rough. We tried on three mornings in a row and eventually I had to turn around and come back.'

I walked back to the ship along the waterfront feeling hopelessly trivial.

In the afternoon there was a fire drill which ended in farce when it took one of the Burmese guys fifteen minutes to be installed inside his heatproof suit, and everyone forgot to check the engine room where the hypothetical fire raged unheeded. A long and complicated discussion ensued – all of it in English, thankfully, since English was the language of the ship's manuals and procedures – in which Mr Kadirgamar, as chief officer, argued heatedly with a surprisingly obdurate Mr Mahmood. Mr M wanted the second of two fireproofed seamen to accompany the first halfway into the engine room so that he could ascertain whether he was needed; Mr Kadirgamar insisted that the manual required the first fireman to report back to deck if he found the fire to be out of control. Only then would further measures be taken. The entire ship's complement – apart from the captain, who supervised from the bridge via his radio – stood about on the main deck. Diesel fumes and the smell of hot paint rose up from the deck. Sweat poured down my legs. The crew stood around the inner circle of officers, grinning at each other, keeping quiet. The argument warmed up and took on a life of its own, staggering across a series of unrelated subjects. Then the second engineer, who had been ruminatively picking his teeth with a piece of copper wire, suddenly lost it. Apropos of nothing, he shouted: 'They will soon burn the fucking mosque down and the sooner they do, the better as far as I am concerned! I am not giving a fuck to it!' He stormed inside. If the fire had only been imaginary so far, then this inflammatory remark seemed certain to ignite a real one. In fact, it seemed to surprise everyone so much that it had the paradoxical effect of calming everyone down. 'Time is money,' giggled one of the oilers, mimicking what I assumed to be one of second engineer's favourite phrases. Even the grave Mr Kadirgamar laughed at this.

BOLLYWOOD BABYLON

We hove into view of the Tanzanian port of Tanga in the mid-afternoon of another day of glassy heat, anchoring about three kilometres from shore.

All I knew about Tanga was what I had read in Bulpin and on Dominic's pirated copy of *Encyclopaedia Britannica*. When Swahili sultans ruled the Zanj coast centuries ago, building lavish palaces on the proceeds of trade with Arabia and India, Tanga was the region's largest ivory port. It was reduced almost to nothing by the continuous pillaging of Omani pirates by the turn of the nineteenth century; thereafter it scrounged a living from the proceeds of Arab slavers who used it as a base for inland raids. A hundred years later, under German colonial rule, harbour facilities were modernised and railways built connecting it to Dar es Salaam and inland plantations. Today it is one of East Africa's larger ports, but from the ship it looked like a small village whose low tin roofs were trying to push their way through the dense foliage to the sunlight. The still water was breathtakingly clear. It was like gazing down through a vast pool of sapphire gin. The harbour was dotted with the beautiful raked sails of local fishing boats, which tacked back and forth like skaters on glass.

That, as it happened, was all I was ever going to learn of Tanga. If there was an exciting nightlife ashore, only seamen working on coastal freighters and fishermen know about it. No-one on my ship had ever been ashore there because it didn't have a deep-water harbour. Instead, tugboats would tow a pontoon out to the anchorage, tie alongside and then the ship's cranes would transfer containers back and forth.

Around midday, the port authorities and stevedores motored out to the ship aboard an ancient wooden tug which was visibly sagging in the stern. Several dhows made elegant passes below the gunwales, getting a closer look. I found Thomas, Moses and Teng fishing off the stern with hand-held lines. According to Thomas, you could catch tasty red snapper there, though he admitted he'd never caught one himself. Moses explained that was because Thomas used thawed-out frozen shrimp. Thomas pointed out to Moses that his credentials as a fisherman were not widely revered aboard the ship. Teng was using flies for bait. The secret, Moses believed, was strips of pork, though under direct questioning he admitted that he hadn't ever caught anything there either. 'The sharks have got them all,' Teng said sadly.

Nothing bit for a long time. An outrigger canoe with a sail sewn out of fertiliser sacks eased alongside the stern. One of the fishermen aboard held up a magnificent silvery fish by its bloodied gills. Its scales shimmered as he turned it for Thomas' inspection.

'Can't the blinking idiot see we're trying to fish?' Thomas growled.

The fisherman called out, still grinning. 'You want him, my friend?'

Thomas told the man to piss off, dumped his reel in an empty bucket and went back inside. The fisherman persisted with his smiling and waving. Teng turned the pockets of his boiler suit inside out to indicate that he had no money, and shortly after, Second rattled down the external steps from the bridge and shooed the dhow away. The fishermen flipped him the birdie. 'It's very dangerous to come in close,' he told me. 'They must keep clear. It's international law.'

'Okay then,' I said.

'And they climb aboard and steal things.'

I assured him that I wouldn't aid and abet any more pirates.

Any social progress made in the smoke haze of the Queen's Club had quickly stalled. I had trouble following the conversations in the officers' mess, which were the only ones I had. Even when they weren't in Hindi, they seemed to be conducted according to rules that I didn't understand.

The thing about conversation on this boat was that when they disagreed, and they disagreed all the time – about the quality of shirt manufacture, the true cost of a computer, phone rates, how a fish curry should taste (nothing like they tasted aboard the *Anna Böhme*, I presumed) – they argued over what was 'accepted' to be the case, rather than what they thought themselves. While discussing the gradual decline of Bollywood product at dinner one night, the Golden Age of cinema came up and Mr M mentioned that Errol Flynn had come from Tasmania, congratulating me in effect for having been born so near him. 'I have read Mr Flynn's book,' Mr M said. 'It is called *My Wicked Wicked Ways*.'

Chatterji leaned back in his throne and scowled. 'What is it called?'

'*My Wicked Wicked Ways*.' Seeing Rakesh smile and raise his eyebrows, Mr M rocked his head from side to side in that amiably insistent way of his. 'But oh yes, it is a very interesting book.'

There was a giggle from the junior officers' table. Mr M turned on them good-humouredly. 'I assure you, it is recognised as quite fine literature.'

By whom he didn't say.

The previous day Mr Chatterji and Mr M had grilled me on my future. They had wanted to know what I intended to do next; I'd said I'd probably try to get a staff job on a newspaper somewhere. Not surprisingly, Mr Chatterji had thought this was a very good idea: it accorded with his twin goals of money and children, neither of which seemed to be progressing far in my freelance state.

Mr M had considered this point of view, but disagreed in a most agreeable way. 'Perhaps the money is a little better in a staff job,' he'd said. 'But I dare say that the life of the freelance is more interesting. If you had been working nine to five, you would never have come to spend this time with us.' He'd beamed at me.

Exactly, Chatterji's scowl had seemed to be saying.

If I could have, I'd have wrapped Mr M up and taken him home with me. With his softly rocking head, his mellow consonants and his utterly unhurried world view, Mr M was a rare treasure. He was an engineer who loved dolphins.

Apart from Rakesh, who kept inviting me to card games and then forgetting to tell me where they were being held, Thomas was my main source of company. He was a swarthy man with a trim moustache and slightly scarred cheeks. He had flashing teeth and a convulsive laugh. He fished with the optimism of a saint in the brackish, bull shark-haunted harbours of every port we visited. We were the only people on the ship with an interest in drinking, so he had, once or twice, smuggled a couple of beers up to my cabin. I liked him; he seemed to like me, but finding some common ground was like feeling around in muddy water for an object I hoped I would recognise from feel. Quite often he talked about Jesus. I tried to turn the conversation around to something else. A typical exchange would be:

> THOMAS: How is your book going?
>
> ME: Fine. (Pause) I guess you miss your family?
>
> THOMAS: Yes, but my wife talks too much. Mostly I miss television. And going to church.
>
> ME: Do you play table tennis?
>
> THOMAS: I used to. (Long pause) Do you want another beer?

But something had been keeping him quiet since Madagascar. One night I was being punished again with barely edible Western-style cafeteria nonsense – some sweet'n'sour chicken thing – while Chatterji and the other officers got to eat curry and chapatti.

Thomas, who was seated next to me for all meals, broke the silence by asking me what religion I was. Religion wasn't the kind of thing ordinarily discussed at the captain's table. I glanced at the captain, who ignored me. Mr M seemed eager to hear my answer. None, I confessed. Agnostic. Ah, Thomas said.

Mr M piped up. 'Are you agnostic or an atheist, Mr Neil? Because often people will say they are atheist, when in fact they are agnostic. Or vice versa. That is quite common.'

'I'm agnostic.'

Mr M rocked his head amiably and resumed eating.

Thomas was considering me gravely. I asked what his religion was.

'Catholic,' he said. 'And most people in Australia – they are Catholic?'

'Er, no. Some are. But most aren't.'

'No?'

'I guess a majority would describe themselves as Christians, but hardly anyone goes to church any more. You'd have to say that organised religion is on the decline there.'

I could see now that Thomas' interest in this wasn't merely anthropological. He gave me a meaningful look and tore a piece of chapatti with his thick fingers. I signalled urgently to Nyem, who was picking wax out of his ear behind the captain's left shoulder. 'Er, some curry, Nyem?'

'Curry?' he asked, startled. 'Chef says there is no curry.'

Chatterji looked up, pleased as punch. 'Mr Neil, you should try different food.' He smiled around the table. 'He is a traveller. I think he should try different foods. But he only eats English food!'

'That's only because –'

'I wonder,' Thomas interrupted, 'did you hear about the tragic story of an Australian missionary in India, a very good man. He was a Catholic. He had a big family.'

I hadn't.

'He was very tragically killed in India.'

'Oh yes. I think I remember reading about that. Terrible story.'

'He was Australian. He was a very good man. Very good man.'

I picked a lump of stock cube out of my dinner and kept quiet.

'I met his wife once at church, ' Thomas went on, with a pained smile. 'She was a very good woman.'

I nodded, but racked my brains for an alternative topic. For once I longed for the usual salival quiet of the captain's table. Mrs Patel emitted some delicate squeaks when some part of her vegetarian curry went down the wrong way. Mr M passed her some grapefruit juice. 'You must always eat with small bites,' he advised her. 'After all, what is the hurry in life?'

'Excuse me,' said Thomas, still with that hurt smile, 'but you can see, it's a jolt to hear an Australian saying he is agnostic when such a man died doing good with the poor.'

Jolt was right. A non sequitur of this magnitude was almost enough to jolt me out of my seat. 'Why?' I asked, more hotly than I intended. 'What has not being religious got to do with it?'

'Please don't take me the wrong way,' said Thomas, lowering his eyes. 'It is just sad, for me, as a Catholic. A man bringing the word of Christ is killed for his efforts and no-one in his country is caring about it.'

To Thomas – who was, as far as I knew the only Christian aboard a ship full of Hindus, Muslims, Buddhists and Jews – Christianity had a monopoly on goodness and charity. Faith made it simple for him: while one Australian was dying in his courageous efforts to save heathen Indian souls, the rest of Australia was wallowing in ignorant sin. I guess that would be a jolt.

I spent most of our first morning in Dar es Salaam trying to get hold of some American dollars to pay my debts aboard. I met a South African businessman who was also getting stressed running around town on a Saturday morning looking for a place to buy American dollars on his credit card. The difference between us being that he was driving a shiny black BMW from closed bank to closed bank, and I was on foot. He offered me a ride. Together we visited four more banks before we finally found one that could give us cash advances on Visa.

He stuffed the greenbacks in his wallet, then took a ten dollar note out and held it up; a pretty risky move in Dar es Salaam, I would have thought. He sighed through his nose. 'They're little exiles aren't they? They're like people who go bush.'

I looked around to see who he might be referring to. He gave me a thoughtful little smile. 'I mean, how did they get here in the first place? Some of them probably haven't been home for years and years.'

He was talking about the notes. Here was a man who anthropomorphised tenners. I looked at him more closely. He was neatly dressed, with a tucked-in button-down shirt, beige chinos and tightly combed grey hair. Suddenly I was curious to know what he was importing. 'Livestock,' he said.

Dar looked hot, dusty and run down. The city was founded by the sultan of Zanzibar in 1862, but there was no sign of the Swahili architecture – the timber balconies, carved doors and stone houses – that makes Zanzibar, only four hours away by ferry, so popular with tourists and publishers of coffee-table books. I saw Indian men huddled over Singer sewing machines in the shade, working the treadles with bare feet. Friendly young African men touted for business from their thirty-year-old Citroëns. Every street had an Islamic bookshop and a travel agency with chalked signs for bargain safaris. But I saw very few Europeans. There was no sign of the gun-toting grandees who used to stay in the grandly shabby Kilimanjaro Hotel when there was still big game to hunt in the countryside.

No longer Tanzania's capital, Dar is still its biggest city. Its port is the largest in East Africa, providing sea access to its landlocked neighbours – Burundi, Malawi, Zambia and Uganda. But the action is at Dar's local waterfront, a wide and dingy beach overlooking the narrow channel through which ships pass on their way to the freight terminal. It has a thriving, much older, local economy of its own. Exquisitely beautiful dhows and feluccas with classic raked sails come right up to the beach to unload their wicker baskets full of silver fish as shiny and bright in the sun as freshly minted coins. Fish are dumped in piles right on the beach. Auctioneers sell them to crowds of women, who push past one another with children on their backs and plastic buckets on their heads.

The bidding was quick and impossible to understand. Some people had only three or four fish to sell, a few yellowtail or sole, and they sat in the sun crouched over their catch, waving flies away with strips of cardboard. One guy sitting under a parasol had a plate of sad little fish with long snouts exactly like soft trumpets. They had oddly anthropomorphic faces and seemed faintly startled, as if they'd died puckering up for a kiss.

Further around, where the waterfront faced the commercial port, was a small ship-breaking operation. Woebegone coasters with piebald hulls of patched iron were being carefully disassembled by men working bare-handed with hammers and pulleys rigged from trees. Behind the waterfront, modern hotels and government buildings were clearly visible; here, the kiosks and outdoor kitchens of the waterfront area seemed to have been improvised from driftwood and broken-down trawler cabins.

Stalls above the beach sold key chains with miniature tusks, food and drink, and books in English and German. These bookstalls seemed to be the only places in town you could find books on subjects other than Islamic prophets and East African politics and history. A seasoned connoisseur of other peoples' bookshelves, I quickly saw that this was the usual mix of abandoned holiday reading and unlicensed printings of airport thrillers, the same collection of tattered leftovers you got in Dahab or on the *Van Riebeeck*.

But there was something out of place here. It took me a moment to realise what it was: Ayn Rand. There were several books by Ayn Rand available new or second-hand in a number of different editions. What was she doing here, in the warm shade of concrete balconies and rubber trees, in a country which had, during the 1960s and 1970s, been a Maoist republic? What did Howard Roark and his glass shibboleths have to offer a city like Dar? I associated Rand with my slide-night period, the early 1980s, when I spent a few months pushing uncomprehendingly through those thousand-page tracts she disguised as fiction – *Atlas Shrugged* and *The Fountainhead*. For me, this was proof that Tanzania was stuck in the discriminating time warp of globalism. For several centuries the West had treated Africa as a dumping ground for obsolete rubbish: the dodgy rifles left over from the Napoleonic wars, outdated medicine and crap cars, but the Ayn Rand collection seemed crueller than any of those. Rand and her ideas went out of fashion years ago in the West, but were, to judge from the piles of her books on sale, hot items on the Dar waterfront.

Still, I liked the idea that an illiterate stallholder might squeeze a few shillings out of Rand's *Introduction to Objectivist Epistemology*. Rand herself would have to approve. I picked up a copy of *Atlas Shrugged* and the stallholder hurried over, his palms pressed together. 'Excellent choice, friend. It is a very fine book,' he beamed.

'Have you read it?'

He laughed pleasantly and spread his hand in a gesture of mercy. 'Please. It is too big for me.' The man was wonderfully fat and smiley. His genial bulk reminded me of Mr M.

He took the book, glanced at the price and breathed in sharply. 'It says three dollars. That is a very low price. But for you, we can make it one dollar.'

I bought a Barbara Vine instead. I also bought a coffee mug with a million-dollar greenback printed on it. I thought my Indian buddies might like that.

The following night the shipping agent gave four of us a ride into town to the notorious Casablanca Bar. We passed the ship-breaking beach where men and boys were patiently gutting a beached tug by the light of oil lamps. Families crowded around coal fires for a plate of fish and squid.

Several other ship's crews had already found the place by the time we arrived. At one long table under a pergola in the courtyard some Filipino guys had settled in, singing songs, thumping the table with their beer bottles and tossing cigarette packets to one another across the table. Girls wearing gold hoop earrings and brightly coloured miniskirts had made themselves comfortable on their laps. The place was full, but there were only a few tourists. When I accidentally caught the eye of an attractive young woman sitting with some friends, she returned my gaze with more ardent interest than I could reasonably expect on a non-paying basis. Remembering Florida, I quickly looked away again.

We had a beer each then crossed into the casino next door. Second suggested we stop in at the bar for a game of pool before we went on to the disco. I hadn't played pool for several years, but as soon as Moses lined up his first shot and I saw the cue slip off the clumsy bridge formed by the knuckles of his left hand, I knew I could give these guys a caning with both eyes shut. While these guys had been serving out officers' cadetships on derelict freighters in the backwaters of South Asia, I had passed my university years in a fug of smoke and late essays at the university of life, which was how I liked to think of The Red Triangle pool hall in Melbourne's Brunswick Street. Those wasted years were finally going to pay off: I was going to hustle a bunch of sailors, albeit a bunch of amiable and totally harmless sailors, on their own turf.

Here was a chance to earn some respect. There was something emasculating about sitting around all day on board while the others worked up an honest sweat in their boiler suits. I was the only person on the ship with no useful skills. I was painfully conscious of the fact that if the *Anna Böhme* was wrecked on an uninhabited atoll on our way to the Seychelles, I would be the first to be eaten. After tonight there would be no more sniggering about my unworldly handling of the girls in Madagascar – my pool skills would be the toast of the officers' saloon. I might even get some crab curry.

Moses' hapless break somehow resulted in one of the balls dropping into a pocket. He missed the next one. My first shot was tricky. It choked in the corner pocket. Never mind. The effect of my subsequent dazzling play would be all the more striking.

Second had teamed up with Moses. He mangled a gimme. I smoothly pocketed my first and then turned a predatory eye onto a cluster of balls in the centre of the table. Conscious of my rapt audience, I chose the toughest shot. I missed. Just.

Moses duffed his shot. Mr Kadirgamar, who was sitting out but watching with polite interest, handed me my beer.

'You don't play pool?' I asked him. I was suddenly high on the anticipation of success. Like a minor baron returned from the

Crusades, I drank in my homecoming: the pastures of iridescent baize, the dusty smell of the chalk, the softly lit cumulus of cigarette smoke. It was bliss.

'No,' Mr Kadirgamar said. 'I have never played.'

'Really? You should have a go.'

'You have played before, Mr Neil?' At least I think that's what he said. Had he been watching? Perhaps I hadn't heard him correctly.

Time to get this over with. I lined up a shot which demanded a fine degree of cut. I sent the white down the table with a delicately weighted tap, then watched in alarm as it sailed past its target without touching it.

'Foul!' cried Second with pleasure. Second was one of those people who liked to play games and umpire at the same time. Now I was forced to watch while he used his extra shot to pocket two lucky balls, not at all helped by Moses, who crouched behind the pocket, calculating the angles with his forefinger and moaning and clutching his head in frustration when Second ignored his advice.

Over the next ten minutes, the sweet rout I'd planned failed to materialise. I mangled my way to a lead, but it was an ugly contest, what with Moses' rank mishits, Second's uninspired tootling around the table and my increasingly unhappy search for form. I tried several different cues. I checked the legs of the table. No evidence of skulduggery. At least, I consoled myself, I was going to win. Perhaps the next game would pan out more justly.

Moses and Second still had three balls on the table when I lined up my last shot. The black ball sat out from the bottom cushion at a teasing angle to the far corner pocket, but it didn't present a serious problem. The sweet click of white on black. The black slunk towards its exit, where, like a diva making an interminable farewell, it quivered for a moment on the lip before dropping into the pocket.

'Yesss,' I sighed, more with relief than triumph. We all watched the white ball rebound off the cushion; we were still watching as the white made an agonisingly steady return journey back up the table where it rolled into the pocket below me.

'Yes!' screamed Moses.

'That's it,' announced Second smugly.

'He wins, is it?' Mr Kadirgamar had been passing me my beer in congratulation, but now his hand was stayed in midair.

Second smiled sternly. 'No, no, no! Mr Neil's white ball followed the black so he forfeits the game. Which means we win.' He offered me a consoling handshake. 'Sorry,' he beamed.

'Is that true?' Mr Kadirgamar asked.

For a millisecond, and that's all it was, I considered inventing an obscure rule, let's say, the little-known Poughkeepsie Challenge Rules on which I'd been raised and in which following the black with the white earns the player double points – but I didn't. Not out of honour; just because I knew I wouldn't get away with it. Other sailors would be consulted at their tables; Second would table the poll results and prove that the Poughkeepsie Challenge Rules had never been heard of by any of the other sailors in the bar. Besides, I reasoned, it wasn't necessary. I was going to clear the table in the next game.

In the meantime, however, I had to watch while the usually phlegmatic Moses pumped the air with his fist like he'd just cleared a hundred minivans on a 500cc motorcycle.

I could taste the sour need for revenge in my throat. 'Another game?' I said thickly. I took a coin from my pocket.

Second shook his head and placed his cue in the rack. 'Let's gamble.'

'But we just started! I'm just warming up. Just one more?'

Moses had already led them into the next room. 'Mr Kadirgamar?' I shrieked, louder than I'd intended. But he was gone.

From the dock, the *Anna Böhme* gleamed like a giant Chinese lantern. There was no sign of the hawkers who'd been camping on the deck for the past two days.

The officers' mess was deserted. I could hear the telltale melodic clang of another boy-meets-girl-and-buys-her-a-palace blockbuster playing in the officers' saloon. Chatterji, presumably, giving his brains a rest in the technicolour universe of the talkies. I wouldn't be welcome there. The corridors were empty. I wandered into the crew's mess and found one of the Indonesian oilers mixing himself a Horlicks. It was Manuel, a man whose fleshy jack-o'-lantern face always seemed lit by the inner glow of a private joke.

He offered me a Horlicks. I shook my head. 'You have a good night? The California ladies get you?'

'No. But I played some pool with Moses.'

His smile went all confused. 'Poo?'

'Eight Ball. You know, snooker.'

'Ah!'

'He'd never played before. He beat me anyway.'

Manuel giggled. 'Rakkie and Sparks are playing poker upstairs if you want. But be careful with you ro'!'

'My what?'

'You ro'.' He rubbed his thumbs and forefingers together. 'You money, man.'

My *roll*. I'd be careful with my roll all right.

I climbed the stairs to the fifth floor and knocked softly on the door to Rakesh's cabin. There was a faint groan – I thought – and the sound of a newspaper being quickly folded away. I could have imagined it. I knocked again. Nothing. I took the stairs back down to the messroom, my Silk Cut lungs struggling with the exercise. Manuel was watching a video. On the screen a thin girl with long red hair was having sex with three men at once. She was honking like a goose. Manuel turned down the sound with the remote.

'You wanna watch?' Manuel asked.

'Can't find the card game. No-one's up there.'

'Try the weights room.'

There was nothing going on in the weights room either, which wasn't surprising. I faced the staircase again. I heard low voices, a couple of decks above me, and footsteps on the landing. Just as I arrived on the fourth deck I heard a door latch close and some quiet laughter.

I went to bed, but I couldn't sleep. At around three in the morning, I crept downstairs and found the officers' saloon empty. I made myself some noodles and cued up *Sleepless in Seattle* on the DVD player. How could I have ever thought Meg Ryan was a boring actress? I watched, entranced, until the final harrowing scene atop the Empire State Building. I climbed up to bed, planning to raid the fourth-deck video library the next day and put aside every Meg Ryan movie I could lay my hands on.

The *Anna Böhme* took about an hour to cover the last six metres or so as we shunted sideways into the dock at Zanzibar. There were no tugboats in Zanzibar harbour, so we threw our lines overboard to a couple of wharfies in a motorboat who, after a couple of comical attempts, managed to transfer the lines to the bollards on the quay. Then we dragged ourselves alongside with the huge winches on the main deck ratcheting us in, a few centimetres at a time. The fifteen-centimetre-thick ropes visibly thinned under the strain.

Arriving in Zanzibar was a lesson in the relative economics to be observed on a ship trading in this region. In Zanzibar, they don't get many big ships. The *Anna Böhme* was the biggest and she pulled a big crowd. Before the ship finally touched, sending a shudder through the entire dock, a large crowd of men had gathered and perched themselves on stacks of aluminium sheeting and large tubes of rusting scrap iron.

By the standards of the island, every crew-member on this ship was rich. The ship itself looked like a millionaire. Even though the decks and railing were caked with a rime of diesel fumes and oil spills and the hull could used a lick of paint, the ship looked like a wonder of pristine technology next to the *MV Mapinduzi*, a coastal passenger and cargo ferry just returned from Dar es Salaam.

Immediately, *Anna Böhme*'s wealth began to soak into the town. Traders were permitted to come aboard and set up their wares on threadbare mats in the shaded areas behind the superstructure. Highly polished conch shells appeared and were neatly arranged on batik cloth. A couple of entrepreneurs stood on the dock and began negotiating cigarette sales and money-exchange deals with members of the crew well before the gangway was unpacked and bolted into place.

The meeting between the captain and the Zanzibar customs officials was a riot, like a scene from a slapstick comedy with product placement from Stella Artois and 7UP. The officials high-fived one another, laughed generously at the captain's jokes, drank his beer and tried to recall whether cousin Thomas preferred Johnny Walker or Bell's. Until then, I'd assumed that the briefcases these officials seemed to carry as part of their uniform were simply tokens of status. I was wrong. When they came aboard, the briefcases were empty, except for a couple of rubber stamps. On the way out, they each contained the stamps and inkpads, two bottles of whiskey, a carton of Marlboro cigarettes and cans of beer.

'If you don't give, then it takes days and days for the loading,' Mr Chatterji explained. 'If you give, then everything goes very easily.'

At the railing, I saw a tall European man in a red checked flannel shirt come trotting down the dock, his face angled up to the sun. He was tall and thin. His teeth shone white when he grinned up at a group of us lounging on the railing. He had one of those sunburnt European complexions that looked like it had been steeped in tea for a month. From my position at the railing, it looked as if his pupils had been bleached. 'Where are you going next?' he called up.

'Mombasa,' replied Mr Patel, who was trying to listen to something being said on his walkie-talkie.

'Mombasa?' said the man. 'Terrific. I'd like to go to Mombasa.'

Mr Patel smiled politely. 'Yes, it's very interesting there. Kenya.'

'Are you taking hitchhikers?' asked the man.

Mr Patel assured him that we weren't. 'We are not allowed to. It's impossible.'

The man in the red shirt gave me a long, suspicious but quite friendly look. I sympathised: this was how the world should be, of course; travellers ought to be able to talk their way onto freighters, for a fair price. But they can't. Not on a freighter that has any kind of insurance policy, anyway, which includes all but the most pitiful rust buckets afloat. The world is getting smaller and travel is becoming smaller-minded.

Still smiling, the man said: 'It's just that I've been trying to get a lift, but no-one is going there.'

Mr Patel nodded sympathetically. 'Unfortunately, it is quite out of the question for you to come with us. It is against the law, you see. In Kenya they be wanting to know how you are going to leave again and the captain will be in big strife.'

'Not that much strife, surely?'

'A very big strife,' said Mr Patel.

'I could hide in the lifeboat.'

The guy clearly hadn't seen a freighter's lifeboat. 'It is not possible,' Mr Patel repeated. Eventually the guy gave up and wandered off.

I couldn't understand why he'd want to leave. From the lifeboat deck, Zanzibar had one of the most tantalising seafronts you could hope for. A broad promenade of Moorish palaces and hotels with ornate Indian-style facades faced a shallow bay where children were fishing with broom-handle rods and line. In the distance grey tenements rose out of the suburban sprawl.

I wandered around the docks for a while. The opposite side of the pier was where the dhows were moored in a tight clump of more than fifty boats, so densely roped to one another they actually formed an improvised pontoon, over which fishermen from the farthest boats climbed over to the shore and back again, clinging to masts and shimmying along booms. During Zanzibar's slave-trading heyday in the eighteenth and nineteenth centuries, the dhow season brought up to 15,000 traders and mariners to the town, almost doubling the population. The place was so backed up with sewage when he arrived there in the 1850s, the British explorer Richard Burton nicknamed it 'Stinkibar.'

But of all the priests, crooks and seadogs who'd stepped off these dhows over the years, the one I was most interested in was the sixteenth-century Portuguese spy Pero de Covilham, whose extraordinary travels in the Indian Ocean are still obscure, but mind-boggling enough in outline. At the time when Portuguese fleets were beating ever further south down the African coast looking for a southerly sea passage to the Indies, de Covilham was sent by his king, John II, to discover the Arabs' northerly trade routes to India and China and, while he was at it, to make contact with Prester John, the legendary Christian king of Ethiopia who might be persuaded to lend his support to a combined Christian assault on the rich ports of the Arabian Sea.

A fluent Arabic speaker, de Covilham set out from Lisbon in 1497, travelling to Alexandria disguised as a Jewish merchant. For the next four years he made a systematic study of trade routes and culture in the Indian Ocean, visiting Calicut and Goa on India's south coast and returning by way of Hormoz and Cairo; then travelling with Persian traders down the coast of East Africa to the wealthy Swahili trading ports of Mogadishu, Malindi, Mombasa, Zanzibar and Sofala. Four years after he left Lisbon, he was back in Alexandria, exhausted and keen to return home to his wife and children and, no doubt, rich rewards at court.

It wasn't to be. In Alexandria he received instructions to continue the search for Prester John. So de Covilham sent an account of the things he had seen back to Portugal with agents of the king, then, following orders, accompanied a Portuguese rabbi to Hormoz and Mecca before finally setting out for Ethiopia. He entered the country through Massawa and found the royal court under permanent siege from Muslim enemies. When he arrived he was told of the Ethiopian law which forbade any foreigner who entered the country ever to leave it again in case they were tempted to betray the secrets of the Christian defences. De Covilham was still there thirty years later when a delegation of Portuguese Jesuits arrived to argue theology with the Orthodox priests of the court. He never saw Portugal again and was soon forgotten in the rush of Portuguese voyages which had begun after Bartholomeu Diaz 'discovered' a southerly sea route to the Indian Ocean in 1488.

In his brilliant *Empires of the Monsoon*, historian Richard Hall muses that by the time de Covilham got stuck in Ethiopia, he had probably amassed more knowledge about the culture and history of the Indian Ocean than anyone had managed to fit inside one brain before or since. What de Covilham made of Zanzibar will never be known. The evidence suggests that as well as being a convincing actor, de Covilham was a talented linguist and a witty conversationalist, so the disappearance of the report he sent John II has to count as literature's loss as well as history's.

I headed into town with Manuel and Teng, who were on a mission for floppy disks. We strolled down a long, dusty road bordered on one side by a football field and on the other by a ragtag market selling fresh produce, battery-operated plastic starships, hairdryers and fake Swatches. Rakesh had extolled the virtues of Zanzibar's women and open-air food market, but couldn't come ashore, he told me, because he had to work. Manuel snorted. Rakesh wasn't coming ashore because he was terrified of the girls, he said.

Actually, Manuel explained, as Teng stopped to inspect a range of Swiss Army knives, it was one girl in particular. Rakesh had been seeing one girl here regularly for three trips; then, a few months ago, he'd found a girl he liked better. When she found out, the girl he'd spurned marched down to the docks with some friends. As luck would have it, Rakesh was hanging in a safety harness off the wall of stacked refrigerated containers, checking the motors on their cooling systems. He had to hang there for several minutes while she stood on the dock and bawled him out. Everyone within a mile heard exactly how she intended to castrate Rakesh if he ever set foot in Zanzibar again.

'The problem was he didn't respect his woman,' Teng said gravely.

'The problem was,' Manuel explained, with flawless seamen's logic, 'she was very ugly.'

I spent the evening wandering the narrow streets of Stone Town, carefully watching the surface of the streets as I went. In one square lit only by a hurricane lamp and the light spilling from the open windows of houses above, boys kicked a plastic football in the sand. A poster on one wall proudly announced that last year's Festival of the Dhow Countries was sponsored by Salama condoms, a company which must have felt it was time to give something back to the sea trade. I didn't see any craters. I had read that many of Zanzibar's famous carved wooden doors had been sacked by American antiquities dealers, but quite a few remain. Some of the streets were so narrow I had to duck into doorways so that people could pass; Muslim clerics with embroidered hats, women lugging string bags fat with shopping.

I wheeled back to the waterfront where the evening food market was getting into full swing, sat on the sea wall behind the market, lit a cigarette and watched the sea change colour as the sun disappeared. Men urinated into the harbour from the bottom stair and excused themselves politely when they brushed against me on the way up. When Zanzibar was the Indian Ocean's principal slave market, the limbs of dismembered slaves were fed to the sharks in this bay.

I bought some fish and sat down on a log among the stalls. A gaunt man with a shaggy goatee sat down next to me and quietly asked for some money for food. I gave him my samosa. He accepted it, looked at it carefully for a minute, then began to nibble at it cautiously. It occurred to me that perhaps he was truly starving and that he was eating so delicately because his stomach wouldn't be able to handle large lumps of food. I finished my disks of chopped octopus, spat out some grains of sand and lit a cigarette, carefully blowing smoke in the other direction. Behind us, cane-juice vendors ground split lengths of cane through a hand-driven press that seemed to work much like an old-fashioned iron clothes-wringer. Bits of crab shell hit the rocks around us as vendors tossed the sucked-out discards over their shoulders.

My new friend was down to the last corner of the samosa. I offered him a cigarette, which he accepted in a way that managed to imply that any decent human being would just give him the whole pack. He waved away my lighter with an irritation bordering on disgust. 'Food!' he said, shaking his last tiny morsel of samosa in my face like I was the dullest moron he'd ever had to dine with. 'Not smoking when eating!'

It seemed impolite to leave until he had finished. Eventually I stood up to go. I smiled goodbye. He simply shook his head at me in amazement, like he couldn't believe that people like me were allowed to exist.

In the morning I called home from an Internet café in Stone Town run by two young Indian women. As I was sitting there with my earphones on watching the expensive seconds tick by, the guy I'd seen on the docks came in, smiled and waved at me. He obviously wanted to chat; when I was finished, he introduced himself. 'I saw you from the street,' he said, gripping my hand firmly.

'I really can't help you get on the ship,' I said. 'There's no way they'll let you come aboard.'

'No, no,' he laughed. 'Forget about that. I just want to say hello.'

We went down to the waterfront and had a cup of coffee at a place where he knew all the waiters and the proprietor as well. The *Anna Böhme*, easily the largest built structure in the city, loomed over our view of the seafront. Jamie had been there for a couple of months, on and off. It turned out that he was getting by loaning money to local entrepreneurs who used the money to buy marijuana off the docks, which they then sold on at prodigious profit to tourists. It was highly convenient, he admitted. No-one had defaulted on a loan yet.

I couldn't believe he'd take a risk like that. What if one of them turned out to be an undercover cop?

'In Zanzibar?' he mocked. 'Don't be ridiculous. Anyway, you've got to trust people, man. And it's good money. I came here to teach English, but I'm making plenty of money out of this. People here are very cool and relaxed. Different to Africa. But now I want to move on.'

Jamie had the kind of easy charisma you can't learn from self-help tapes. He had flashing white teeth offset by his deep tan and careless mop of enviable hair. He had long, sensual fingers. He used them to roll messy cigarettes using tobacco from an old lozenge tin. I guessed he could have been as old as thirty-five, but he looked much younger.

When I told him why I was there, he took it upon himself to act as guide. That afternoon we toured the old slave quarters and the natural history museum. In the evening, we met up with a friend of his called Diane, a short girl from Boston. She wore a beret despite the sticky heat. She had been teaching English in Poland for the past three years and was now working her way to Hawaii where her estranged father lived. It occurred to me that if she was heading for Hawaii, she'd taken a wrong turn somewhere. 'I'm in no hurry,' she shrugged. 'What is there to get back to?'

The following night I met Jamie and Diane and some expatriate friends of theirs at a pub on the waterfront. There was obviously quite a big travellers' community there. It felt older and more grizzled than the summer backpacker scene in Europe, though. These travellers had been here longer; some of them had almost settled.

While Jamie was working the room like a student politician, Diane and I got talking about the places we'd been. I told Diane I thought the only way you could get away from the disappointment of travelling to imagined places was to try to travel to the past instead, where the tour groups couldn't go.

'You mean, in the mind?'

'Well, sort of. Yeah.'

'But you can do that from home,' she pointed out.

'Precisely,' I said, neatly losing the argument.

The night wore on. I asked Diane if it was true that half the time the inhabitants of Zanzibar lived by the light of oil lamps because the electricity constantly cut out. I told her what I'd heard about sailors breaking their legs in unexpected potholes. She'd never heard of it, she said. Then, perhaps encouraged by my credulity, she told me a story of her own about a local superstition: an evil man-bat called Popo Bawa ('Bat's Wing' in Kiswahili) who slipped into the homes of the sleeping and viciously sodomised them, their children and their animals. All that victims could remember when they woke was that he smelt horribly and that the stink of his terrible sins clung to them afterwards. Popo Bawa had arrived in Zanzibar from Pemba Island during the winter monsoon of 1995. Before that, apparently, he'd been doing unspeakable things to livestock on the mainland.

I assumed from the totally absurd content of what Diane was saying, and the playful expression on her face while she was saying it, that she was speaking in code about something else, something more plausible than a goat-buggering man-bat, but somehow less speakable. What could that be? I looked around the room: three German hikers on the balcony trying to write postcards in the lamplight; a pair of Israeli girls laughing with a grey-haired hippy from New Zealand who was trying to light a suspiciously thick rollie with the oil lamp on the table. 'Are you talking about drugs?' I asked in a low voice.

She blinked at me, then laughed. 'No, you idiot, I'm talking about Popo Bawa, the man-bat. It's true. Whole villages around the island sleep outside because they say that he only does his thing inside.'

'They say he arrived on a boat,' Diane said meaningfully. 'Just like you.'

'I doubt he arrived on a container ship.'

'Dracula arrived in England on a cargo ship,' she pointed out, rather cleverly, I thought.

Jamie wandered by our table looking for his tobacco and confirmed the story. I watched Jamie chatting in several languages with various people in the bar, I realised that he was utterly at home here with his permanent dissatisfaction. He was a younger version of Miguel, but essentially the same person: they were both attractive men drawn away from the places they were born by a compulsion that probably didn't make them any happier.

I arranged to meet up with them again the next day – we'd go for a dhow ride, Diane said – but it didn't work out. The *Anna Böhme* sailed ahead of schedule and I didn't see them again.

PLAYING BACKGAMMON WITH THE PRIEST

> You know as well as I do that everyone on board
> gambles – whether playing cards or backgammon –
> some even travel for this very purpose. But take note
> – if you care for your honour, never gamble . . .
> While others gamble set about reading one of the
> books that you will take with you. And if sometimes
> you want to spend time doing something other than
> reading or writing, young man, play backgammon
> with the priest.
>
> Fourteenth-century Venetian merchant

When I returned to the ship, Mr and Mrs Patel were enjoying their customary late-night cup of tea. I took a slice of chocolate pound cake into the crew mess. Nyem, the steward, and Jackie, one of the Burmese seamen, were watching something called *Titanic II: The Britannic*, a straight-to-DVD shocker someone had picked up in one of Singapore's pirate CD emporia.

Titanic II was certainly one of the very worst films I'd seen in my life. But at least the words rolling across the screen were in English. 'England and Germany have been at war for two long years . . .' rambled the preliminaries. Nyem was struggling to read it, so I read it aloud for him.

'Ah yes, thank you,' he said. 'Second war.'

'First,' I corrected.

'Yes, thank you. Can I have a cigarette?'

I pushed the packet over to him and watched while he delicately removed two smokes and placed them carefully parallel on the table in front of him. The first one was barely alight when he frowned. 'Did you buy these ashore? In Zanzibar?'

'Madagascar.'

'They are very weak, aren't they?'

'Are they?'

'Not good, sorry. African cigarettes are not good.'

But he smoked the other one nonetheless. By the time our heroine's repressed experiences aboard the first *Titanic* began to resurface, Nyem had helped himself to three more. He offered the pack like it was his to two other guys who stepped into the mess for some noodles.

We were having some difficulties, Nyem and I. Whenever he got the opportunity, Nyem made a point of telling me how little money he earned. Since he trained as a steward on passenger ships, where the base salary was even meaner than it was on cargo ships, he saw a passenger – a novelty on this kind of ship – in the same way that a suckerfish might view a fat shark: an opportunity not to be missed. Since my first day aboard he had delivered the same speech several times about how hard he worked – *So busy, so busy* – and how he had six beautiful girls, his babies, at home who were a source of delight but also a serious financial drain, since they ate all his money. He would love to come out with me in port some time and show me the sailor's life; sadly, however, he could not afford it. If I wanted him to go out with me to the Florida Bar in Mombasa, he said, I would have to pay.

'The *what* bar?' I asked, fighting back a vision of Florida from Madagascar turning up in Mombasa and chasing me around the back streets with rolling eyes and that mocking smile.

'Florida Bar. Is very good. There are many girls in Mombasa, so many girls . . .' His eyes started to mist up, but he wasn't going to budge. If he and I were going to have some girls and some good times, then I would have to pay. It was up to me to make the right decision. 'But people from Burma always say, "charity is a joy". I always like to give my moneys to orphans.'

His only mistake was to tell me how much he was getting paid: US$900 a month, with overtime included, a sum which put my own earning capacity into sharp relief. He had detected, I think, my reluctance to pay for his 'girls', whether daughters or hookers. Toilet paper had become strangely difficult to come by. Coat hangers mysteriously disappeared from my wardrobe and replacements had to be laboriously arranged by Nyem himself – *Very difficult, very hard to find, but I try for you specially* – and the small fridge in the galley containing snacks and leftover fruit and cakes was frequently locked now. Bin liners had become a luxury impossible to replenish. My soap supply had run out. 'Soap?' shrugged Nyem, as if he'd never heard of it. So we were in a stalemate for the moment, and Nyem was holding all the keys to the cupboard.

Mombasa was the field where the battle would be decided.

The next evening, the officers' mess was in a state of uproar, which was inconvenient because I was trying to follow an episode of 'Inspector Morse' taped off South African cable television by the agent in Dar es Salaam. Mr M came in first, his normally amiable features darkened with displeasure. He shouted in Hindi, banged the doors on the video cupboard, raked through a pile of board games and videos, and left again. Then two of the junior engineers came in and had a quick-fire argument with Second, who was also watching 'Inspector Morse'. After them it was Mr Patel and Mr Kadirgamar, both in boiler suits; Mr Kadirgamar scratching his chin nervously with the antenna of his walkie-talkie and Mr Patel shaking his head sadly. There was more quick, unhappy talk in Hindi. By nine o'clock most of the officers had been through the saloon to ransack the cupboards and to shout at one another. The cadet steward stood in the doorway, looking on slack-jawed. I felt a presentiment of disaster. Clearly the ship was on fire. Perhaps pirates had caught up with us at last, or water had breached a bulkhead. But Morse was just getting to the heart of the matter in Oxford, so I decided to ignore the commotion until someone told me what the problem was in English, or until I saw flames.

It wasn't a fire, as it turned out. Or pirates. It was worse than that. The DVD player had disappeared. Stolen, probably in Dar es Salaam, presumably by one of the guys who'd been hawking ebony statuettes and ivory knife handles outside on the main deck. The officers couldn't believe it. The terrible news that the new Bollywood releases the crew had picked up in Singapore on pirated DVDs were no longer showing in the saloon cinema and that the bass amplifier would boom to the tune of latest-release Bollywood no more ripped through the ship like flu. By breakfast the next day, hope had given way to despair.

No-one likes a thief, but I have to confess I wasn't entirely unhappy about this development. No more Bollywood for the time being. More Meg.

Depending on whom you ask, Mombasa is one of the great flesh-pots of the Indian Ocean, a sink of vice beggared by Aids and poverty, or an atmospheric little town with an historic fort.

Mr Chatterji was suffering my presence on the bridge as we waited for the pilot to board outside Mombasa harbour at six o'clock in the morning. We could see a sprawl of yellow and white lights a few miles up ahead. I tried to connect the dots in my head to form the city I'd been reading about.

Mr Kadirgamar should have been in bed, but for some reason was perched on the captain's stool, drinking tea and monitoring bursts of static on the radio. Chatterji was in the chart room, perhaps sleeping. I was swallowing large mouthfuls of instant coffee from the million-dollar mug I'd bought in Dar es Salaam.

'Have you been to Mombasa before?' Mr Kadirgamar asked me.

'Never.'

Mr Kadirgamar's eyes glinted. Like Mr Chatterji, the placid Kadirgamar seemed to live in a permanent bubble of fear about what could happen to you ashore, and he enjoyed spreading the terror. 'You must be careful. It's very dangerous.'

'I'll be fine,' I said.

Chatterji darted out of the chart room, his pink tongue peeping out from between his lips. 'You talking about Mombasa?'

221

'I am telling him about the mugging and murdering,' Mr Kadirgamar said.

'Ha!' Mr Chatterji's favourite subject. He agreed that yes, people were frequently mugged in Mombasa, but it was still much better than the coast of West Africa. 'There you come from the shore with nothing wearing but only your underclothes!'

For a meek man who spent all his time in his office or cabin, the captain seemed to have been involved in a suspiciously large number of security incidents. He certainly claimed to have been whacked, dropped, stripped, tripped and beaten in every port you could name.

The chief officer was more matter-of-fact about the dangers that lurked ashore. 'It is better to go in a car at night time,' Mr Kadirgamar said. 'But of course, everywhere is dangerous these days. The United States even are dangerous. Last year in New Orleans, two Bangladeshi sailors went on shore leave and disappeared for two days. When the police mounted a search for them, their bodies were found under a railway bridge. Because they didn't have any money, you see, they were raped and stabbed and their bodies cut up.'

The captain exclaimed in Hindi.

'Yes, yes,' confirmed Mr Kadirgamar. 'I read it in *Sailor Today*. Both were raped and *then* cut up.'

'Oh dear,' Chatterji beamed. Chatterji was the kind of person who died a thousand *petit morts* of pleasure contemplating all the dreadful things that could happen to other people.

'That is why,' Mr Kadirgamar said to me, 'you must always have twenty dollars or thirty dollars to give, because it may save your life.'

But I didn't have any money at that moment. I was out of American dollars and struggling to get any on my credit card. 'Do you know if it's possible to get US dollars on a credit card here?'

Mr Kadirgamar just shrugged. The captain tut-tutted through his teeth. 'Besides, ' Chatterji added helpfully, 'I cannot guarantee you a shore pass.'

I'm wasn't so sure now that I wanted one. The more I listened to these guys, the more tempted I was to remain on board with my Meg Ryan videos and Tom Bulpin's reassuringly historical account of the region, in which all the cut-throats have been dead for at least two centuries.

While I was waiting for the shore pass to be issued, I stepped into the galley for a snack. Nyem was in there stacking plates. He poured some water into a cup for my morning coffee. 'We going into Mombasa tonight? I show you the nice ladies. I am working very hard. All day, all night. We have some dancing . . .'

'Don't you want to call your wife and children?'

Nyem's smart eyes narrowed. Maybe, his eyes seemed to be saying, he had underestimated his opponent. 'I have no money to call my babies,' he growled.

'Well, maybe tonight you and I can go out with the others.'

'In Burma, people are very nicely. They say giving to charity is lucky for the person. I like to give money for peoples' babies.'

I nodded brightly. 'That's excellent. Me too.'

'It's very hard working on this ship. Up at six, then working-working until bedtime. No time for dancing.'

'Still, if there's no money . . .'

Nyem tipped the hot water for my coffee into the sink. 'No time for coffee now,' he said, turning away. 'Busy so busy.'

Morning was over and still heat had settled in the streets by the time I reached them. My taxi dropped me off at the pair of monumental elephant tusks in Nkrumah Street. I was irrationally terrified. As soon as I had purchased my $120 from Barclays I went to a café where I hid in the toilet and stuffed the greenbacks into my sock.

My first destination was the old dhow harbour, deep inside the Old Town where beautiful hand-carved balconies sagged over the dirt streets. Much noisier and more lively than the Stone Town of Zanzibar, it nonetheless looked just like it. Despite the fragrant dilapidation of the houses, few of them were more than a hundred years old.

Not gifted with maps, I somehow failed to find the dhow port.

Instead, I ended up taking a staircase down into a gully above the beach which the locals were clearly using as a rubbish dump. Some vicious-looking sea birds picked among the empty cans and broken prams. I headed back to Fort Jesus, getting lost among the cul-de-sacs and smelly alleyways. It was the sort of place where you found yourself glimpsing private scenes through open doorways and windows with no glass: two children sitting quietly on either side of their grandmother accepting in turn spoonfuls of yoghurt from a tin; an elderly man with a peacock feather in his fez quietly urinating against the tyre of a hand-drawn wagon; a boy leaning out of a window with a plastic model aeroplane in his fist.

I lost myself in the travellers' fantasy of becoming someone else altogether, someone who had known these streets from birth, someone who belonged there. Most of the houses were only 150 years old at most, but some of the narrow byways must have been ancient. These were the same streets once trodden, perhaps, by Pero de Covilham on his way to Sofala, about 2000 kilometres further south. Unlike me, de Covilham was here on serious business. But as the years wore on he must have been forced into that same fantasy, becoming his disguise in the long years he'd spent pretending to be an Arab merchant, eavesdropping and lurking among the godowns and taverns of the Indian Ocean.

I emerged, finally, into the sunshine on a wide street full of little shops selling ebony figurines to mobs of skittish tourists.

In the afternoon I toured bookshops. There weren't many. The Christian publishers seemed to have a stranglehold on the market here. I browsed among such titles as *Why You Should Speak in Tongues* and *No Sex Please: We're Not Married*, the cover of which showed four cardigan-wearing youth-groupers with arms linked, gambolling across a meadow. There were guides to countries that didn't exist any more, including Zaire and Yugoslavia. They were not discounted.

Later I met Thomas and Rakesh at the Casablanca Bar where I was introduced to a friend of Rakesh's, a tall and lean Swahili man with spivvy good looks. His name was Wes and his delight at seeing his old buddy was clearly at least partly professional.

'How long, my friend, how long?'

'Who knows?' Rakesh shrugged. 'Maybe two days.'

Wes slapped his hand to his forehead in mock horror. His copper bracelets jangled together. 'Only a couple of days! Man, they've gotten too fast down there. I tell them to slow down, but they're all efficient. Everything has to be efficient.'

It was only six o'clock in the evening, but the night's work had already begun for the friendly ladies of the Casablanca Bar. As soon as we sat down, several women invited themselves to our table. As in Madagascar, the girls here seemed to choose their names using a blindfold, a pin and a map of the United States. 'Anything you like Mister Harry,' Dallas whispered. 'What you like?'

Dallas had a narrow face and clever, humorous eyes. But the truth was, I didn't want anything and said so. 'Don't be messing with Dallas' head, baby. No like massage?'

Rakesh took a photograph of us all with a disposable camera, then led the way to a bar in the Old Town. From the outside, it looked like a typical two-storey stone-and-timber house, complete with dilapidated latticework balcony. Inside it was dark and smoky. The set-up reminded me of one of London's pathetic illegal drinking clubs that fill up when the pubs close, places where you sit at card tables in someone's bedsit above the streets of Soho savouring the illicit atmosphere and the smell of wet gaberdines and beer breath, drinking warm beer and no-name spirits. There was a wooden table in one corner of the front room with an ice chest on it, and loud Bob Marley music. On the wall behind our tiny table was a poster of Che Guevera. On another wall was a poster that looked like it had been torn from *National Geographic* of a vicious-looking shark, all bloody gums and brainless jaws.

'What is this place?' I whispered to Thomas.

He shrugged and grinned. 'Shark Bar,' he said.

'I saw a shark eat its own intestines once in a film,' said Rakesh. 'A diver cut its belly so that its guts fell out. The shark gobbled them up.'

Thomas rolled his eyes.

'It's a shame you're not here for long,' Wes said to me when I explained what I was doing there. 'The port is too efficient. Not so many ships now. Kenya is going kaput,' he grinned, then contradicted himself when he explained that last year, Mombasa port handled eight million tonnes of imports, most of it transhipped by rail inland to Uganda, the Congo or Rwanda. The Ugandan president had recently threatened to start importing goods through Durban in preference to Mombasa and Dar es Salaam if handling delays in Mombasa weren't sorted out. It was a fairly hollow threat, Wes pointed out, since bringing things in through Durban would add two days to the four days it usually took for goods to be trucked from there to the Ugandan border.

I told Wes I was surprised by how small Mombasa seemed, how beautiful the balconies and alleyways were in the Old Town. How like Zanzibar, really. It was the Muslims, Wes explained. 'The Arabs. They run this place.'

'And the Indians,' added Rakesh. 'Bloody Indians everywhere, and everywhere they go they're owning shops. Have you noticed that?'

'Gujaratis,' said Thomas. 'Like our millionaire. You know second engineer?'

I nodded. The second engineer was a small, sarcastic man of about thirty-five. He had a mouthful of broken teeth and his Bakelite glasses were held together by a piece of copper wire. He was the man who wanted to burn down a mosque somewhere.

'He is a millionaire,' Thomas said. 'I am talking US dollars here. His wife is a doctor and they are saving up to buy a hospital. He's from Gujarat. They are all tight there. Tight shopkeepers. He always uses his teabag twice at lunchtime. You watch. That's how they get rich.'

Wes and Rakesh disappeared upstairs, and Dallas and her friends drifted away to a more promising-looking table in the next room where some Korean sailors appeared to be enjoying themselves. 'That guy is loopy,' Thomas said. He meant Rakesh. I realised I'd never really understood where Rakesh fitted into the ship's chain of command. 'Don't ask me,' Thomas said, holding up two fingers to the owner, who rummaged around in his ice chest and brought us two more unlabelled brown bottles. 'He does a bit of this and a bit of that. I think he is the officer in charge of bullshitting.'

I was feeling fine, now. Watching Thomas light a cigarette on the hippo-shaped candle in the middle of our table, I felt glad to be sitting with my sailor pal in what appeared to be a Swahili speakeasy, only yards from the old dhow harbour where Arab seafarers have been coming ashore for prayers and sin longer than anyone could remember. I thought of Tristan; how we'd plied Neptune's favours with a few Tunisian coins on the yacht marina at Ajaccio, and how well it had worked out. He would have loved this. I took a swig of beer in his honour.

The beer was horrendous. I tried not to wince.

'I know,' said Thomas. 'They brew it themselves. It's probably poisonous. But it's cheap.'

Thomas didn't want to talk about beer though. He had a lot on his mind. He was worried that I was offended by Chatterji and the fact that he clearly didn't like me.

There are of course people who love stoking a smouldering unease between others into a blaze of hatred so they can sit back and enjoy it from neutral ground; Thomas wasn't like that. He was genuinely worried that I felt abandoned on the ship. At the same time he didn't want to be disloyal to Chatterji, whom he claimed to hold in high regard. Our skipper, Thomas informed me, was one of the smartest men in India. As a boy, he had won a scholarship offered to only ten students across the country. 'He has a very high IQ,' Thomas said.

'Who says so?'

'Everyone knows this. He comes from a poor family, you see. He has earned everything he has with his brains. Still, I am afraid that he doesn't like white people. I think he feels that white people have caused a lot of problems in India.'

'Well, I guess I can understand that.'

'You mustn't take it personally.'

Of course I took it personally. But I assured Thomas that I didn't.

'Sometimes if you make enemies on a ship it is dangerous

because they will push you over the side one night and pretend it was an accident.'

'What?'

'But you don't have to worry. It's a lot of paperwork when someone goes overboard. Too much paperwork for Chatterji.'

I wasn't entirely sure that he was joking.

Satisfied that I wasn't suicidal over Chatterji's low opinion of me, Thomas now felt free to sink into his own slough of despondency. He had problems of his own. His dear wife talked too much for starters; she embarrassed him with her strident opinions in front of his Muslim friends in Mumbai, whose wives were much less verbal; he had a number of gambling debts which he could pay for, but would nonetheless have to be explained to his wife. But mostly, he was troubled by his sins.

'Where does it say in the Bible to drink lots of beer?' he demanded to know. 'It says to drink wine for health; but nowhere does it say you have to fall over drunk. It doesn't say you have to have fun with another man's wife, does it? Look at you,' he blubbered miserably. 'You don't drink much. You don't play with girls. I've never heard you swear –'

'Bullshit!'

Thomas smiled bleakly. '. . . You hardly even smoke. The point I am making is, you're a better Christian than me and you don't even realise it!'

It seemed ironic that in the year 2000 an Indian Catholic sailor should be torturing himself on his private rack of faith, particularly in an exhausted seaport on this ocean, of all oceans. For most of its long history as a trading basin, the Indian Ocean has been a place of unusual religious tolerance and pluralism. Freedom of movement was sacrosanct: it had to be so that sailors of all nations and religions could safely trade their way among the ports between China, Arabia and the East African coast. A thousand years ago, in the great city of Hormoz on the mouth of the Persian Gulf, this tenet was said to be enforced by a law which forbade anyone to insult another's religion.

That changed after Vasco da Gama beat his way around the Cape.

The next morning I accepted a taxi ride from Carla, a middle-aged woman spruiking for customers at the port gates. She was reading a magazine called *Love Dust: The Magazine That Tells Real Intimate Stories*. Carla wailed about Kenya's disappointing performance in the Olympic Games. The only bright spots for her, a loyal East African, were the Ugandans, and – spreading her loyalty a little further afield here – the Cameroon soccer team. She dropped me off at Government Square, behind which, she assured me, I would find the old dhow harbour.

She was right. The old harbour was the sort of place that travel fantasists like me should only ever see at dusk. I perched on some steps and drank in the scene. I counted three largish dhows and several smaller fishing boats of different kinds, and one ark-shaped wooden coaster that looked like it hadn't traded anything for a long time. For at least a millennium, in dhows and teak coasters sewn together on India's Malabar Coast, Arab traders and pirates had sailed here on the winter monsoon, bringing their carpets and dates, leaving with slaves and ivory. By the time the Portuguese arrived in 1498 Mombasa had outstripped in size and trade all the other ports on the Zanj coast. They found 'a very fair place with lofty stone and mortar houses . . .' wrote the Portuguese traveller Duarte Barbosa twenty years later. 'This is a place of great traffic, and has a good harbour, in which are always moored craft of many kinds and also great ships . . . The men thereof are oft-time at war and but seldom at peace with those of the mainland, and they carry on trade with them, bringing thence great store of honey, wax and ivory.' I stayed for a while, letting my mind wander. When the writer Alan Villiers arrived here on a dhow in 1939, his ship moored among ships from Oman, Muscat and Sur. He noted the sweet smell of copra by the customs steps I was sitting on; the harbour itself was full of 'picturesque and so varied ships, all sailing vessels, all sweet of line and graceful as a crowd of costly yachts at some anchorage in the Mediterranean, and the white lateen sails always seemed piratical and picturesque'. The big dhows carried on their trade, he wrote, as if da Gama had never rounded the Cape. And as if iron hulls had never been invented.

I found a café whose espresso machine was visible from the street, and settled at a table with a copy of that day's *East African* and my dog-eared *Economist*, the same one Florida had watched me buy in Toamasina that was now going on six weeks old. Across the street a group of school kids stood watching a television through the glass of a shop window.

The *Economist* had a special about the impact of globalism on the Third World. The World Bank, it seemed, had made an offer to cancel Mauritania's crippling US$2.6 billion debt, on the condition that the government embark on a reform program and promised to tackle official corruption. The *East African* carried an article reporting the press statements following the World Bank meeting in which several senior American economists named corruption as the principal cause of poverty in Africa, effectively washing its hands of five centuries of profit taking.

But was it only about corruption? I'd seen enough of these ports to know that the spirit of the market was thriving on the shores there. It always had. Ports are hothouses of barter and exchange. In Dar the streets were full of unemployed young men, like the guy who showed me where international calls could be made, tried to sell me his sister, then, failing that, a woofy sea bass, and finally, having sold me nothing, argued coherently for several minutes in favour of a payment for his time. He probably could have gotten a job in PR anywhere in London, yet somehow he couldn't get any capital to stick to the palm of his hand.

Of course, global capitalism had been going on there for a long time and rarely to the advantage of ordinary Africans. The seventeenth-century Neapolitan traveller Giovanni Careri was amazed at the number of African slaves from Mombasa and Sofala to be seen in Goa. The slaves were so cheap – only '15 or 20 crowns of Naples a head' – that there would surely be more, he thought, if not for the African superstition that the Portuguese were buying them to turn their bodies into gunpowder.

What struck me was the pretence of equality between the boy in Dar and me; we were both happier to pretend that the desperate poverty on display in Dar was the same everywhere. From television, he must have known differently. Television has to be depressing for people like him. Not because it broadcasts images of consumerism and junk culture into Tanzanian homes, but because broadcasting is all it does. It offers tantalising images from the distant West of a happy consumer lifestyle, of consumer goods like McDonald's or Game Boy which simply don't exist in Dar. Why didn't he just threaten to beat me up and take all my cash? Dignity, I supposed. Perhaps his faith. Whatever the reason, this adherence to the basic contract of civility between dirt-poor locals and First World tourists never seemed more irrational or humbling as it did to me in Dar es Salaam and Mombasa; me with 100 dollars still sweating guiltily in my boots.

Carla picked me up outside the Internet café on Nkrumah Road where I'd sent a message to Sarah. As we drove, she gave me a shrewd going-over in the rear-view mirror. 'You call your wife?'

I nodded.

'So, you want to go see some nice girls before the ship?' She glanced across, gave me an indulgent wink. 'I know some places for sailors.'

'Think I'll give it a miss.'

'But they really want to meet you. I tell them you're big and handsome.' Carla laughed slightly too hard at this for my liking. 'So we go?'

'No, we don't.'

At the gate to the docks she gave me her copy of *Love Dust*. 'It's nice to read,' she said. 'I'm finished. Take it. Maybe cheer up on ship.'

Most of the officers were seated somewhere beneath the cigarette cloud in the officers' saloon watching some Olympic highlights on KBC.

The mood was subdued. The DVD player had not been found. It had gone forever. We watched some men's discus highlights; then a women's basketball quarter-final between Brazil and Russia came on. People shifted in their chairs. When Brazil snatched victory with a basket in the last three seconds the guys

231

were out of their seats with excitement. Not so much because they cared about women's basketball, but because Brazilian women were winning. Those girls from Brazil had a real grip on the seaman's heart – they were the sirens that lurked in the race memory of all merchant seamen – even these really tall ones who would be twice the height of any man in the room except Rakesh.

Back in my cabin I flicked through Carla's magazine, which turned out to be a supermarket confessional blended with a bizarre strain of sermonising. One reader had written in to tell readers all about her wild affair with her wealthy boss. She wasn't, she told us sternly, taking any nonsense from the old bloke, notwithstanding his 'constant horniness':

> Sensing his climax at far, he stopped his lustful acts and, after making arrangements of where to pick me, I left. Sincerely speaking, my crotch was all wet and I first made my way to the ladies where I wiped it dry but the wetness prevailed. That evening we had a good time in a tourist-infested Italian hotel in town [Nairobi]. I enjoyed the Italian delicacies to my best level.

Every few pages there was a public warning about the dangers of Aids. On a page headed by the title 'Landlady is given sex for rent by two boys', the banner read:

> IMPORTANT NOTICE: Never trust anyone no matter how healthy she/he appears to be, death could be lurking behind that beauty. TAKE CARE!

There were no stories fantasising about trysts with sailors, or, for that matter, the truck drivers who were generally blamed with freighting Aids around the continent. In Tanzania 8 per cent of adults are infected with HIV. Médecins sans Frontières estimated that up to 20 per cent of patients in some African hospitals were misdiagnosed as HIV-infected and so left untreated because drugs required to treat Aids were too expensive. Still, according to the story the landlady in question had no complaints about the unusual method of payment. Carla was right. It was a good read.

I watched our departure from the main-deck railing. Before we left, a lot of local men – not stevedores, not vendors, just men with nowhere else to be – were sitting around on coils of rope and stacks of tiles just gazing at the ship. Several sailors stood at the railing along from me, smoking in silence, gazing down at the dock. Scraps of dirty paper blew across the concrete.

That night a movie called *The Parent Trap* was showing in the officers' saloon. The movie was about sickeningly adorable nine-year-old twins who brought their separated parents together through lots of ingenious ruses. It was a kids' movie, basically, but the officers loved it. Mr Chatterji, whose taste was usually for Bollywood extravaganzas, particularly enjoyed it. He was sitting next to me in the dark of the saloon and I could hear him tut-tutting at the parents' fighting, and gurgling with pleasure when the parents realised what had been obvious to everyone else for the last hour of the movie: that they still loved one another. When the credits finally rolled, he flicked off the television with the remote. There was an abrupt quiet, like the kind you get when someone storms out of a room and slams the door behind them. 'I must ask you,' said Chatterji, addressing the room at large, 'what was the moral of the movie?' No-one said anything. Then I realised everyone was looking at me. So was Chatterji.

'What's the moral?' I squirmed. There was a joke here, and I was missing it. 'Er, not to have kids?'

'No!' Chatterji laughed uncertainly. 'No, no the moral is you must have children. You *must*. Children bring happiness, you see.'

That's certainly what the movie had implied. 'I see.'

'Without children, life is nothing, nuh?' Chatterji continued. 'That is why it is important to have a family. And not too late. Because you never know what's going to happen.'

Mr M had to agree with his colleague. 'So then, Mr Neil, you see it is time to get on with it. We are none of us getting younger.'

233

I glanced around the other officers for looks of support, but saw none. Rakesh was laughing softly to himself. Only Thomas looked at me, with a pious expression that seemed to say: *Save yourself while you still can.*

I felt a flicker of panic. Here were witnesses to my passing youth. I'd meant for this to be a young man's trip; a journey taken for the plain joy of getting away as much as anything else. Instead, here I was being hurried through the turnstiles to middle age.

I struggled to get to sleep that night. I realised that no DVD player meant I wouldn't be able to see the rest of Meg Ryan in *Hanging Up*. Oh well. There would be some of her older work in the VHS library on the fourth deck. A copy of *When Harry Met Sally*, perhaps. I'd even settle for *Joe Versus the Volcano*.

The little red frame that travelled so slowly across the face of the calendar in the officers' mess finally dropped onto a new line, the last one for this voyage.

I wasn't sorry. I was tired of staring at containers through my porthole, and the food had declined even further. The curry which flowed from the galley was still apparently out of bounds to me, no matter how often the skipper gleefully insisted that I try some. As part of our ongoing battle, Nyem had taken to leaving the long-life milk out of the fridge to stew in the humidity of the galley. Whenever I came downstairs to make myself a coffee in my million-dollar mug, I ended up carrying coffee with spoilt milk back up five flights of stairs. Somehow, terrible flavours ended up infecting everything I ate. Everything tasted of last week.

Sometimes I sat out on the deck next to the swimming pool, basically a grimy metal sink hammered into the deck next to an extraction fan outlet on the starboard funnel. Here, surrounded by iron – iron walls, metal seats, the iron deck – the universe seemed to just grow hotter and hotter without any prospect of relief. The concept of the universe expiring in a heat death seemed less an astronomical abstraction and more like a very real possibility. Drops of my sweat vanished within seconds of hitting the deck.

One afternoon I read an item in *Sailor Today* magazine about a ship which had been abandoned five nautical miles offshore from Mumbai harbour. The ship, the Honduras-flagged freighter *El Hamas*, had left Singapore for Mumbai earlier in the year. When it arrived, the agents decided to sell the ship to a ship-breaker in Alang, further up the coast. None of the crew had been paid for four months. The ship's captain went ashore in Mumbai, shortly followed by Filipino and Indian crew-members. Twelve Indonesian and Burmese seamen were left behind. *Sailor Today* painted a bleak picture of conditions aboard: dwindling supplies of water and food, no fuel to drive the generators and so no electricity and worst of all, little prospect of help. The article said 'considering that the agents have abandoned the ship because they could not find a buyer, and the crew's wages are unlikely to be paid unless the ship is sold, relief for the crew might take long to come'.

I found it almost impossible to imagine living in a ship without any power; a lifeless hulk of rusted metal swinging in silence on its anchor chains, nothing inside but darkness, foul air and a coolstore full of spoiled vegetables. Dominic may have been right when he told me that the Filipino guys lived like swells in three-storey condos in Manila. But it hardly seemed to make up for the possibility that you could end up like that, scrounging for survival on a forgotten ship like a rat.

We tied up on the docks in Victoria, Seychelles' capital, on a flat, airless morning. The rainclouds that had threatened to produce a downpour finally let go just after the customs officials came aboard. By now I wasn't terribly interested in exploring the character of Victoria's port district. I just wanted a swim.

Unfortunately, there was no hope of a shore pass. Chatterji called me down to meet the agent, who told me that alas, since he hadn't been informed that I was on the ship, he hadn't arranged to have an immigration official come on board, and since it was Sunday there was no hope of getting one in. The captain, whose responsibility this clearly was, shrugged his shoulders. I wanted to hit his little smirk as hard as possible, but didn't. I stormed around the ship a couple of times, unable to believe what was happening.

Not for the first time, it was Mr M who came to the rescue. He arranged to forge his pass for me. 'Just tell them you are the ship's radio officer,' he said. 'Usually there is no problem.'

I walked out past the guard box an illegal immigrant. It was raining lightly. I used an ATM machine to get some rupees, hailed a taxi to Beau Vallon, and spent two hours watching a ferocious downpour from a stool at the beachside bar at the Coral Strand Hotel. I hired snorkelling gear and walked around to the rocky point to the south-west, together with two French guys also carrying gear. The streams of rainwater cut bulging canals through the sand, turning the bay brown. When I wasn't looking around the edges of my mask for sharks, I tried to sidle up to some fish for a closer look, but my lungs were obviously feeling the impact of my new smoking habit and I found that I couldn't stay down for long. I noticed a little turtle scooting along the bottom. I dived down to take a closer look but I just made it nervous. It cleverly headed deeper, where, it must have realised, I was too cowardly to follow.

I returned to the Coral Strand Hotel, ate a soggy pizza and went for another swim when the sun came out again. I was drying myself on a picnic bench when I spotted Mr and Mrs Patel arriving in a taxi. Among the sunbroiled nakedness on the beach, they looked like royal visitors: Mr Patel in his crisply pressed trousers and button-down shirt, Mrs Patel in a shimmering sari. Mr Patel waved. After a brief conference, they came over and invited me to come with them. I was reluctant to cramp their time together but I accepted, mainly because I thought it would be handy to have Mr Patel with me when I tried to get back into the port.

The Patels had hired a taxi for the day and were on a strict sightseeing schedule. Mr Patel and I *Mr*'ed one another all the way around the island like a couple of genteel retired dictators. *Would you please take a photograph, Mr Neil? With the casino in the background please? Certainly, Mr Patel. Thank you, Mr Neil. After you, Mrs Patel. Thank you, Mr Neil.*

We were driven back through Victoria, thence to the Berjaya

Hotel which the Patels wanted to see because it had hosted, over recent years, a run of victories for Miss Indias in the Miss World competition. The hotel had become a kind of pilgrimage for the Indian officers on our ship. As if in a sacred temple, the Patels stepped gingerly across the pool deck. This was why they'd come ashore and from their dreamy, disappointed faces, I could tell that they were struggling with the curse of all travellers who travelled to feel closer to the past: they couldn't believe they were actually there. It was impossible for them to believe that if they could have stepped through the television and into the Miss World broadcast, they would have found themselves in this pleasant but thoroughly ordinary place. They hid their disappointment behind the camera and took some more snaps, carefully including a staircase down which Indian Miss Worlds had floated, and had a drink on the pool terrace.

Time ran out before we could go and see the coco de mer trees in the botanical gardens. The female coco de mer nut is supposed to look startlingly like the female pelvis, so I was fairly glad I didn't have to see that in the presence of Mrs Patel. She would have borne it with graceful calm, no doubt, but I would have been mortified. As it was, the oddly phallic ice blocks in her drink put an embarrassing silence into our conversation on the pool terrace at the Berjaya.

'How long does it take a ship to sink?' Thomas asked. I was trying to teach him how to play Spite and Malice over a six-pack of Heineken (me) and a bottle of Jamieson's Whiskey (him), both from the ship's slop chest. He was sweating heavily, as he often did when he drank. His mind was beginning to range across a variety of depressing topics; another symptom of Thomas in his cups. 'Not as long as you'd think. You run into something big and all that will be left of the ship after ten minutes will be a few bubbles on the surface. And if you don't act fast, you will be at the bottom.'

He was appalled to hear that no-one had shown me how to fire a flare or how to clear for automatic release the position signalling devices stored at the very top of the ship on the monkey's island. Here was yet another instance of the captain's unspoken contempt for his only passenger. 'I tell you, the captain has it in for you royally. Has someone shown you your seat in the lifeboat?' They hadn't. 'Come on,' he said, dragging me up. 'Bring your beer.'

Thomas unpinned a seating plan from the corkboard on the landing and stood under the bare globe on the boat deck trying to make out the names and numbers. We staggered about a bit despite a calm sea. The lifeboat was exactly the same as the one on the *Anneke Schliemann*, a part submersible painted a vibrant shade of International Orange, the universal colour of life jackets, buoys and life rafts, whose properties included, among high visibility in a search situation, a noted tendency to attract sharks.

Thomas showed me where I should sit. 'Always put on your belt. The impact when it hits the water can be quite a shock for the neck.'

I nodded. 'Don't worry. I've done lifeboat drill on another ship.'

Thomas took a swig of Jamieson's from a plastic cup. 'All you have to do if there is an emergency is get here,' he said. 'These beauties are unsinkable. There is nothing to worry about.'

Unless, of course, you didn't get to the lifeboat. The only man aboard who had ever had to abandon a ship in a genuine emergency – and I found this a little unnerving – was the captain himself. Here's how the story went.

In the early hours of the morning, one day nine years before, Chatterji was on the bridge of a bulk freighter drifting outside Kuwait. The ship was quiet, most of the deck crew were asleep below; there were a couple of oilers in the engine room carrying out maintenance. Looking up from his paperwork, Chatterji suddenly saw a flash of hot white and red light away to port. Before he had time to wonder what it was, there was a terrific explosion. So loud, Chatterji said, the noise stunned all three officers on the bridge for several minutes. When he recovered, Chatterji saw that a ragged bite had been torn out of the hull and deck on the port side. The ship was on fire. He ordered the crew to prepare to abandon ship. He radioed for help, grabbed his favourite pair of binoculars, and scuttled through the hatch and out onto the bridge deck. When he circled around behind the bridge deck, he could see that his crew was hastily launching the lifeboat several flights

of stairs below, having apparently decided to disregard the con-
vention of waiting for everyone else. Chatterji screamed at them
to stop. They didn't hear him. Luckily, they still hadn't worked
out how to launch the boat by the time Chatterji reached them,
having half-scrambled, half-fallen down the stairs.

As dazed sailors in T-shirts and boxer shorts scrambled for
seats in the boat, Chatterji's chief engineer realised that the men
who had been working in the engine room were missing. Chatterji
and the chief engineer took the external stairs to the main deck,
opened an external hatch leading to the engine room and started
down. Just then the ship was rocked by another explosion, much
less violent than the first, but enough to convince Chatterji that he
was out of time. They bolted back up to the deck and rushed to
the stern. The boat was gone. There was no time to lower one of
the open boats. Chatterji and the engineer pulled on their life jackets and jumped overboard. They swam an interminable distance
in the black water to reach one of the light buoys marking the sea
channel. They pulled themselves up onto it and listened in despair
to the fading sound of the lifeboat's motor. Before long, it had
motored out of earshot.

Chatterji's throat was parched. His eardrums felt muffled.
There was nothing to disturb the shocked silence but the slap of
the sea against the buoy and the distant scream of military aircraft
high above.

When the sun came up, Chatterji could see that though it was
mortally wounded and listing gravely, his ship hadn't yet sunk. It
fact, it wasn't even on fire.

Sometimes I liked to dwell on this scene. Chatterji, the man
born to rule, accustomed to ripping apart fiendish crosswords
with the sharp mandibles of his intellect, who liked to feed his
prize-winning mind with dense economic history and quizzes on
Bollywood trivia, had somehow come to this, clinging to a
Kuwaiti buoy in his sodden whites, his favourite binoculars somewhere at the bottom of the Persian Gulf and his sodden captain's
cap shrinking around his oversize brain. What ran through his
mind as he gazed at the smouldering hull of his ship? Were the

two oilers dead? Had they gotten aboard the boat? And where had the bloody chief officer gone with the lifeboat? He didn't know. What had hit the ship? He didn't know that either. And on top of all that, I imagine he was slightly galled that he had abandoned a ship that had failed to sink or even to burn to the water line. That wasn't going to look good on the report.

Around midday they were picked up by a coastguard helicopter. The men in the lifeboat had been able to radio for help and were picked up mid-morning. The two missing crew-members were also found. Realising they'd been left behind, they had grabbed lifejackets and pitched themselves into the sea. During the night they had drifted away from the ship with the surface current, and by the time they were picked up by another merchant ship in the early morning, they had floated a few kilometres closer to shore.

It was only when he got ashore himself that Chatterji realised his ship had been struck by a stray Iraqi missile. Thanks to that missile, Chatterji liked to say, he was one of the first people in the world to learn that Iraq had invaded Kuwait.

Thomas and I climbed the external stairs all the way to the monkey's island.

There was enough moonlight to make out the rim of the sea, where water ended and night sky began. Ahead, the riding light lit the edifice of containers. Thomas showed me the flares and beacons which would activate themselves automatically if the monkey's island sank below the surface.

My friend gazed up at the sky and shook his head slowly. 'And you tell me there is no God,' he sighed. He raised his free hand as if he might yank a star out of the night sky and show it to me. Most sailors, I knew, would look at the stars and see the cosmos from which Erich von Daniken's pyramid-builders had come, not evidence of God. For some reason, I thought of the Bangladeshi sailors who'd gone ashore in New Orleans for shopping and a taste of Cookie's girl-gumbo and never come back. And then of Said, the electric eel, with his brown eyes peeled for a reappearance of the *Flying Dutchman*.

We didn't talk for a while. It occurred to me that the closest I'd yet come to finding the missing second volume of Marco Polo's voyages was Chatterji's story about Kuwait. My Marco had gone to sea for adventure and ended up floating into a cartoon spice port after a cartoon pirate attack; I realised that was how I imagined a younger Captain Chatterji, my pint-sized nemesis, waiting for help on his fibreglass light buoy just out of Kuwait harbour. He, too, had ridden into an exotic Eastern seaport on a barrel of luck. But I still didn't know what happened next.

Two nights out from Kochi, Chatterji declared that there would be a party. Like a maharaja declaring a feast day, he ordered large quantities of meat, fish and potato salad to be prepared in the galley and then carried up to the boat deck, four flights of stairs away. A modest quantity of beer was put on ice.

Nyem came up to my room to take me to the party. I got up to go. 'Not yet,' Nyem said, perching himself on the bed and eyeing the bar fridge. 'Perhaps you don't mind if I have one beer?'

So we drank a beer together. I had slowly warmed to Nyem. He still talked incessantly about how hard he worked; I still let my eyes glaze over. In his previous career as senior waiter at a five-star hotel in Yangon, Nyem claimed to have personally served Myanmar's president at table and several other presidents, including, if Nyem recalled correctly, leaders from South Korea, Thailand and Cambodia. No wonder he considered cleaning the captain's toilet a come-down.

Out on the boat deck, the party was in full swing. The barbecue was an ingenious custom job made out of half a 44-gallon drum sliced through the middle and cradled on a stand improvised from welded iron scrap by some handy sailor long ago. The whole thing was brown with rust. Under the grill, which was encrusted with the grease of a hundred barbecues, a shovel-load of coals exhaled dense brown smoke. Generous quantities of beef sausages, whole tuna wrapped in silver foil and steaks were blackened on the grill.

I stood for a while at the railing and inhaled the atmosphere. It had been an airless day, the heat penned in by low, gauzy clouds. Now the air was cooler and fragrant with fruity aftershave, whiskey and smoked meat. The boys had all turned out in striped short-sleeved shirts, which looked like they'd all come from the same Singaporean emporium specialising in fake Tommy Hilfiger. The officers were wearing soft leather shoes; Thomas' had tassels. The captain sat alone at the head of a long, empty table along the portside railing. He was picking at some coleslaw and smiling a lot. He looked miserable.

It felt like the spinning world had gone into slow motion. In the western sky, the sun fattened, turned red, then dissolved into thick sashes of pink and orange which clung to the sea's edge for what seemed like hours. Everyone danced except the captain and Mrs Patel, who sat to one side in her beautiful cream and ivory sari, smiling tightly. The sailors rumbled in a tight, sweaty knot. Now and again someone slipped on stray grains of fried rice. Watching all this, I remembered that night in the crew's mess aboard the *Anneke Schliemann*, where I had sat, with Nadia and Dominic, among a roomful of Filipinos drinking warm beer and watching Johnny's video of the party on another, happier ship. Here there was even a token 'girl' – one of the Filipino guys, an oiler everyone called Jimmy – who was famous for the feminine flourishes of his disco moves. He gyrated like a showgirl while everyone danced in a circle around him, whooping and clapping. 'He has rubber hips!' Thomas shouted in my ear. 'I tell you he could be in the Folies!'

Rakesh had pretty rubbery hips himself. Pairs formed for the slower numbers – Rakesh leading Teng through a series of elegant dips and twirls, and second engineer, the Gujarati millionaire, cradling Jimmy tenderly under the bare light globe. Mrs Patel escaped to her cabin as soon as politeness allowed.

The highlight of the night was provided by Nyem. It turned out that Nyem was an amazingly good breakdancer. The crowd brayed for a solo. Nyem, who had been skulking around the edges of the party, didn't need to be asked twice. He dropped his pan and brush, and instructed the DJ to cue up 'It's My Life' by Bon Jovi. Then he stepped into the space cleared for him and began to breakdance.

I may never see anything like it again. Nyem could breakdance like a 22-year-old Michael Jackson. With his limbs jittering and ratcheting like they belonged to an experimental washing machine, Nyem enacted the rituals of his day as a steward in an electrified parody, jerkily placing a plate in front of the captain, whirring an imaginary vacuum around the deck and refusing a beer offered by a shipmate – *Too busy, too busy!* 'It's very brave,' Thomas shouted in my ear. 'You see, he is moonwalking the tightrope between what is okay and what is not okay for him.'

Everyone screamed for an encore, except the captain whose shifty eyes roved across the faces of the crew, a fixed smile on his face. Flushed with his triumph, Nyem begged off with a typically egregious and pitiful remark about having to vacuum a carpet somewhere in the ship. Everyone forgot about him and went back to their own dancing, including the Divine Mr M who delighted the crowd with his own attempts at moonwalking.

At one point, the Gujarati millionaire came up to me with a dreamy smile on his face and a glass filled to the brim with Scotch. His eyes were swimming in his head.

'I don't drink Scotch!' I apologised. He insisted that I must. 'If you are a sailor, you drink Scotch. Do not be worried. It is mostly water.' It tasted like petrol.

For a while Thomas tried to organise a prank in which the Gujarati millionaire, who was due to sign off in Kochi, would be told that the company had refused his application to sign off. Everyone thought this would be a capital joke but it was decided to put it off until tomorrow when he'd be less likely to suspect foul play. Besides, it looked like he was enjoying himself in the arms of the highly flexible Jimmy, and it seemed mean to interrupt.

When the party petered out, I went downstairs and watched *When a Man Loves a Woman* in German, regretting again that I hadn't watched *You've Got Mail* or *The Doors* before the DVD player was stolen. Still, it was better than nothing.

THE SECRET OF CARDAMOM

The captain didn't want to go into Kochi at night because of the risk of piracy, by which he meant old sailors who stole aboard to nick the paint, rope and tools they knew where to find. We stayed offshore. Kochi lay sixteen kilometres away in the darkness. The lights of other ships drifted nearby. Some of the guys were fishing over the side with hand-held lines and a floodlight. The floodlight illuminated the water to a depth of a metre or so. Plankton swirled below the surface like dust motes caught in a shaft of sunlight. At the edge of the darkness, clumps of fleshy green matter drifted by on the surface current.

I was on the forecastle deck at six in the morning. We nosed our way through the scattered riding lights of the other ships. Dawn came slowly, held back by a low bank of thundercloud which steamed across the sky from the north, closing overhead like a giant cataract. Warm, ropy rain pounded on the forecastle deck. It bounced off the winches and drummed the surface of the water white.

Two tugs led the ship through the narrow harbour mouth. In the pre-dawn gloom I could just see the islands to our left fall away, opening out into a wide estuarial lake. Then the cloud bank shifted away and I felt the rising sun like a steaming cloth on my face. The harbour surface turned pink. Raindrops hung in the air like glass beads for hundreds of metres above. The harbour was streaked with wreaths of water hyacinth.

Here it was at last – Kochi, or Cochin as it was formerly known. A city of the sea whose docks and fishing nets are fed by the inland waterways which run for hundreds of kilometres through the hinterland to the sea, bearing barges loaded with pepper, coir, cloves and cardamom. In the distance I could see the spiky skyline of downtown Ernakalum; to the left, the lush forest spilt into the sea around the jetties of Vypeen Island. Immediately to my right lay Fort Cochin, the city's ancient trading heart. Along its western shore were stone houses and sagging wooden jetties, and in the distance, picked out by the slanting light, the soaring teak cradles of the Chinese fishing nets. Further around the island's nub, opposite our berth at Willingdon Island, the timber and stone godowns of Mattancherry's ancient spice markets grew taller in the sunrise, their faces flushed pink and yellow and eggshell blue.

We berthed at Willingdon Island in a paddock of gently rocking weeds.

Chatterji was counting bundles of fifties in his stateroom when I went to say goodbye. He let me shake his hand. Nyem was nowhere to be found. I left him a tip and then left quickly, before he could find my offering and declare it wholly inadequate for the support and upkeep of his babies.

Thomas, who had come to regard me as his brother in sin, had declared his intention to ensure that my stay in India got off to a good start. While I was being dragged through the interminable customs and immigration process at the port, he went ashore to smooth my path.

Immigration spat me out onto the doorstep of the Seaman's Club – the first stop for any self-respecting mariner in Kochi. I ducked into the shadowy doorway of the crew's bar to get out of the rain. A shipload of Chinese sailors sat around tables with bottles of Indian beer, smoking, laughing and singing along with Bon Jovi on the jukebox. There was a strong and pleasant smell of marijuana and fried eggs.

Thomas was waiting for me in the clubby gloom of the officer's bar further inside. It was difficult to see in the darkness, but this looked like my first glimpse of lingering Raj chic: leather settees in racing green which creaked like an old ship when I sat down, mahogany card tables and ceiling fans stirring the cigarette smoke above. A waiter in a white jacket with a mandarin collar served us Kingfisher beers.

We left during a brief intermission in the rain. Thomas paused outside and peered into the crew's bar. He inhaled dreamily. 'The ganja in Kerala is the best stuff in the world,' he sighed. Surprised, I asked if he was a regular smoker. 'Blinking hell, don't ask,' he said. 'Where I ask you in the Bible does it say a fellow should be smoking spliffs all the time?'

Thomas piled my bags into an auto-rickshaw. We climbed in on top of them, me cradling my model *Confiance*. First stop was the office at an export quality-assurance business based in Kochi's Willingdon Island. Thomas' friend, one Mr Samuels, had been ringing around local hotels at Thomas' behest. He had arranged for me to stay in the Seagull Hotel in Fort Cochin overlooking the water. 'That's where all the history is,' Thomas said, pleased. 'That will be most perfect for your book.' I thanked Mr Samuels profusely. But wait – we had been granted a rare honour. The boss wanted to see us.

Mr Sengupta welcomed us into his office like we were his dinner. 'Please, please,' he drawled from behind a mahogany desk at the far end. His office was the size of a tennis court. There was a Manchester United pennant on the wall behind Mr Sengupta's desk, which was made out of some beautifully polished dark wood and had a soft leather surface the colour of dried blood.

Thomas made an odd jerky motion at my side. He may have been genuflecting. He introduced me. 'A journalist,' murmured Mr Sengupta, rubbing his hands together. 'You don't say?'

I seated myself in an overstuffed wingback chair. Across the room I could see a plaster plinth on which stood a display of the products out of which Kochi had been built: neat cardboard packets of tea, cashew nuts, cloves, cinnamon, cardamom and a symbolic hank of coir fibre. Mr Sengupta was in his forties, I guessed. He had a round, shiny face. He looked like he had long been able to afford to see the humour in all situations.

Mr Sengupta was, he explained without any beating around of the bushes, one of the richest men in the state. 'It's true that despite my various faults – and my wife says that I am the world's biggest bullshitter – that I have enjoyed some success in the practical area. But,' he said, looking at me keenly, 'any business, and I think journalism must be the same, is about learning the nitty-gritty.

'When I began here as a young man, I went to a cardamom farmer and I said, "I want to learn how to tell good cardamom from bad cardamom. I want you to teach me the secret."' He paused here, leaning forward to accept a cigarette from Thomas' outstretched packet. The lid on his chrome lighter clicked shut like the door of an expensive car. 'The farmer was happy to help. He told me that the good cardamom was the cardamom grown on *his* farm and the mediocre cardamom was the stuff grown on the farm next door. Of course, the farmer next door said the same thing!' Sengupta chuckled. 'You can imagine. But eventually, I *did* learn. It's the only way. You can tell the quality from the size, of course; anyone can learn the premium varieties. But how can you teach someone the *smell* of premium cardamom? I ask you, how can this be taught?'

Thomas and I exchanged dumb looks.

'It can't! You have to learn it from experience. One might as easily say that you can learn swimming from a correspondence course!'

Thomas fell about with obliging laughter. I could tell from the tears of sweat on his cheeks and forehead that we were in the presence of an important man. Either that, or the Kingfisher beers at the Seaman's Club were taking their toll.

Over the next hour, Mr Sengupta spoke of many things. He smoked, too, all the remaining cigarettes in Thomas' packet. 'I don't mind telling things to an Australian,' he said pleasantly, 'because I think it's fair to say that the Australians are the only ones who haven't fucked us over at one stage or another.'

It was late in the evening by the time we got to my hotel. Thomas installed me in a cuboid room with concrete walls. There were two narrow beds shrouded in a grey mosquito net and an air-conditioner jammed into the single high window, its fan grating unhappily in the heat. 'If you have any problems,' Thomas said, 'you know who to call. If there is any trouble with the police or if the air-conditioning breaks down, just call Mr Sengupta. He is best friends with the police. He can sort anything out. Anything at all.'

At the docks we had a sweaty and tearful farewell, moistened by the several Kingfishers we'd drunk in my room. Then I watched him go, one of God's gentler soldiers, striding unsteadily towards the great metal edifice of the *Anna Böhme* with a bottle of Famous Grouse Whiskey under his T-shirt. I was going to miss him.

I ate that night at a small family-run place next door. The tables were set out beneath a pergola. In the walled garden which surrounded it, there were miniature grottoes and statues and temples representing every religion I could think of. This place felt like a magical garden perfumed by the smell of fresh mud from the afternoon's downpour, frangipani and the oily smell of mosquito coils smouldering in clay pots on the ground.

As usual, I was seeing the city through the pages of a book: Salman Rushdie's *The Moor's Last Sigh*. Probably worse, I was seeing through the nostalgic recall of its unreliable narrator. I'd heard Rushdie reading from this book at the Royal Court Theatre in 1995, one of the first public appearances he'd made since the fatwah had forced him underground. It had been a soggy London day and peoples' umbrellas kept setting off the metal detectors specially installed in the foyer. The book had stuck with me ever since, particularly the parts set among the spice docks of Ernakalum and Fort Cochin. The family of Rushdie's anti-hero built a fortune in the spice godowns of this very island. On the ship that morning, I had steeled myself for disappointment. It wasn't necessary. What I'd taken for Rushdie's magical realism now seemed like a frank depiction of reality. I could hear the warm sea slapping on the jetty at the bottom of the garden, the same night water on which Aires da Gama had rowed away from the family palace in his wife's wedding dress, his beloved Prince

Henry the Navigator at the oars, leaving a lingering smell of jasmine and cardamom in his wake.

This was the life. Not only was I installed above Fort Cochin's magical harbour in an exotic parallel universe and eating food that had been prepared with the eater's pleasure in mind, but I was enjoying the protection of the local maharajah.

I had asked to see one of Mr Sengupta's godowns in Mattancherry, half an hour's walk from my hotel in Fort Cochin. 'We call them warehouses,' Mr Samuels told me the next morning. He had been deputised to keep me amused until lunchtime. He was a quiet, personable man in his late forties. He had the air of a powerful lieutenant, a man who had God's phone number programmed into his mobile phone. 'Of course, our warehouses are in Ernakalum and Willingdon Island now. But real business is still done here.'

The narrow streets of Mattancherry's Jewtown spice markets were a miracle of timelessness. The godowns were a mix of architectural bloodlines: terracotta tile roofs, Malabar teak ceilings, Arabic-style carved wooden balconies tacked to Portuguese-style timber and plaster walls and then, closest to the ground, stone shop fronts pressed into the ground by the piled weight of history above. In the slanting shadows between them, a fabulous carnival of Eastern commerce went on. Workers humped sacks of chillies to and fro, wholesalers bartered over samples of tea. Goats nosed the garbage and drank muddy rainwater from the gutters. Lost-looking cows got in everyone's way. Wholesalers conducted their business in cool shop fronts open to the street. A few were doing business on laptops and mobile phones, but most of them were haggling over cups of tea and sacks of spices, doing their deals like they'd been done since time began.

There was no sense that things needed to change. Through my Westerners' eyes, though, I gazed at the scene and couldn't help thinking that here, the sooner things changed the better. The men lugging sacks of cardamom and cloves off wagons were probably the poorest working people I'd ever met. It's difficult to stop looking at any place that doesn't have rippling skyscrapers as a prospect for development or, if you're a sentimentalist, as a place waiting to be destroyed by it. But this was a functioning economy with an unimaginably ancient history of religious liberality and profit and loss, a story which ran all the way down from the early Arab and Jewish traders through to the Chinese, Portuguese, Dutch and British. Mr Sengupta sat at the bottom of this rich flow diagram through history like a figure from the sprawling Mahabharata murals in the Mattancherry Palace, a portly deity with many arms, all of them firmly grasping the great pepper mill of the Malabar Coast.

As well as cardamom, pepper and tea, Mr Sengupta's business was in cashew nuts. 'As you know, Kerala is famous for its cashews,' said Mr Samuels, scooping his hand into a sack of lentils, there being no cashews handy. 'The best cashews in the world. The Arabs love our cashews. The only problem is, we don't grow enough here. So we have to import some from Africa so that there are enough Kerala cashews to go around.'

'But how do you make money out of that? By the time you've brought them over to India, how can anyone here afford them?'

Mr Samuels laughed without showing his teeth. 'Oh no, Indians don't eat them. Too expensive. All the cashews we import raw we export packaged to Europe and the Gulf. It's very good business.

'You see if an African peels a cashew, the nut comes out broken,' Mr Samuels sighed. 'This is a sad fact of life. Here we can do it cheap *and* the nut is preserved whole.' The only problem with this splendid scheme was that the charterers in African ports used the good-quality containers to ship coffee to North America and Europe; the old ones with dicky refrigeration systems went to India, which meant that the top layer of nuts often arrived spoilt by exposure to moist air. He made it sound like a form of racism.

'It *is* racism,' Mr Sengupta snorted when he dropped by in his BMW to take us to lunch at the Seaman's Club. 'They think because we're poor Indians we can have the crappy containers.' He shooed away a goat that was trying to eat one of his car tyres.

Mr Sengupta's first job in Kochi harbour had been to check the levels of heavy fuel in tankers that came into the port to discharge. 'It was called "lightening", because you're lightening your ship by pumping fuel out into holding tanks, and my job was to come aboard at the end of the procedure and make sure that the tanks were fully empty. In other words, ensure that my clients had got all of the oil they'd paid for.

'I began to notice an attitude problem among the ship captains and senior officers. At the time, you have to remember, India didn't have a tanker fleet of her own. Until 1978, India had no access to her own oil supply, there were just small feeder vessels. All the oil came in on foreign tankers. And these captains treated us like we were nobody. Why? If there's one thing I cannot tolerate from a visitor, it's lack of respect.'

I sat up straighter. Now and again during lunch Mr Sengupta tapped me on the shoulder, the sign that it was time for me to offer him my pack of Silk Cuts again. 'You should smoke Marlboro,' he told me. 'The taste is superior.'

'I prefer them mild,' I said.

'Ha!' Mr Sengupta slapped me on the back. 'Excuse me but these are ladies' cigarettes. Where was I? Oh yes. So if a captain was arrogant with me, I made a special effort to teach him a lesson. The measurements they used to test the depth of remaining oil in the hold was only accurate to within seven centimetres of the bottom. In other words, you couldn't actually tell how much was left below seven centimetres and anyway, it was impossible to get all of the oil out. You just can't do it. But if one of these guys was rude to me, I would say: "I'm sorry, captain, but I see from the readings that there is at least seven centimetres of fuel left in the hold. I'm afraid I can't sign your papers until I'm satisfied that it's all been pumped out."'

'Gradually,' Mr Sengupta finished, 'they got the message.'

I could imagine the scene so perfectly, the dawning realisation of the German, British or Kuwaiti captain that he had made a costly mistake; then the humiliating strategic retreat to abject politeness and possibly even prostration on the greasy deck. It wasn't just Chatterji who bore a vestigial grudge against Europeans: Sengupta did too. For him, the story of Kochi was a triumphalist narrative in which centuries of exploitation was ended by the nous and sheer ballsiness of Keralan merchants like him.

Mr Sengupta clicked his fingers for the bill. 'Did you see that big anchor outside the front of the Seaman's Club?'

'Yes, I think so, I –'

'That, my friend, is the history of Cochin. If you want to understand the history of this place, go back there and study it. It belongs to the ship that dredged the channel into the modern terminal. The silt it dug out was used to create Willingdon Island, where we are sitting right now. Before that, ships had to anchor out in the harbour. Cochin was nothing then. We were at the mercy of foreign fleets. If you are serious, I tell you go back there, and take photographs. Study it closely. That's the beginning.'

Alastair turned up in a pair of Swedish sandals which, he informed me, were made out of the same material that was used by NASA to insulate the space shuttle. Despite the sandals, he loped out of the sweaty fug of a Keralan afternoon looking like a bespectacled Mowgli, his ragged shorts and grimy T-shirt suggesting a long sojourn in the Western Ghats. In fact, he'd just gotten off a plane from Melbourne.

I was delighted to see him. Al was the perfect person to have along on a sentimental adventure. He knew the ethos of running away to sea by heart. It was a language he picked up reading himself through a neo-Edwardian boyhood, stuffing his young head with Buchan, Kipling, Stevenson, Cooper; the sorts of books boys were meant to read in an age when boyhood was a chance to familiarise future explorers and infantry officers with the tactile world of guns and timber, nails and emergency fastenings. Perhaps because of all this reading, Al sometimes had the bemused air of someone who had had an agreeable accident with a time machine.

We celebrated his arrival with a drink in the bar at Brunton's Boatyard, an expensive hotel built above an old shipyard facing

Vypeen Island across the harbour. From our table on the upstairs terrace we overlooked the muddy bus terminus, lots of busy goats, and beyond, the Chinese fishing nets raking fish out of the current. On the way out, Al showed off by describing the origins and development of the antique firearms mounted on the wall behind the downstairs bar. Flintlock, matchlock, percussion lock. Three hundred years of increasing firepower hanging on a wall.

In the fifteenth century, the Venetian traveller Nicolo de' Conti wrote that if China was the place to make money, then Cochin was the best place to spend it. Along with Calicut (Kozhikode) and Cannanore (Kannur) further north, Cochin's spices had supplied Arab and Chinese needs for at least a thousand years before that. Arab booms and ocean-going dhows loaded deep with dates, frankincense, myrrh and carpets followed the monsoon here to trade for spices. Jewish traders established a community here as early as the fourth century AD. But the traffic also came the other way. Chinese 'treasure ships' called here too, the massive ocean-going junks described by travellers like Marco Polo and the Muslim merchant and traveller Ibn Battuta. These ships were the marvels of their age; they carried upward of 600 souls, cisterns of fresh water and vegetables planted in wooden tubs. They offered unparalleled comfort to merchants like Polo and Battuta, both of whom sailed in treasure ships. Ibn Battuta noted with pleasure that the private apartments allocated to him aboard comfortably accommodated his harem of slave girls.

The tourist-magnet fishing nets are all that survive of that Chinese influence. We spent a morning with a crew of fishermen who saw us coming a mile off and kindly offered to let us help them operate its heavy counterweight pulley system. The fishermen introduced themselves by age and religion – two Muslims, a Christian and a Hindu. The rectangular net was strung like a trampoline from a frame of supple timbers which reached thirty metres into the air. These guys rented the apparatus from a fishing net supremo who owned several others.

Our new buddies took the chance to smoke our cigarettes and watch us. We strained on the ropes and picked at the blisters which instantly appeared on our palms. 'Soft hands!' they giggled. 'But if you are used to it, this is very good work,' one of them told us, reclining on the deck of his machine and lovingly smoking one of my cigarettes. 'You can be outside all day long. Very healthy. Very nice.'

'You have to wonder,' Al remarked later as we made our nightly search for bargain seafood, 'what those guys do for free labour when there are no tourists around.'

It rained steadily for the next ten days. My trip, which had begun in a dry heatwave in the Mediterranean, was coming to its end in a soaking of warm rain.

We got up very early one morning and hired a rowboat from behind the spice market in Mattancherry. We asked the rowboat wallah to do a lap of the harbour for us. Rashid was a fount of harbour lore. He was struck by Al's apparent likeness to one of Rashid's favourite Bollywood stars – 'the skin and the features are identical' – and warmed to him further when he found out that Al was a lawyer. Rashid kept an address book in a little locker in the stern for just an occasion as this one: the locker was already full of lawyers' business cards. Now thirty-four, he had been doing this job for twenty-one years. He married at twenty-one a girl of fifteen. 'I never go school,' he boasted, 'but I speak seven or eight language.'

Rashid tied up to a stone wall on a small, uninhabited island across the harbour. This, he explained, was the place where he brought prostitutes and their johns. 'You want to see?'

'Not really,' said Al.

'Of course,' said Rashid, leading us to the spot where his clients lay out the groundsheet supplied by Rashid, got naked and got on with it. Usually old men and young girls. With money, he reflected, anything was possible. I got the impression that Rashid felt obliged to witness these trysts, presumably with an expression of disgusted forbearance on his face. Rashid whacked the bushes with a sapling branch as we went. 'Lots of poisonous snakes,' he explained. 'Living in trees. Dropping on head.'

Within seconds of arriving at this muddy clearing in the undergrowth, we were ambushed by mosquitoes. Lots of mosquitoes. 'But never before have I seen mosquitoes here,' Rashid marvelled, as Al and I yelped and swatted at the humming clouds; then he recalled that government helicopters regularly sprayed the island with 'anti-mosquito' oil. In his mosquito-friendly black shirt, Al suffered the worst. He dug at the welts that sprung up all over his arms, legs and neck.

'Don't worry,' Rashid said. 'No malaria here.' No mosquitoes had bitten Rashid.

'They'd only be spraying for mosquitoes if there's malaria,' Al grumbled. We were left to wonder how the sailors coped with the mosquitoes while their naked buttocks were flailing in the tropical dusk.

It was only when we got out on the water that we realised what an extraordinary range of boats there were afloat in this harbour. When the Dutch garrison surrendered to the British in 1795 there were at least ten shipyards in Fort Cochin. There are modern shipyards on the mainland of Ernakalum now, but most of this ancestral skill has devolved into backyard ingenuity. We saw boats so strange it looked like an imaginative child had drawn them. These boats looked like they'd been improvised from patched-up snake boats or restored dories, and though they nominally derived their propulsion from lawn-mower motors or motorbike engines or even curtain rods and tarpaulin sheets, they seemed to be powered by sheer optimism. Most of this motley fleet was being used for line and net fishing, but some probably moonlighted as the 'pirates' Chatterji feared. A few boats scrambled out of the way of a navy frigate steaming past Willingdon Island on its way into base. 'Indian,' Rashid nodded. 'Sometimes Italians. Sometimes French.'

I asked if they got many American warships in Kochi. Too many, he said, through clenched teeth. One group of American navy sailors had ruined his opinion of Americans forever. They'd hired Rashid's boat to take them and their dates to snake and mosquito island, but soon nicely liquored up, began bantering with Rashid about his refusal to drink some of their beer. Rashid's shiny face crumpled in revulsion as he recalled how the sailors had taunted him, how their girls had sat in his boat virtually naked, with their shirts unbuttoned, smoking – 'The *women* too, smoking!' – and how the sailors had sprayed beer in his face, presumably to emphasise the great pleasures he was missing. 'I prayed to God that he would understand that I didn't want to drink it. But they sprayed it right in my face . . . I couldn't do anything . . .' He shook his head, regretting perhaps the fate of the sailors' souls. 'No, sorry. Americans are no good.'

In the main, Rashid was an insanely jolly individual. Everything he saw between waking up and going to bed at night seemed to remind him of his incredible luck. But he couldn't conceal his unhappiness when Al the lawyer confessed that he drank alcohol. 'Quite a bit of it actually,' Al admitted, honest to a fault. He wasn't invited to leave his card to be added to the collection at the back of the boat.

During the days we left tracks of sweat across most of Kochi's historic landmarks – the forts that have risen and crumbled there, the churches, the famous synagogue, the Dutch cemetery. The city's European remains, in other words, most of it chaotically overgrown by foliage or else obsessively retained in all its out-of-place colonial glory.

With the fixed smile of a sea-facing town with a lot of stuff to sell, Kochi has tolerated the arrivals of a lot of different creeds over the years. Locals seemed to extend the same liberal bemusement to backpackers, whom they accepted as the badly dressed acolytes of a strange, itinerant sect. In Jewtown, a jewellery wholesaler told us that forty or fifty passenger ships called at Kochi each year, all of them during the cooler months that follow the winter monsoon. The anxious wait for tourists had made the shopkeepers cranky and we kept having to extricate ourselves from groups of overeager salesmen.

In the evenings, we doused ourselves with mosquito repellent and sat on stools in the decommissioned bar in our hotel. The bar was in an enclosed second-floor verandah which overlooked the narrow gap between Fort Cochin and Vypeen Island. From here, on my second day, I had watched the *Anna Böhme* being guided out through the harbour mouth, Lilliputian tugs straining at its monstrous bulk on the end of ropes. We watched the descendent of the great *Lord Willingdon* ploughing in and out again, a steady stream of silty muck snorting from its bilges as it made the harbour safe for intercontinental shipping.

Just along the waterfront from our raised verandah view were the jetties that reached out into the harbour from Kochi's coastguard headquarters. A twelve-metre cruising catamaran was tied up among the official powerboats. Patches of barnacles and several years' worth of water hyacinth had gathered between its offwhite hulls. Quite a bit of dockside mythology had clung to it as well. According to Rashid, this boat belonged to some Frenchmen who had been caught several years earlier by the coastguard trying to smuggle a load of hand grenades and other assorted weapons out of India to clients in the Red Sea. The manager of the hotel, a very young and eager-to-please man called Raoul, told us that the Frenchmen had simply failed to get their papers in order before they'd arrived, and someone – some Sengupta in immigration, probably, spying a rare chance to give another former European power a kicking – had impounded it.

This seems to happen quite a lot in Kochi. From the bridge spanning across the canal between Willingdon Island and Ernakalum on the mainland, I could see an entire flotilla of rotting Sri Lankan fishing trawlers manacled to the navy docks. The fishermen who strayed into Indian waters are fined and deported; their boats get to stay for good.

According to Raoul, the catamaran's owners had recently returned to Kochi to petition the state government authorities to release the boat. Evidently to no avail.

This catamaran became our obsession. During the long evenings of heavy rain, we spent a lot of time idly wondering how we might possibly steal it. It wasn't being used for anything, we reasoned, and if we were caught, Mr Sengupta would bail me out of strife in a jiffy. Maybe Al as well, if he was lucky. Al's plan involved hot-wiring the engines or, if that didn't work, going aboard with a big outboard stolen earlier, bolting it on and bursting out of the harbour before the coastguard had time to scramble together its fleet of patrol boats.

I pointed out that someone would surely notice.

Al brushed this aside with the confidence of one who had read a lot about piracy and smuggling. 'We'd wait for a cloudy night.'

'What about engine noise?'

He thought about this. 'Well we could sail it out, though that would take a long time.' He pondered the problem. 'I could just wave grandly like the film star everyone thinks I am and they'd just assume I'd bought it.'

'Have you ever actually sailed anything Al?'

'No. Have you?'

'No.'

Still, the idea lingered. We could hear the boat's hulls slapping on the strengthening current as we lay in bed at night.

After a week of this, we decamped for Kozhikode, 200 kilometres to the north.

For most of history, Kozhikode, or Calicut as it was previously known, was Malabar's most important port. No longer. Unlike Kochi it has no deep-water harbour and its port is closed during the monsoon season. The only shipping that calls there now is coastal. These days, its chaotic city centre bustles with other concerns: its university and the timber, textile and coconut industries.

We stomped through the mud of the bus station and found ourselves a bracingly dismal hotel which stank of rising damp. We dumped our gear and headed for the waterfront. It was Sunday afternoon and most of Kozhikode's citizens seemed to have beaten us to it, cooling their ankles in the limp surf and savouring the evening breeze rising off the Lakshadweep Sea. We sat for a while among the rime of sea scurf, the plastic bags and cigarette ends.

There were fewer travellers around and so a correspondingly greater interest in Alastair's legs. Several people came up to say hello and make conversation, some of them mistaking Al for the movie star, some of them just eager to know where we were from. A band of boy cricketers still sweaty from practice wanted to know who our favourite cricketers were. They were flatly unimpressed with my choice – the Pakistani Inzamam-ul-Haq (captain of Tristan's Fatties XI) – but warmly congratulated Al, who knew less about cricket than your average Inuit fisherman, on the name he plucked from the air: Australian captain Steve Waugh, whom the boys praised as a philanthropist and cricketing genius.

We returned later after a meal. The beach was deserted. We pulled ourselves up onto a derelict pier and walked to the end. The pier continued on the other side of a gap where it had obviously collapsed at some point. A long-disused section of railway line suggested that there had once been a steady trade of goods flowing in and out of the nailed-up godowns on the shore behind us. No more. It looked like a bomb had broken the back of the pier. A pier from another time. My last pier, on a trip of piers.

A Portuguese fleet under the command of Vasco da Gama anchored here in 1498 after the longest continuous sea voyage in European history. From the poop decks of their leaky caravels, the sailors got their first glimpse of the fabled Indian subcontinent. They looked across the harbour at the city described by Nicolo de' Conti as being eight miles in circumference and 'a noble emporium for all India, abounding in pepper, lac [red dye], ginger, a larger kind of cinnamon'. To Calicut came cloves and cinnamon from Ceylon and cloves and nutmeg from Malacca. Everything Pero de Covilham had reported to John II appeared to be true.

Sadly, any hope of a mutually beneficial friendship between Calicut's Zamorin rulers and the Portuguese soon faded. The city's Arab merchants were unimpressed by the samples of trade goods da Gama had brought with him. When the cagey admiral finally went ashore, he was briefly detained by the sultan who would come to regret his whimsy. Four years later da Gama was back, armed with an impressive fleet, inflamed righteousness and 'a great desire to go and make havoc' with the local ruler and his town.

Da Gama's countrymen had been continually surpassing themselves in their violence around the Indian Ocean since they first arrived – in one of the history books he'd bought in Kochi's Jewtown, Al had found a story of a Portuguese captain who fired the severed heads of prisoners out of cannon over the walls of a besieged town on the Zanj coast – and they would continue to do so for another two centuries. But in da Gama, righteousness mixed with ingenuity to produce extraordinary results.

He began by brushing aside the heathen sultan's request for a negotiated peace, preferring instead to bombard the city with cannon for three whole days, smashing the walls and municipal buildings of the great city to rubble. A Brahmin was sent out by the sultan to plead for peace. For an answer, da Gama had the man's lips cut off. His ears were also cut off and the ears of a dog sewn on in their place, and then he was sent back to his sultan.

Warming to their work, the Portuguese then pillaged all the merchant ships at anchor in the harbour. They took 800 prisoners from among their crews. These unfortunates had their noses, ears and hands hacked off. They were piled into a ship with their legs tied together and their teeth smashed in to prevent them gnawing through the ropes. Da Gama ordered the ship's sails be set for the shore and the ship set alight. This hellish pyre drove onto the shore where the victims' horrified relatives tried in vain to douse the flames.

The noses and ears were sent ashore separately, in a small dory, with a note from da Gama to the Zamorin, suggesting that the sultan might like to make them into a curry.

I often wondered whether people knew this stuff when they shuffled respectfully by da Gama's empty grave in St Francis Church, Kochi.

Still, it wasn't only the Europeans who traded in brutality. The great French-trained general and Raj of Mysore, Hyder Ali, attacked the city in 1752 and razed it to the ground, which is the main reason why there are relatively few historic buildings left in town.

Before long we were joined on the pier by a dark figure visible only by the glowing tip of a cigarette. The figure had a flashlight as well, which it shone in our faces. The beam lingered on Al's legs. 'Hello!' Al said, in his most chipper style. 'We were just admiring the pier. Can you possibly tell us what happened to it?'

Up close, there was enough moonlight to make out the man's face. He was short, with a neatly clipped moustache. He was dressed in the standard Keralan mufti: neat cotton slacks and a button-down shirt, untucked. He seemed puzzled, but quite pleased, to find us here. 'Nineteen-fifty,' he said after a long while.

'I see, yes,' Al said, nodding and smiling at his ambassadorial best. 'But do you know what happened to it exactly? Why was it . . . *ruined*?'

The man tilted back his head. He didn't say anything. He seemed to be drinking in the black quartz of the night sky.

'Why is it kaput?' I added, recalling how useful 'kaput' had been in Beirut.

The man squinted at me in the dark, then looked back around him at the row of godowns from which he had emerged, perhaps trying to find the person to whom I had addressed my question. He turned back and flicked the stub of his cigarette into the sea. 'Cargo?' he said, with a questioning inflection, as if he wasn't sure he had the right word.

'Not fish?'

'No no no.' He jerked his head at the godowns. 'Cotton.'

This was interesting – Kozhikode was, after all, the home of calico – but hard to reconcile with the strong stink of rotten fish that seemed to radiate from the cluster of buildings along the waterfront.

'Pepper also?'

'Pepper, pepper.'

Al pointed at the missing section of pier. 'Perhaps it was bombed?' he suggested hopefully.

The man smiled, waggled his head and gazed out to sea. We stood around companionably, listening to the sea sucking on the barnacled posts below. Finally the man said, 'Prohibited?'

'I don't know,' I replied. 'I didn't see any signs.'

'Yes,' he nodded. 'Prohibited.'

Al caught on first. 'Is it? We didn't realise.' He smacked his forehead with his palm. 'Sorry about that.'

'Prohibited!' the man repeated. He smiled, pleased, and prowled the beam from his flashlight along the full length of the pier to emphasise that every last inch of it was indeed prohibited.

'Oh dear,' said Al pleasantly. 'We'll just finish these cigarettes then, and we'll be off.'

'Now,' said the man.

'Okay then,' said Al.

The man escorted us off the pier. He led us along an open sewer and out through a body-shaped hole ripped in a mesh fence topped with barbed wire. We waved; he waved back. Then we watched as he picked his way back to his lookout above one of the abandoned godowns. His window flickered with the bluish light of a television.

We ranged up the coast from Kozhikode to Thalasseri (formerly Tellicherry), to look at the fort and the overgrown European cemetery where swarms of mosquitoes kept a smug vigil over the graves of all the whities they'd killed with 'marsh miasma'. Then we returned to Kozhikode and headed for Beypore, thirty minutes down the coast by auto rickshaw.

The village of Beypore has one of the few surviving traditional boat-building industries on the Malabar Coast. Hulls built there by hand are famous for their unusual joinery: the teak timbers are not nailed or bolted together – they're sewn. Until iron was used to build hulls in the nineteenth century, all the fleets of the Arabian Sea floated on Malabar teak. No other wood suitable for building ocean-going vessels grew on the Arabian Sea littoral: nowhere else on the west coast of India, not in the Persian Gulf, not in Arabia. There were usable forests in Africa, but they were too far from the coast. During the eighteenth and nineteenth centuries Indian sultans supplied teak and jackfruit wood for Omani slave ships. Marco Polo didn't like the look of the sewn boats he first saw in Hormuz, in the Persian Gulf. 'These ships are wretched affairs,' he opined, 'and many of them get lost, for they have no iron fastenings and are only stitched together with twine made from the husk of the Indian nut . . . The ships are not pitched, but are rubbed with fish-oil.' In fact, the designs he saw in Hormuz were used throughout the Arabian Sea for the next 600 years. The ships built there by hand are still used by traders in the Arabian Sea; the finished hulls are towed to the Gulf where they are fitted with diesel engines.

We stepped onto the breakwater in Beypore and were instantly accosted by a very thin young man in stovepipe trousers and pink shirt. He welcomed us to the beautiful Malabar Coast. He was an assistant film director, he explained, working for a very famous Malayali film director from Canada. This director's first film, we should know, had been a big hit. Had we heard of it? We hadn't. And what were our jobs? He was quite pleased for me when I told him I was a journalist; he was thrilled to the point of disbelief to hear that Alastair was a lawyer. He pumped Al's hand again a second time and vowed to help us find the boats we were looking for.

We eventually found a boatyard and got ourselves invited in. In the yard there were two thirty-metre, ark-shaped boats raised on stilts. To my layman's eye, both of them appeared to be riddled with iron bolts and nails. 'The sewn boats of Malabar, eh?' Al muttered. We badly needed someone who knew boats and could speak English at the same time; instead we had a film director who was eager, but of no use whatever. He did, however, find some shabby models for sale in a tin shed behind the workshop. We crept away and stood under the hull of one of the half-finished ships.

'Well,' said Al, 'it's beautiful wood.'

'Malabar teak,' I whispered. 'The real thing.'

'Looks like it.'

'To me, however,' I said, 'these look like iron nails.'

Al ran his hand over the smooth hull. This was his area of expertise. Al may be a lawyer, but he was born speaking the language of carpentry and creation. Awls, rivets, planes, nail punches: these were his area. Watching his face puzzling over the gap between what our books told us and what he was seeing, it occurred to me that people like Al were once required to run an empire, matching book-learning to the slippery facts of India: puzzling over the problem of gunpowder gone damp in the coastal humidity; watching people drop dread from mysterious fevers; and wondering what would be a good time to stop drilling the sepoys and have a gin and tonic in the shade.

My friend tapped his chin with a forefinger. 'That,' he announced, 'is because they *are* nails.'

Raoul, our young hotel manager, was glad to see us back in Kochi. He was always glad to see us. He'd been extremely solicitous since I first arrived and Thomas had warned him that if he didn't look after me and ensure that my stay in Kochi was filled with positive experiences, Mr Sengupta would personally string him up from the spire of St Francis Church by his scrotum.

'How is your book going?' he asked anxiously.

'Fine.'

He grinned, showing his attractive teeth. 'I suppose you are famous author in England, is it?'

'No, not at all.'

'Ha!' He winked at Al. 'I suppose he is being too modest, is it?'

'No,' said Al. 'He's not.'

Raoul seemed to take this in his stride.

Rashid rowed us out to the five-star Taj Malabar hotel on the tip of Willingdon Island for our farewell dinner. He had been treating us like a pair of fallen women since he learned that we were both drinkers. 'Are you drinking many beers tonight?' he asked, in the too-casual tone a cuckold might use to ask his wife whether she intended to sleep with the entire village this week. 'I suppose you will be becoming like drunky men?'

'I expect so,' said Al thirstily.

'Maybe you will fall into the water!'

'It's possible,' Al agreed.

Rashid made a point of showing us the slashed remains of a three-metre water snake which had perished in the screws of a freighter and had floated in the wash below the Taj Malabar's jetty ever since.

We took a table right by the water in a pavilion enclosed in transparent plastic. Heavy rain for the past few days had washed a fresh invasion of water hyacinth into the harbour. An electric bug-zapper radiated the pleasing smell of burning mosquitoes. Ferries passed a hundred metres away; then came the delayed aftershock as the widening ripples struck the rocks below our table and splashed drops of water across our view of Fort Cochin.

'If we did nick the catamaran,' Al mused, 'and managed to get it started, and then headed straight out to sea, what would we hit first?'

'The prow of a very large container ship.'

'Assuming we weren't run over.'

Mm. 'The Lakshadweep Islands probably. A national park. Coral shelves teeming with rare and exotic species.'

Al didn't think that sounded half bad. 'Excellent. And after that?'

'Somalia, I guess. Do you want to go to Somalia?'

'Maybe next time.'

Rashid dropped us back at Customs Jetty a few hundred metres from our hotel. In the narrow lane leading from the jetty up to the main street, we passed an auto-rickshaw. There was a man sitting in it. 'What you want?' he whispered, *sotto voce*. 'Smoke? Marijuana smoke? Not smoke? Girl? You want girl? Come on, tell me. You tell me, it's okay, say whatever you want.'

We'd stopped. He slunk over. In the faint light that reached down from the street, we could see that he was a very old man. He had a slightly crazed, ferrety look. His collarbones cast shadows. It looked like he must have been living off whatever nutrition you could suck out of a bedi cigarette.

'Anything you want, just say me.' He took a plastic sachet out of his trousers and dangled it in front of us. 'Grass, you want? Or girls. Say me now. Anything okay. You want boy maybe? Is okay, tell me what you want.'

All men of the world here, his tone implied; among scoundrels all judgement is suspended. If we'd told him we wanted to have our way with a goat he would have organised it in a jiffy.

Then we heard people coming along the main street at the end of the lane. 'Shhh!' the man hissed. '*Pretend, pretend.*' He put his hands behind his back and thrust his chest out like a lord taking a turn in his gardens. 'What is that star?' he mused in a theatrical voice, gazing up into the heavens. 'Oh yes! Big star! Very nice. I love star. Very good!' He glared at us. 'I pretend, *you* pretend – *pretend* see?'

'Oh yes, look at that,' declared Al, arriving stage left in the nick of time. 'My word. Mm. Very interesting.'

A family in saris, jewels and flip-flops passed the lane. They peered suspiciously at our shadows.

When their footsteps faded away, the man clapped his hands and hissed with pleasure. 'We fool them,' he said. 'I just playing, see? So no problems with police.'

Back to business. *Anything you want.* What did we want? 'Maybe he can get us the keys to the catamaran,' Al muttered. 'And some showgirls to go with it.'

I couldn't resist, in my Kingfisher-fuelled state, interpreting this decrepit apparition as a kind of Old Man of the Port, a spirit of a lost world. Nothing we asked for would surprise him, because he'd heard of every known desire already. Perhaps if I told him I was looking for Marco II, a ten-year-old who'd drifted into a port just like this one twenty years ago and never been heard of since, he might have whipped the missing book out from behind his back right there and then.

Of course, he wasn't a genie or spirit, he was just a poor driver who probably owed money on his rickshaw and made a few rupees on the side selling marijuana to tourists. We ended up walking away with some surprisingly expensive medicinal cigarettes wrapped in a strip of newspaper. 'If this is anything more than cheap tobacco, I'll eat my shorts,' said Al. He'd only brought one pair of shorts.

'And you a lawyer and everything,' I tut-tutted. 'What would Rashid say?'

'He'd probably say he could have gotten me a better deal.'

Al flew back to Melbourne. I flew to Mumbai where I had a 24-hour stopover before I went on to London.

I'd never been to Mumbai, but I was anxious to get home now and didn't have the energy to dig any further into the city than Colaba. So I passed my afternoon dawdling among the bookstalls tucked in the alleyways and between the porticoes of the neo-Gothic buildings. The heat in Mumbai was even more intense than in Kochi. Now and then I felt the sting of cold water dripping from air-conditioning units hanging on walls high above the street.

You could buy virtually any book you could think of here. There was science fiction, pot-boilers, Stephen Hawking books, a complete edition of the *World Book Encyclopaedia* from 1984, Anthony Robbins' guides to ways of finding lots of money inside you where you thought there was none, guides to ways of finding inner peace and guides to finding Jesus. There were editions of *Harry Potter* in hardback, printed in India at a fifth the price you'd pay in London. I flicked through dusty piles of *LIFE* magazine. On the evidence of these photographs, the world was a different colour in the 1950s and 1960s. Movie stars' lips were redder; the khaki uniforms of African rebels were shinier; and cities photographed from the air always looked dusty and brown.

I found myself gravitating again towards the fat stacks of Ayn Rand. Sweating anxiously, suddenly more homesick than I'd ever been, I felt as if I were standing in the middle of a metaphor I couldn't shake. I could have been back on the waterfront in Dar es Salaam. Why was I surprised to see Ayn Rand here, right here – yes – next to her old shelf-mate, Erich von Daniken? The sea's edge is where people have always gone to peddle their cracked wares, the place where the ideas of revolutionaries and crackpots enjoy a permanent twilight. That was the idea I'd hoped to find alive and well when I set out, and here it was: evidence that when ideas ran out of steam or truth, they were chased down to the sea by new and better ones, like black rats fleeing the brown.

In the evening I sat on the roof of my hotel chewing through a plate of greasy pilaf. The food was bad enough to remind me fondly of Cookie on the *Anneke Schliemann*, but the view was fine. From here I overlooked the triumphal arch of the Gateway of India, and beyond it Mumbai Harbour where an ill-assorted flotilla drowsed at anchor. There were small freighters, pleasure yachts, a couple of lost-looking trawlers with their nets hanging out to dry on their booms and, farthest from shore, the blunt silhouettes of bulk carriers. Somewhere out in the night, beyond the farthest freighters I could see, was the ghost ship *El Hamas* and her complement of forgotten men.

Tomorrow, I would smoke the last cigarette of my life. Then I would board my plane for the last leg of a sea journey which must have set the record for air miles covered by someone writing about the sea. I would clutch my fragile *Confiance* in my lap all the way through the night to Heathrow. After meal service, they might show *Hanging Up*, the Meg Ryan film I'd missed seeing on DVD on the *Anna Böhme*. Perhaps after that I would sleep fitfully and dream edgy, aeroplane dreams. With any luck, I would dream of a day when this humble book might find a place on the bargain bookstalls in Dar es Salaam and Colaba, next to Rand and Robbins, or maybe sandwiched among pictorial guides to Ceylon and Abyssinia, and all the other places that no longer exist.